Environment, Politics and Activism

The Role of Media

Editor

Somnath Batabyal

Routledge
Taylor & Francis Group

LONDON AND NEW YORK

First published 2014 by Routledge

2 Park Square, Milton Park, Abingdon, Oxfordshire OX14 4RN
711 Third Avenue, New York, NY 10017

Routledge is an imprint of the Taylor & Francis Group, an informa business

First issued in paperback 2018

Typeset by
Glyph Graphics Private Limited
23, Khosla Complex
Vasundhara Enclave
Delhi 110 096

British Library Cataloguing-in-Publication Data
A catalogue record of this book is available from the British Library

ISBN 978-1-138-79563-1 (hbk)
ISBN 978-1-138-37938-1 (pbk)

Environment, Politics and Activism

To the unsung activist

Contents

PART III: CASE STUDIES:
INDIA AND THE WORLD

Acknowledgements

This volume would not have been possible without the generous funding of the Cluster of Excellence, Asia and Europe in a Global Context, University of Heidelberg. The editor is also indebted for support to the Centre for Culture, Media and Governance, Jamia Millia Islamia. Prof. Madeleine Herren-Oesch supervised the work and gave freely of her time, advice and encouragement. Finally, a big thank you to all the contributors for their diligence, patience and above all, indulgence.

Introduction

Somnath Batabyal

From the fringes where it lurked for decades, concerns around the environment entered the political mainstream around the 1980s. Today, in both the Global North and South, environmental rhetoric is built into political campaigns. It competes for attention with every other governmental terrain – internationally and within nation states – be it issues of economic growth, development, poverty alleviation or even defense strategies. The Conservative Party in the United Kingdom (UK) promise the "greenest government" (*The Guardian* 2010) ever, Obama marks his victory speech as the night "when the rise of the oceans began to slow"[1] and BRICS (Brazil, Russia, India, China and South Africa) nations try to negotiate environmental concerns along with their need and right to develop.

Yet it is our preoccupation with the modern state as the "single most effective medium for influencing people's lives and by extension the only route to genuine environmental protection" that has led us to the brink of a crisis of survival (Wapner 1996: 18).

The problem is simple and it seems, intractable. Environmental degradation and its effects do not obey human cartography and imperatives of national economies. The repercussions of the operating of a coal mine in New Castle will not be limited to the UK. Similarly, the illegal mining of minerals in Orissa, while wrecking immediate havoc on the forest tribals of the region, may be felt as a rude cyclone in Florida. Yet in international meets where our elected governments decide our futures, it is the interest of the nation state that is put first. At the overhyped Copenhagen Climate Summit in 2009, a Chinese negotiator told a colleague that the climate negotiations by its very logic were designed to fail. "Each country sends its best negotiators to the summit. Each of us is trained not to lose. If we do not lose, environment will." Joseph Heller could hardly ask for a better Catch-22 moment.

Environmental negotiations between nation states today and aid flow for the poorer countries from the rich in order to adapt and mitigate the devastating effects of sinking farmlands and disappearing water bodies have pretty much followed the same post-Second World War patterns of "development." Climate change is just the latest package in a long line of reform choices. And here it is necessary to understand, if briefly, 20th century's overwhelming political paradigm; "development" and its toxic legacy which has brought us to the brink of an ecological disaster. Yet, such is its dominance over our intellectual and moral landscape that, though discredited, it is by no means declining.

"Development as we know it – a continuous drive towards more and more economic prosperity – was literally invented post Second World War and announced on June 9, 1949 by US President Truman" (Esteva 2010: 1).

> We must embark on a bold new program for making the benefits of our scientific advances and industrial progress available for the improvement and growth of underdeveloped areas.
>
> The old imperialism – exploitation for foreign profit – has no place in our plans. What we envisage is a program of development based on the concepts of democratic fair dealing (Truman 1949).

No longer will the former colonies be exploited. They will receive "the benefits of our scientific advances and industrial progress," and be aided to become more like "us" – in this case, the United States (US). In this speech, Truman sets up the American lifestyle as the benchmark of aspirations, a phenomenon that is backed by Hollywood films depicting country ranches and farms, fast cars and trawlers, washing machines and dishwashers, and later through multimillion dollar advertisement campaigns and multinational brands as they enter the "underdeveloped" world.

"It is the legacy of the 20th century," Wolfgang Sachs points out, "that the desires of nations for a better tomorrow are predominantly directed towards development-as-growth. However, the multifaceted crisis of the biosphere turns this legacy into a tragic liability" (2010b: x). The last 50 years have seen an alarming depletion in ground water levels, greedy exploitation of minerals, denudation of forest cover and a hole in the ozone layer; the human race is at the brink of a catastrophe from which there might be no recovery. It is here that we arrive at one of the central dilemmas of the development ethos. The ethics of development is based on a founding principle: the idea of "comparative equity" – that the earth's resources be divided and shared in equal measure by all. Into the second decade of the 21st century, there is almost no contesting that the earth has limited resources and a major share of it has been used up by the rich nations. Indeed, no more industrial revolutions can take place; the earth simply doesn't have enough in its coffers. If all of the world were suddenly to reach a Western level of living standard, we would need "five or six planets" to take the load (Sachs 2010a: xvii). There can be no comparative equity.

Yet, the common refrain heard at every climate summit from every Southern corner is their "right to develop." Poor countries contend, and justly, that they must be given their due share of the resources and the atmosphere to develop.

> The longing for greater justice on the part of the South is one reason for the persistence of the development creed – even if, in this century, neither the planet nor the people of the world can any longer afford its predominance (ibid.: xvii).

The pursuit of "economic justice," the realignment of the financial world and the insidious forces of globalization have helped the rise of the Southern powers – China, Brazil and India being at the forefront of a Gross Domestic Product (GDP) driven revolution. For them it is as if President Truman's promise at the birth of the development period in 1949 – that poor nations would catch up with the rich – had finally come true.

As a result of this shift development came to mean the formation of a global middle class alongside the spread of the transnational economic complex rather than a national middle class alongside the integration of a national economy. Seen from this perspective, it comes as no surprise that the age of globalization has produced a transnational class of winners (ibid.).

Today Indian tourists book out Thomas Cook charter flights to Paris and Beijing's cheap workforce keeps the global consumer industry afloat. But it is problematic to celebrate this as a "revival of the South," when it represents a shift and not an end to inequality. This, as Sachs and Esteva argue, is the legacy of development policies which have espoused a notion of comparative equity, where nations should have a fair share of the world's wealth, and not absolute equity which recognizes the individual's right to a fair share.

Indeed, southern countries have managed to raise their economic profile significantly, but development policies, falling short of absolute justice, have left more than half of the world's population still without the right of access to food, shelter, clean air, water and basic health care. In Sach's stark words:

> The globally oriented middle classes, although they push for development in the name of greater equality, largely disregard the plight of the poor . . . In just about all newly industrialising countries, social polarisation has been on the rise along with growth rates over the past thirty years (Sachs 2010b: x).

The earlier victims of inequality were the poor nations; today when money and influence are turning increasingly transnational, the dominated are the global poor. As Esteva explains in the same volume, the poor are not simply left poor; their means of resistance to hegemony is simultaneously undermined:

> Redevelopment implies the economic colonisation of the so called informal sector. In the name of modernisation and under the banner of the war on poverty – pitting as always the waged against the poor, not a war on poverty itself – redeveloping the south involves launching the last and definitive assault against organised resistance to development and economy (2010: 13).

By the 1980s, development had lost its sheen. The assorted crisis of the previous 40 years provided overwhelming evidence that we were headed towards a catastrophe. The shift from the discourse of development to climate change in the mid-1990s was therefore enthusiastically received. By the turn of the century, Southern countries were clamoring for more money for adaptation and mitigation rather than for poverty alleviation programs while Northern countries wanted to see significant reductions in carbon emissions instead of photos of happy children receiving food packets. The paradigms – aid flow and access to markets – remained; the lexicon changed.

There were however two crucial differences. First, as stated here, environmental consequences obey no cartographical constraints. This allowed Southern countries, to put it politely, more powers of leverage. A hungry face might prick your conscience; the disappearance of green covers will have a more direct health impact globally. Poor African countries now demand payment not to denude their forest covers, forcing rich countries to act.

Second, the economic situation has changed drastically since the last century. The ascendancy of Southern countries, especially BRICS, has changed global economic equations. Take India for example. In 2005 the Government of India made conscious and drastic changes in the aid framework. The Department of Economic Affairs (DEA), Ministry of Finance, issued the Guidelines for Development with bi-lateral partners. All donors providing more than $25 million of untied aid were welcome in the country. G8 countries continued to be able to operate but in practice most small donors closed their India offices.

While the ramifications of this are too complex and manifold to be adequately dealt with here, it is clear that India's position in the aid market was no longer being determined for it. Following the regulations, and in recognition of continued economic growth, India is now in a position to openly demand specific aid solutions.

India's stance, though on the surface seemingly heavy handed and arrogant for a country where more than 400 million live below the poverty line, is not in any obvious discord with how affluent nation states approach environmental concerns. The Indian government is following its richer cousins in attempting to appropriate the space for discussion on lives, livelihoods, wealth, food and water security, coastal ecology, economic development, bio diversity, energy security and well-being among other things – under the rubric of environmental concerns – to be isolated and managed.

Pigeonholing "environment" as a problem to be solved, isolating it from the larger processes of global economy and demarcating its boundaries, has allowed governments and multinational corporations to appoint environmental governance committees, managers and executives to solve the "problem." This isolation allows our governments to be seen as fighting a particular crisis; it masks the complicated, interconnected nature of environmental degradation that permeates the ordinary everyday lifestyle choices we make, slips past political and physical boundaries and is affected by policy decisions far removed from the environment ministries that national governments set up.

Besides being isolated as a problem to be solved by governments, the environment is also used as a blanket term to cover a host of issues, each with its own urgency. Campaigners fight for the rights of polar bears in the Arctic, others clash with mining companies for tribal rights in Orissa, politicians legislate on protection of forests on the one hand while the poor demand their rights to the same for survival on the other – all under the rubric of environmental activism and its protection. Whose rights are more justified? What can be put in the back burner to be tackled later or maybe never at all?

Debates around the environment is in reality therefore a debate on the state of our democracy, reflecting who we are and the kind of society we live in or want to live in. Isolating it as a problem to be "managed" or using the term for everything – from a cyclone in California to a washing machine advertisement in India, so widely that it becomes an empty signifier – is unhelpful. At the same time, it gives rise to other related problems. Vested interest groups including national governments, activists and academics have employed such umbrella usage to derail policies while corporate houses have lobbied to push for policies to "manage" environmental concerns.

Despite the dominance of the state, its limitations in environmental governance and negotiations are now understood and the last decade of the 20th century has seen the civil society, especially non-governmental organizations (NGOs) marking their presence in international environmental negotiations. The first most visible demonstration came at the 1992 United Nations (UN) Conference on Environment and Development at Rio de Janeiro where over 1,400 NGOs negotiated alternative treaties and engaged in extensive networking (Chatterjee and Finger 1994). In recent years, the debate on the role of NGOs and the state in environmental regulation has intensified with a host of academic writing and media focus making environment, at least in the global North, a mainstream discourse. But in this either/or debate, what gets ignored is a host of other actors, including quasi-state institutions that have jumped on the environmental bandwagon through multiple means to push particular agendas. With rapid strides in communication technology transforming traditional power bases and creating new modalities of power and influence, the state is adopting newer modes of control through various institutions and governmental assemblages (the G8, G20, G77 are examples of the latter). Civil society resistance and co-operation finds new collaborators. The financial system, educational and research institutions, the media – both traditional and new – form part of this matrix that determine global environmental politics and its agenda.

Social research on environmental politics however remains exclusive, focusing on the traditional state or, more recently, on the role of the civil society. This tunnel vision does not account for the complexity of today's environmental politics, the multiple actors and their diverse allegiances.

In trying to organize a conversation around environment, from which this volume springs, the first problem was therefore this: where do we start and what do we include? If environment and environmentalism includes everything, clearly choices had to be made.

Democracy, we know, is negotiated. In the fight for justice, rights and equity, precedence is given to issues; others are put in the back-burner and the media plays an important role in this. Never neutral, the media creates discourses, builds campaign and awareness, adopts and discards issues. Politics is mediated in myriad ways through newspapers and news channels, through mobile telephony and through social networking sites. Twittering brings down politicians and starts careers and conversations. Avant-garde cinema, experimental documentaries along with mainstream Hollywood tackle a variety of political issues, from urban poverty to environmental doomsday predictions. More and more people are made aware of an incredibly broad range of issues today than perhaps ever before in human history and the media and its related technology has played the biggest role in this. As the first decade of the new century draws to a close, environment emerges as the new discourse. It pits nations against each other, the rich versus the poor. Even activists squabble over which environmental issue should be given more prominence.

Using these notions, democracy and the role of the media as a point of entry, this collection is an exploration of environmental politics and activism and of how the media and related technology has aided and influenced the discourse. The collection of essays in the volume brings together academics, activists and practitioners working on a range of topics related to issues of environmental justice, equity, the role of the youth, of newspapers, magazines and 24-hour television – each examining how the media discourse and politics around environment are being shaped.

Emerging primarily out of a two-day conference held in New Delhi in December 2010, the volume has several case studies from India. Yet, it explores the geo-politics of environmental discourse by examining situations in (to use UN abbreviations) Least Developed Countries (Ethiopia) and in Latin American countries (Brazil) which are now joining the emerging economies and thus shifting their political alliances in international meets.

The first two chapters lay out some of the theoretical frameworks. Hanna Werner (Chapter 1) argues that a certain hegemonic notion of development imposes a normative limit to its critique. Articulations of resistance are determined by the limits of a discursive framework that builds its legacy upon positivist developmental politics and alleged contemporary needs are used to justify particular sacrifices in order to serve the greater common good. This, she argues, not only diminishes the range of accountable semantics to speak about the losers of modernity, but also covers the fact that the implicit notions of development and national progress that guideline the hegemonic discourse are conceivably not as self-evident as they appear. This happens not least through the appropriation of language that accompanies the symptom-oriented policy of the new spirit of capitalism and considerably affects the space in which critique can be articulated. Any critique/activism that responds to the pragmatism of developmental politics faces the dilemma of how to engage with its paradigms. Articulation and practice, however, often vary considerably. Environmental activism has undeniably played a significant role in impacting discourses and decisions on development project implementation in India – within but also beyond the realm of mainstream political discourse. The creative performance of socio-ecological movements shows that there are still various substantial possibilities to write – and enact – the history of Indian development. Werner's chapter aims at exploring such spaces of dissent, taking reference to the narration of *Chipko*, one of the most popular environmental movements in post-independent India.

Spurred by his meeting with a fake polar bear at the 2009 United Nations Climate Change Conference (also commonly now known as COP 15) at Copenhagen and its hyper-mediated framework, cultural theorist Matti Pohjonen literally decides to get his hand dirty. His chapter extends the critique of development aid raised in the previous chapter by understanding it in practice. "Counting trees" in Ethiopia, Pohjonen worked on a pilot development project whose aim was to use mobile phones to develop a new method to calculate carbon dioxide sequestration in trees in smallholder farms (Chapter 2). Pohjonen critiques his own practices and the politics of development aid funding which neglects local knowledge and relies on a dominant scientific–technological discourse. Part critique of development theory and part a reflection on practice, Pohjonen's chapter along with Werner's open up the spaces for examination of particular case studies that appear in the final section of this book. The next section deals with the media and environmental discourse, focusing on India in the new century. The rapid increase in the number of private television channels and competition for limited advertising budgets have given rise to concerns and criticism of news channels for abdicating social responsibility and catering to the lowest common denominator. Television journalist Smita Maitra and producer of India's biggest and extremely popular environmental news show *Greenathon* steps into the debate and argues for a middle-class environmentalism articulated through mass media. Maitra stresses the usage of the popular and the recognizable, such as Bollywood and its stars, in the production of socially relevant television content. In doing so, she argues for "reformist environmentalism as an absolute value," seeking a "valid cultural discursive space for the *Greenathon* and all its future avatars" (Chapter 3). The chapter focuses on the program concept and its execution and attempts to highlight how "a dry subject like the environment" can be brought into urban drawing rooms (ibid.).

In my chapter (Chapter 4), I argue to the contrary. It is an examination of how the mainstream media handled two separate, yet interlinked issues, the campaign for Clean Air in Delhi in the 1990s and the drive against the Bus Rapid Transport (BRT) system in 2010. It states that a middle class-obsessed media narrative has shifted the environmental discourse in the country from predominantly an "environmentalism of the poor" (Guha and Martinez-Alier 1998: 70) to urban issues that concern the privileged and the wealthy, thereby limiting the possibilities and the scope of its politics.

The divide between rural and urban India is no more an imaginary trope of poverty versus munificence, calm against pace or the idyllic pitted against a loss of innocence. The Indian Home Minister recently announced that the state wanted rural people to move from their villages to the cities, giving governmental intentions a concrete shape. Pratap Pandey (Chapter 5) visits the mainstream media in his chapter to examine how the rural–urban divide is framed and uses it to analyze India's development trajectory and environmental policies.

The final chapter of this section focuses on the need that the mainstream media has for new stories and spectacles. Taking up the case of the victims of the Bhopal Gas Tragedy, it discusses how protest movements in India use the bodies of victims as sites for spectacles thereby satisfying the media's unrelenting quest and exploiting it. Taking case illustrations from the disaster victims' struggle, Shalini Sharma (Chapter 6) shows how the movement draws on "body" as the message articulating a political ideology and how this politics of representation contests the politics of the state.

The third section, "Case Studies: India and the World," has three case studies, both from India and elsewhere. In the first chapter, Bharati Chaturvedi (Chapter 7), an environmental campaigner, activist and writer, frames the issues of the informal waste management sector against a global backdrop of injustice. She looks at local issues in her daily work at Chintan, an organization which besides other concerns, works with rag pickers in Delhi, and examines the utility of connecting these to existent global networks.

"Our World," ran the slogan of the Youth Campaign in COP 15 at Copenhagen in 2009. The youth are the stakeholders of the future and rarely since the counter culture movement of the 1960s in the US, have they played such a defining role as they are playing in the movement for environmental justice. Kartikeya Singh (Chapter 8), one of the founders of the International Youth Climate Movement (IYCN), examines the processes of a fledgling campaign as it seeks political legitimacy. Through various case studies and his own experience of running a global movement, Singh shows how innovation and zest can attempt to counter pessimism and the politics of the usual.

The third case study examines how the state and the youth movement have collaborated in Brazil – part of the BRICS and one of the most important growing economies in the world with its attendant environmental worries. This chapter analyzes the development of the Environmental Collectives of Youth (CJMAs) in Brazil, detailing the case study of the Environmental Collective of Goiás Youth (CJMA-GO). This particular social movement started with a Brazilian federal government initiative, organizing a national conference that brought young people together. Originally the aim was the formation of a group of young environmental leaders who would take part in this conference that provided subsidies for the formulation of national public policies towards youth and the environment, such as the National Program of Youth and the Environment. However, some other results originating from this conference process went far beyond the original intentions, with the young people involved in the process developing a socio-environmental movement with its own specificities.

It is necessary here to flag a few things. First, given that we have argued that environmental concerns and its surrounding politics should not be isolated or boxed, we open ourselves to everything. Everything cannot be contained in a volume and this book must not be read as a comprehensive guide. Instead, we have dipped into certain snapshots that highlight the book's and its contributors' concerns.

Our concerns might be similar; our politics, not necessarily. In fact, in certain chapters, we forward contradictory arguments. For example, Smita Maitra (Chapter 3) argues for a middle-class reformist environmental agenda. I state that the middle-class discourse risks the pushing of a bourgeois agenda that marginalizes millions. If Kartikeya Singh (Chapter 8) writes about the global movement of the youth which allows the latter to carve out a political space for itself, Tiago Rodrigues (Chapter 9) examines case studies where the state and the youth movement collaborate to create civic and political awareness.

The writing styles too, differ vastly. Hanna Werner and Matti Pohjonen, well versed in the academic language of the best universities, write with caution. They forward arguments carefully with a nuanced understanding of cultural and social theory as well as that of developmental politics. Singh however writes with the enthusiasm and hope that his brand of politics deserves. As an editor, I have not tried to ensure uniformity and instead, welcome the diverse.

The focal point of this book of course is the environment; each of the authors is involved with its politics, be it research or activism. But having drawn from a wide array of interests, we hope to transcend the insularity of the environmental debate and insist on a larger canvas that can encompass the concerns.

What conclusions can we draw from the various viewpoints presented in this volume? First and foremost, our politics are changing even if our politicians fail or steadfastly refuse to see it. The politics of the last few centuries was mainly about power, be it the fight amongst nation states or individuals, the gender battles or sexual discrimination, identity politics or collective bargaining. With the ecological disaster that stares us in the face, power as we have studied it, has been dramatically altered. At least theoretically, the poor or the disempowered can do as much harm to the ecology as the rich and powerful. In fact, the rich – both nation states and human beings – have successfully portrayed the poor as the culprits. In practice, the rich and powerful have done much more damage, simply because they have the resources to do so. The problem lies in the fact that everyone is affected no matter who causes the damage. There are no permanent safe havens. The relationship between the powerful and the powerless therefore has permanently altered. It is in this altered scenario that we must rethink social theory and social activism.

Second, as there are no safe havens, there is nothing that can be excluded. All our actions affect the environment. Much more education, awareness and thought must go into it than the meagre resources now allotted to companies to "green" their product or schools to include "environment" in the curriculum.

Third, and perhaps most importantly, there are no conclusions. It is in fact dangerous to conclude a conversation whose contours have just begun to take shape, whose politics and ramifications we are yet to fully understand. What we as writers of this volume have tried to do is show that there is no unifying, easy singular theme to this debate; no one remedy, no easy solutions.

While this lack of focus has allowed us to prevaricate, searching as we are for an identifiable enemy, what we are today confronted with is a unique set of problems. The old politics are not so much invalid as they are inadequate. As Gilles Deleuze said "[t]here is no need to fear or hope, but only to find new weapons" (1992: 3–7).

Note

1. From Barack Obama's first Presidential victory speech. http://www.youtube.com/watch?v=I0tuAJkbUWU. As accessed on January 27, 2014.

References

Chatterjee, P. and M. Finger. 1994. *The Earth Brokers: Power, Politics and World Development*. London: Routledge.

Deleuze, G. 1992. "Postscript on the Societies of Control," *October*, 59 (Winter): 3–7.

Esteva, G. 2010. "Development," in Wolfgang Sachs (ed.), *The Development Dictionary: A Guide to Knowledge as Power.* London and New York: Zed Books.

Guha, R. and J. Martinez-Alier. 1998. *Varieties of Environmentalism: Essays North and South.* Delhi: Oxford University Press.

Sachs, W. 2010a. "Introduction," in *The Development Dictionary: A Guide to Knowledge as Power.* London and New York: Zed Books.

————. 2010b. "Preface to the New Edition," in *The Development Dictionary: A Guide to Knowledge as Power.* London and New York: Zed Books.

The Guardian. 2010. "Cameron: I Want Coalition to be the 'Greenest Government Ever,'" May 14. http://www.theguardian.com/environment/2010/may/14/cameron-wants-greenest-government-ever. As accessed on January 27, 2014.

Truman, H. S. 1949. "Inaugural Address," in Gerhard Peters and John T. Woolley, *The American Presidency Project,* January 20. http://www.presidency.ucsb.edu/ws/?pid=13282. As accessed on January 14, 2014.

Wapner, P. 1996. *Environmental Activism and World Civic Politics.* Albany: State University of New York Press.

PART I

Theoretical Frameworks

1

The (Im)possibility of Critique in Developmental Debates

*Hanna Werner**

"We are not against development, but . . ." is an oft-heard statement in debates that focus on worldwide economic disparities and the disadvantages of global capitalism. Alleged development critics reassure their audiences that they generally agree with over-all developmental paradigms before pointing out inequalities with regard to resource access and the distribution of developmental benefits. What, by and large, follows this rehearsed structure of argument is the plea for an "alternative" approach. Development is not questioned *per se*, but problematized with regard to the adverse outputs or rather symptoms it produces if implemented inadequately.[1] Hence, the demands for conceptual fine-tuning include criteria such as sustainability, equal distribution of developmental benefits and so forth.[2]

There is no doubt that those voices have been an indispensable – and quite often the only – challenge to post-colonial inequities by influencing decision-making processes and thus ameliorating conditions. Nevertheless, the question arises of why the reaffirmation of the prevailing discourse is apparently seen as a necessary precondition to articulate one's critique. Signalizing general accordance seems to be a prerequisite for any critical standpoint to make itself heard within the statist developmental discourse. The debate often appears as a call and response game, in which mutual concessions are made and adjustments are formulated. The articulation of a straightforward "no" to statist paradigms seems virtually impossible, if they are propagated as inevitable *realpolitik* choices.[3] I will come back to that. To begin with, I suggest that the reason for these (normative) limitations lies neither in the inability of the critics or activists to clarify their position, nor in the forceful oppression of their voices (although that is certainly part of the dilemma), but, if nothing else, in the way critique itself functions as a discursive, historical concept. Critique does not merely denote a constellation of modes of applied dissent, but a theoretical range of potential reactions to disconcerting social realms. Setting aside the question of content for an instant, let us ask: "What is critique?" (Foucault 1992).

This chapter is divided into three major parts. Initially, I will examine the etymological and conceptual trajectory of the term "criticism" and illustrate the "network of idiomatic correlations" in which critique is situated in order to understand its (shifting) functionality within a given social order (Röttgers 1975: 15). Departing from this theoretical contextualization, the second part deals with environmental activism in post-independence India, focusing on the analysis of *Chipko*, one of the country's most popular environmental movements in the later 20th century. The final section of the chapter concludes with some remarks on the political potential of merging strategies of dissent and conceptual meta-critique.

Spaces of Critique

Criticism[4] as a concept is part of a cultural consensus which, in the "West" at least, has been in place since the Enlightenment; however, it has been fiercely contested ever since. This can be seen in the monopolizing tendencies of various theoretical attempts during the last century to "capture" the term, such as Critical Theory, Critical Rationalism and so forth (Röttgers 1975: 1).

Deriving from the Greek root "krino," critique etymologically means "to separate," "to judge" and "to decide."[5] In ancient Greece, the concept of critique was used mainly for the sphere of law and medicine (Röttgers 1982: 651). At the same time, a use of the term in the spheres of grammar and philological textual criticism developed. This emphasis seems to have been dropped altogether in the Middle Ages, and was only taken up again during the Renaissance. From the beginning of the 17th century, one finds a more generalized application of the term in the realms of philology, logic and aesthetics, which significantly alters the function as well as the spatial scope of critique

(Röttgers 1975: 19; Bormann 1976: 1249ff.). This (social) generaliza-
tion culminates in the amplification of the term "Kritik" by Kant, who
elevates critique, or rather the ability of making critical deductions, to
the status of a universal human condition under which every judgment
of the higher human faculties has to be subsumed. Being thought of as
ubiquitous, critique nevertheless remained restricted to the cognitive
sphere, i.e., reasoning. An expansion of the concept of criticism to
the social mainstream did not take place until the beginning of the
20th century (Röttgers 1982: 615).

With the advent of the Enlightenment, a fundamental turn seems
to have taken place as far as the social role or rather duty of the critic
is concerned.[6] Kant states in his writings that the most important
feature that characterizes a responsible stance towards the (modern)
present is an informed, namely "enlightened" attitude and reflection (1996[1783]: 11). To be aware of the present and its needs has
ever since been one of the foremost tasks of the intellectual critic.
Subsequently, social criticism implies a strategic political dimension,
which makes it a "task" located somewhere between theory and practice. It is located in and targets the social realm (as compared to an
abstract philosophical realm), in which the potential and limitations
of its development, the forms of its practical political implementation
and, last but not least, the social role and location of the critic are to
be found and defined.

Since the societal turn has shaped our understanding of criticism, it seems useful to elucidate some fundamental attributes of
critique as an explicitly social concept. The common contemporary
notion of critique implies an essentially destructive notion of "saying no" – no to something, no to someone (Geuss 2000: 274ff.). This
negative connotation is often seen as socially deviant and thus unac-
ceptable. It has become a common place that critical articulation
should be of a constructive nature and provide alternatives to the
criticized subject, if it aims at obtaining a valid status. The demand
of suggesting alternatives is a particularly interesting issue, since it
deludes observers into overlooking the contingent character of the
status quo, namely the fact that it has been the result of a selective
rejection of historical choices. Ultimately, it is the normative precondition of critique itself – as a historically constructed concept –
that restricts the possible scope of its endeavor. Critical evaluations
of performances and accomplishments correspond with "laws" of

cultural taste and value; i.e., consensual societal reference points that limit the possible range of their own articulations. Cultural and political hegemony provide the yardstick by which a critical articulation must prove its legitimacy and is subsequently accepted as appropriate or rejected as inadequate. As we shall see, this has strong implications on the discursive horizon where critique can develop, and this varies considerably over space and time.

Critique seems hardly conceivable without an object of reference that predetermines its form and content. As part of a "language game of reasoning," critique appears as a reciprocal discursive tool that navigates between the ascription of legitimate meaning on the one hand and a reactive act of confession, justification or rejection on the other (Geuss 2000: 249). The social position of the critic seems to be one of the most decisive factors in claiming legitimacy and hints at the often problematized disparity between critical practice and the theoretical formulation of a fundamental critique. In relation to the criticized object, one can distinguish between two contrary locations. It is either "internal," an immanent, interpretive criticism described for example by Michael Walzer, who assumes that social and cultural loyalty is a structural precondition of critical articulation (2000: 709ff.); or else it is thought of as an "external" critique, which claims that the distance of the critic from the criticized society is an essential prerequisite of his objectivity in terms of knowledge, reference and judgment. This, though depicted somewhat simplistically, reflects the position of the early Frankfurt School. Another description that illustrates this distinction is the differentiation between "strong" and "weak" criticism (O'Neill 2000: 719ff.). "Weak" criticism describes a form of dissent that situates an antagonistic standpoint within the given social realm and could therefore be labeled reformative. A "strong" criticism, on the contrary, requires a point of reference that transcends the given social context- and looks for an alternative to the criticized object/ society in the form of an aspired ideal outside the existing (social) order. The ascendancy of Critical Theory is a prominent example of a context-transcending model of critique; by reverting to an extra-social ideal of reasoning, it formulates all points of critical reference as a radical "outside" to the existing society and thus breaks with Hegel's idea that everything that is real is also reasonable (Adorno 1971: 12). Critique is said to be an essential element in any democratic social order, since, following Adorno, the potential of democratic participation lies in the ability to distinguish between knowledge as cognitive realization and the mere acceptance of a conventional or authoritarian imposition (ibid.: 10ff.). In line with Marx's argument, critique is thought to be indispensable for the preparation of action. This form of criticism, which explicitly aims at social change, can be disassociated from another form of critique that is often found in poststructuralist theory, for example in Foucault's adaptation of Nietzsche's genealogical method (Foucault 1974). Critique – as in Critical Theory – consists of exposing ideological delusion; it ultimately aims at transformation, and thus opens the gateway for practical dissent. The main target of this type of criticism is the actually existing social condition and its legitimizing structure in the form of hegemonic consensus. As opposed to that, the poststructuralist model does not make an assumed factual reality, but rather the conditions of its construction and perception its focus. Rather than formulating a critique of reality as such, the categories of its production as essentially contingent are taken into consideration. The result is a "second-order critique" that focuses on the critical deconstruction of the *modus operandi* of critique itself as such, a (historical) concept. Such an approach differs significantly from ideology critique, since it replaces ideology – in its classic, Marxian meaning – with perspective (as social position) and thus considers every position as necessarily ideological; it deconstructs the process of its development as social "truth" as much as it questions the "objective" possibilities of its cognitive perception.[7]

With reference to development critique one could exemplify this difference as follows: a classical critical approach targets development as an ideology which relies on promises of equality, but ultimately benefits only a selected few. The "second-order" approach, on the contrary, aims at illustrating the historical conditions that led to a situation in which development – with all its meta-narratives ranging from progress to sustainability in its later, self-reflective phases – could emerge as an inevitable, largely beneficial concept regardless of "practical failures." The acknowledgement of the contingent and fractional character of developmental perspectives leads to an idea of critique that aims at deconstructing the process of the historical formation of normative concepts of sociality rather than merely criticizing the adverse symptoms of their (insufficient) implementation.[8]

Referring to its conceptual history, critique appears as a deconstructivist approach, an attitude, an action, a pre-theoretical judgment or a combination of these components. Subsequently, a possible answer to the question "what is critique" requires an analysis of the given context. Let us therefore continue with a closer scrutiny of the "practical" side of critique, namely matter-of-fact dissent in the form of social activism against hydropower projects in India.

The Realms of Activism

The following quotation which hints at the limitations of the anti-dam movement in India exemplifies a "classic" model of critical semantics and illustrates the major problem this chapter deals with: "As long as the paradigm of resistance does not base itself on the foundation of economic logic and political organization, the national and sub-national establishments will continue to ignore, resist or evade the anti-dam activists" (Dixit 2007: 20). Many voices, ranging from social activists to intellectuals, subscribe to the same basic perspective. The problem of not obtaining a powerful voice is located in the inability of the critical articulation to adopt the semantic logic predetermined by the given hegemonic discourse. Hence, one needs to ask how the (globalized) developmental discourse – in which social activists participate and to which they respond in their aim of being heard – functions, and what, ultimately, the reasons for achieving a substantial speaker position within it are. Though (the access to) language is the most significant factor, I suggest that a semantic analysis would not be able to explain this quandary entirely and, most importantly, would not include perspectives which would enable us to transcend these discursive limitations. A discursive field, an "episteme," to use Foucault's terminology, consists of more than just speech acts. It is in particular the performative act, in which glimpses of subversion are to be found.[9] Hence, we have to direct our attention to the level of actors.

Activists and social movements play a major role as non-governmental actors that – more or less effectively – impact discourses and decisions of implementations of development projects and/or create public awareness for controversial social issues. Their articulations reflect the amplification of the divergence between the agenda of the state and its subjects. An essential role and function of movements is to confront the state with the "counter-image" of a potentially different society, a vision that might once have been and could still be possible. "Social movement" – with reference to environmental issues also "socio-ecological movement" – is used here as a relatively wide term referring to a more or less enduring conglomerate of political action and articulation by a group of people or a network of groups; an outgrowth of civil society against the alleged misgovernance of the state or its corporates as manifested explicitly in coercively imposed, non-participatory "developmental" programs or projects.[10] A vision of social change is integral to the formation of social movements. I favor such a broad definition, since it is quite often not easy – and analytically not advantageous – to distinguish between movements, agitations, and other forms of protest. I suggest that such a differentiation makes sense only with regard to the analysis of particular histories of emerging protest to understand their implications and to evaluate their scope. By and large, the categorization as a "movement" occurs *a posteriori.* The participant groups can include locally affected people, activists, members of one or the other non-governmental organization (NGO), intellectuals, research institutions and other civic groups; their allies are often overlapping, and their agendas not clearly distinguishable. Yet it is important to make a distinction between different groups and the trajectories they follow with regard to questions of (global) alliances, funding, agendas and issues of political representation.

What has informed the reflections presented here was an engagement with the (historical) legacies and modes of resistance practised by the movements. Socio-ecological movements all over the Indian subcontinent have acquired great significance not least due to the participation of prominent "Gandhian" intellectuals and activists. They draw their legitimization not only from a Gandhian heritage and include notions of belief and practice that are closely embedded in regional histories and trajectories, but also adapt elements of global environmentalist movements and political thought. Thus, there is a connection with specific debates on development and modernity in India on the one hand, but an equally obvious linkage with concepts of transnational social and environmental criticism on the other.

A key example for the analysis of socio-ecological movements in India is certainly the *Chipko Andolan* (movement) and its antecedents in the region that is today the state of Uttarakhand. It still serves as a vital reference point for contemporary local agitations that trace their history and legacy to *Chipko.* Whether in songs, in contemporary political slogans, or in accounts of former leaders and their successes – *Chipko* is part of the collective memory of the region and the resistance against the Tehri dam is explicitly placed in this historical narrative.

The *Chipko Andolan* evolved in the early 1970s and came to be known worldwide as the "Hug the trees"-movement, not least through the involvement of one of its assumed leaders, Sunderlal Bahuguna. The movement was supposedly the first environmental movement of its size in South Asia and has played a pioneering role for later agitations such as the opposition to hydropower projects in the region, and also for struggles in other parts of the country. However, several problematic aspects have been pointed out, ranging from shifting intentions in the course of the movement, namely "environmentalism versus economic welfare of the region" to the deprivation of the local population due to its dogmatic environmentalist approach, the discord among the protagonists and so forth. Well-known authors have documented the history and impact of the social movements of the region, including Bharat Dogra (1992), Ramachandra Guha (1989) and Vandana Shiva (1991), who has become known not least through the strong focus on women in her interpretation of the movement. There are several others, who have written comprehensively about the movement, such as Haripriya Rangan (2000) and the anthropologist Antje Linkenbach (1994).

What is quite striking is the more or less openly articulated asymmetry that exists between academic accounts of the movement and the variety of local perceptions that claim originality. To illustrate the image that *Chipko* has created in the minds of many (scholars), I make use of a longish passage from Haripriya Rangan's "Of Myths and Movements," since it serves not only as a good, though somewhat cynical summary of the movement's reception, but also hints at a number of the theoretical predicaments I am dealing with in this chapter:

> There was a time when the people of the Garhwal Himalaya – through centuries of isolation and learning from their surroundings – lived in harmonious and peaceful coexistence with nature ... Then, more than thirty years ago, after India's war against China, this peaceful idyll was disrupted. The Indian government no longer wished to lose any more territory in the Himalayas and therefore resolved to bring its border regions firmly under its control ... Timber merchants poured in from outside, bringing labourers with them to clear large forest tracts. Single-minded in their pursuit of profits, they soon left behind degraded and barren landscapes ... Soon the people of Garhwal could bear this

destruction no more . . . And so, the story goes on, the people got together and devised a plan. Each time the lumbermen were sent out to fell trees in the forest, people from nearby villages ran out to hug the trees and persuaded the labourers to go away. They gathered together at felling sites and chanted the question, "What do forests bear?"; the gathering gave the answering chant, "Soil, water and pure air." They were successful each time . . . Soon this tree-hugging strategy came to be known as *chipko*, which means stick to, or adhere to, in both Garhwali and Hindi. Gradually, people from the cities − students, activists and intellectuals − began hearing of Chipko. They rushed to support the cause, and spread the message of the movement across the country. They joined the leaders of the Chipko movement in their criticism of the Indian government's ecologically destructive forest policies. The government finally yielded to pressure and acknowledged the error of its ways . . . Chipko was hailed as India's civilizational response to the ecological crisis and became an inspiration for numerous grassroots activities and the emergence of ecologically sensitive approaches to development in the Garhwal Himalaya (Rangan 2000: 4ff.).

The passage not only illustrates the trajectory of *Chipko* from being a local movement to becoming a more or less decontextualized narrative existing of its own accord, it also raises questions concerning authorship, reception and representation of the movement. As the author herself remarks, any critical remark with regard to the *local* reception of the movement and its transformation − from a more or less economically motivated struggle for the improvement of local industry and livelihoods to an environmental movement with a global reach and audience aiming at conservation and sustainability − is absent in the quoted passage. Ultimately, the essential question is: "[h]ow did Chipko come to be transformed from a strategy of protest by groups demanding concessions for forest-based industrial development in Garhwal, into an 'ecological movement of permanent economy'?" (ibid.: 21ff.) According to Rangan, the answer to this question lies in the way in which narratives produce normative effects, claiming authority, morality and authenticity.[11] Environmentalist narratives such as those associated with *Chipko*, Rangan says, are "particular forms through which social power is gained, asserted, and reinforced by narrators in various spaces of political discourse" (ibid.: 19). The implicit aim is to reshape social and material life through modes of deliberate dismissing, inclusion and representation. Rangan argues that by transforming it into a "transnational icon" (ibid.: 15), the meaning of *Chipko* has shifted from a historical event into a myth in the sense Roland Barthes uses the term, meaning it does not refer to a legend, an "untruth" or ideal-typical conception, but a way of constructing images that attribute symbolic meanings to particular objects, places, contexts or social practices (Rangan 2000: 10). Hence, it does not imply an idea of "falseness," but a shift in the allusion of significance.[12] By being narrated like a myth, the story of the movement was detached from its local origin and transcended the geographical and historical context. This often led to a reception that differed significantly from local interpretations.

In their "globalized," decontextualized form, movements or rather the narrations of movements gains a significant role. I think one can agree with Antje Linkenbach, who says in "Ecological Movements and the Critique of Development":

> For two reasons, ecological movements . . . seem to have a great attraction for Western and Indian critics of development . . . For them social movements are testifying to the uprising of the depressed, making audible the voices of those who now can no longer be seen only as victims, but from now on have to be recognized as agents, fully responsible for their future, actively trying to change their situation . . . The interpretation of ecological movements thus leads to mystification, heroization and oversimplification; movements are functionalized and 'used' according to the interests of the interpreters (1994: 68ff.).

The question of representation this quotation poses is essential with regard to the theoretical analysis of social critique: who is the "authentic" (as against the interpretative) voice of the movement and what are its aims? Is it those directly affected, the (assumed) leaders of the movement, the urban middle class or the intellectual interlocutors? And whose voice eventually prevails within the discursive framework which defines the "developmental needs" and influences their subsequent implementation?[13]

In order to address these questions, Haripriya Rangan pleads in "Myths and Movements" for a re-contextualization of movements and the narratives that inform their perception. This approach, however, poses another question: arguably, a number of concerns, i.e., comparative approaches of transcultural importance arise only when the movement and its strategies are dealt with in a de-contextualized setting. To give an example: is Uttarakhand, as Ramachandra Guha asserts with reference to James Scott, a "landscape of resistance" (1989: 5)? These labels sound promising and inspiring, especially for an academic in search of hints and glimpses of "another world possible." But they can be misleading if (political) ascriptions overwhelm a careful differentiation of actual aims and agendas. De-contextualization can easily generate oversimplifications and broad statements which could fail to notice regional particularities. Guha argues that the narrative of *Chipko* which has reached the world is not comparable with what he calls the original "peasant ideology" that guided *Chipko*. For him, *Chipko* is primarily a peasant movement, and although a lot of later analyses have focused on its key strategies under various labels, they did not reflect the movement's internal state. For instance, while *Chipko* may have involved women, adopted Gandhian non-violent strategies and raised popular awareness towards environmental problems in the Himalayas, it cannot, according to Guha, be described as either an environmental, Gandhian, or feminist movement as such. For Guha, *Chipko* is primarily a social movement with the "public" identity of an environmental movement and the "private" identity of a peasant movement (Guha 1989: 187, quoted from Rangan 2000: 39).

What is theoretically highly interesting in this context is how assumptions are turned into somewhat inaccessible statements through narratives that invoke discursive "historical common goods"[14] like "Gandhian" principles and allegedly universal environmental and developmental concerns. One might ask from where "Gandhians" who are using labels ranging from "Indian spirituality" to "environmentalism," from "spiritually informed science and technology" to Christian sermon obtain their legitimacy. Within such an abstract reading, Gandhian philosophy appears as a transcultural array of thoughts and practices, expressed in performances of dissent, at times customary, at times unconventional, but continuously integrated in a discursive framework that guarantees the consistency of their argument within contemporary political thought. With reference to these "meta-narratives" one might, for instance, ask for the case of *Chipko*: were the strategies of dissent used by the movement "Gandhian" and are therefore the movement's protagonists such as Sunderlal Bahuguna Gandhians? Was *Chipko* the first and most influential eco-feminist movement in the world, since it appears that women played the major part? The answers to such considerations obviously correspond to prior definitions.

The study of contemporary forms and acts of resistance in the region shows that there is still a strong reference to such narratives. Environmental activism still plays a vital role in the region of Uttarakhand. Many of those who have been actively or passively part of *Chipko* still subscribe to a "Gandhian" ideology and methods of resistance, and bolster their conviction regarding the efficacy of the movement with references to the successful history of the (supposedly) Gandhian independence struggle and other social movements that followed in its wake. As with earlier movements, one has to carefully distinguish between different groups and agendas within newly emerging oppositional movements. One of the most striking incongruities that shaped internal conflicts in *Chipko* as well as contemporary environmental conflicts is the disparate interest between an ecological protest aiming at environmental sustainability, and being informed by a "modern" idea of conservationism on the one hand, and local striving for economic development on the other. Ecological protectionism has often been regarded and opposed as hindering economic development.

These observations show that acts of dissent and their perception often differ so severely from each other that they require acts of translation. Hence, the question arises *how* do we translate – between different visions of a desirable society – and *why* do we need to translate? Because of assumed and enacted knowledge hierarchies between experts and laymen or because of acts of deliberate and involuntary re-distribution of resources?[15] Moreover, conflicts between short- and long-term developmental aims often reflect dissimilar understandings of democratic participation, i.e., immediate benefits locals might aspire to versus imposed sacrifices for the (future) greater common good. Quite often these conflicting visions lead to acts of victimization or rather incapacitation through the ascription of "backwardness" and the political representation of the locally affected by self-appointed developmental "experts."

A "subaltern" state of marginalization is obviously not only defined by an actual social location, but primarily by the perception of this location by the "mainstream." Social stratification is not a material fact in the first place, but rather an ascription that locates different groups according to *a priori* defined criteria of what development signifies within the hegemonic opinion. Hence, the important question is: which "tools" – and discursive positions – are available to different groups within developmental debates and political struggles? It is mainly due to particular political motivations, whether to achieve social legitimacy or for other strategic reasons, that social movements are given labels such as "tribal" in the case of the *Narmada Bachao Andolan,* or "peasant" as stated here for *Chipko.* Interestingly, the tools and methods used in the case of both movements – such as addressing the media, or, more importantly the legislative – could with some justification be labelled "middle class strategies," which are seldom within the reach of the economically and socially marginalized. Indeed, the steps of addressing certain institutions have often been taken (or at least initiated) by the movements' assumed "leaders" and/or other "external" critics. This observation does not, of course, disqualify their involvement *per se*: "The intervention of an urban, intellectual critique is an intervention, and yet it is not necessarily a corruption" (Jairath 2010: 77).

However, it raises important questions with regard to issues of representation and unrestrained speech acts. The question of representation gains particular significance with regard to the differentiation between a theoretical "meta-critique" and the typical requirements of grassroots' activism. While visionary meta-reflections about a desirable society are necessary to transcend limitations produced by the – normative and normalizing – effects of power within the hegemonic discourse, one has to be careful not to dismiss the actual needs and demands of those whose empowerment is the declared aim of this critical engagement. The use of resources that exceed the local availability and, more importantly, knowledgeability,[16] can serve as useful tools to strengthen a struggle. Conversely, their implementation can change the face of a movement to the extent that agendas are transformed and those originally affected are bypassed. In this context, the very role of the public intellectual/activist is at stake. This aspect shall not be discussed here at length, since it would transcend the scope of this chapter. It is nonetheless important to emphasize that dissent does not imply the same meaning for every social position, since the potential consequences that subversion bears with regard to questions of identity formation – and more severely physical integrity – are ultimately not the same. What I mean to say is, simply, that different social positions imply different levels of risk and potential punishment.[17]

As mentioned here, the (analytical) de-contextualization of movements might not only be justified, but desirable. On the other hand localization, i.e., re-contextualization as suggested by Rangan indeed proves its importance, since it highlights the predetermined range of tools, instruments and means that are accessible at a given time in a given space, i.e., the respective social context. Only when seen in this context, do specific acts of dissidence gain their particular meaning.

This does not only account for practices but also for knowledge, and hence we can finally pinpoint the merging point of knowledge and practice, i.e., not only *what*, but also *how* a certain thing is known, reflects its cultural embeddedness and prescribes the limits of agency.

Future Visions?

The creative performance of social activists posing a political challenge to hegemonic development patterns and the realization of social visions beyond the mainstream understanding of development show that there are various substantial possibilities to write – and enact – the "history of Indian development." But how can we conceptualize the space in which the "struggle for modernity" takes place? Whose voices have a decisive or negligible impact on debates in which developmental perspectives and social visions are negotiated?

The ensuing resistance against large scale hydropower projects in India – in Uttarakhand closely connected to the *Chipko* heritage – serves as a perfect example to elucidate these considerations: the arguments in favor and against large dams are well known. While the arguments of proponents include food security, drinking water and power generation, opponents are concerned with social issues, namely involuntary displacement, the unsatisfactory compensation and resettlement practice, adverse ecological consequences, and the simple falseness of the cost–benefit–statistics.[18] For the contested field of large dam building the fundamental challenge, however, can be summarized as follows: numerous environmental impact assessments have shown that large and mega-dams do not fulfil the promises that have legitimized their construction in the first place. They generally meet neither ecological nor social demands and seem to partake of the modernist euphoria that marked the early 20th century. Even official records show that the performance of such installations often falls short of expectations (WCD 2000; Dharmadhikary et al. 2005). Still, large dams are being continuously built. Hence, as naive as it might sound at first, the question remains: why are the critics, though clearly outnumbering the proponents by a wide margin and building on decades of struggle, not being listened to?

In answer to this question, the consequences of economic globalization are often exclusively referred to. Although this is certainly an important part of the explanation, I have suggested that the (im)possibility of social critique is intrinsically connected with the historical persistence of normative paradigms in developmental debates. One needs to consider the hegemonic language of legitimacy that sets the criteria and marks the limitations for what are acceptable speech acts in a given social context. As P. Chatterjee rightly remarks, if the only language available is that of "Western modernity," incidents which cannot be described or rather "named" in this language, will not be recognized as being modern and thus be rejected as historically inadequate (2008: 49). To overcome this dilemma it seems essential to invent a new "grammar," since a social vision requires first of all an adequate language in which it can be articulated (ibid.: 48). This reflects a political rather than an etymological problem. It is debatable, however, if one actually has to invent a novel language to describe features newly (re)discovered as objects of transcultural social theory or if this language already exists amongst those using – or rather inhabiting – their own categories of a desirable future. This, I would like to add, does not only apply to the sphere of language, it also includes the practical side of dissent, i.e., the use of certain practices and strategies. Whoever is labelled "backward" is likely to face difficulties in intervening in mainstream definitions and practices.

The observation about the adequacy of language implies a number of crucial questions for the articulation of resistance: what is up-to-date protest? Does an up-to-date articulation of resistance require an up-to-date semantic framework? Classic descriptions of social inequality have, over time, lost in rhetorical and subsequently political strength. The "grammar of revolution" appears as an anachronistic nostalgia for a bygone age and vision the practical infeasibility of which has been proven. As mentioned in the beginning of this chapter, the articulation of opposition against hegemonic developmental perspectives regularly refers to a normative framework that has been accepted as legitimate by both sides of the contested field. The consequences are obvious: any critical (speech) act bears the risk of being actually affirmative of hegemonic parameters, since it responds to normative principles that remain (historically) unchallenged. If the historical legacy of "development as improvement" remains unquestioned, critique cannot be more than an *a posteriori* correction tool, which aims at the amendment of adverse developmental symptoms. Critique being reduced to a veto function, however, is problematic, since it subscribes to a discursive framework, in which the limitations of its potential articulation have already been accepted.

Paradoxically, cost-benefit critique in that sense could even be harmful vis-à-vis other types of critique, since an affirmative acceptance of hegemonic ideologies facilitates their declaration as incontestable axioms on other similar occasions. Non-conformist types of critical articulation which do not respond to this logic can then easily be discredited not only with regard to their content, but even for being supposedly irrational or illogical with regard to the *realpolitik* requirements of the *status quo*. This, ironically, entails the instrumentalization of reformist critical voices, whose viewpoints are declared to be acceptable – by virtue of being controllable – dissensions. The reconsideration or rather readjustments that are undertaken when integrating those latter critical voices come in handy, since they do not require the reassessment of any fundamental decision. Coming back to the large dams' debate, the obvious consequences of such a "gated discourse" can be observed throughout recent debates; they are reflected in opponents' statements as well as in company policies. Arguments for better compensation, rehabilitation or ecological adjustments appear as rhetorical figures that are being employed by both sides, and which serve situational agendas on one or the other side, but do not necessarily result in reconsidering the project proposal itself.

What are the conclusions to be drawn? Development critique is obviously more than a demand for good governance. If one wants to criticize the developmentalist paradigm, one must start by understanding its historical legacy. Consequently, the task is to explain how developmentalist ideologies emerge, and, further, how they achieve a supposedly self-evident and thus paramount status within a larger discourse that sets the parameters for what a desirable society should look like. Taking this suggestion as a point of departure, the challenge is to formulate viable arguments that counter the statist developmental agenda *and* the ubiquitous legitimating framework it is embedded in. This exercise however, remains incomplete or even redundant, if actions regarding immediate livelihood issues are postponed for ideological reasons. Returning to what has been said here, let me conclude with an appeal for the mutual enrichment of critique as dissident practice and discursive strategy. The statement that the critic (academic or not) has to be aware of the present and its needs consequently requires an attitude which involves critical engagement at the level of daily practice as much as it entails the deconstruction of assumed developmental imperatives.

Notes

*I am grateful to Benjamin Zachariah for helpful discussions and comments on an earlier version of this chapter.

1. It is precisely in their ahistorical abstraction that terms like "modernity" or "development" have achieved a status as incontestable frames of reference within the realm of politics, which remains powerful regardless of the critical transformation those categories have undergone in the last decades (largely within academia). There is no space to provide a history of the term "development" in this chapter. Others have done so in an elaborate way. For the grounding of development within the establishment of modern categories see Arndt (1987).

2. This observation should illustrate the tendency of the developmental discourse. The aim is not to judge or discredit particular – situational and not necessarily consistent – positions, but to contribute to a general analysis of the construction of discursive hegemony. It would require a thorough discourse analysis of numerous individual contributions to distinguish between "conformist" and "non-conformist" approaches with regard to prevailing development paradigms. Yet speech acts are often ambiguous and claims for consistency thus fairly inadequate.

3. One is tempted to suggest that developmentalism still serves as a major driving force for statist endeavors; nationalist claims are far from disappearing in the "age of globalization" and the persistent perpetuation of modernization theory in the realm of politics seems to be at odds with the disapproval lavished on it by the post-colonially informed academia. More importantly, it still provides the hegemonic discursive frame of reference for the critics of developmentalism that partake in a debate on the adverse impacts of development implementations, which does not seem to have altered significantly since its heyday in the 1980s. The content of development debates has altered insofar as claims for economic growth have been balanced with demands for equity, sustainability, and so forth. The self-evidence of the foundational principles of development – namely the unquestioned assumption that progress however defined is "a good idea" – has hardly been challenged. Hence, I suggest that there is a significant "non-simultaneity" (*Ungleichzeitigkeit*) between academic and

public debates on the subject. Intellectual critiques of modernity seem not to have significantly altered concepts of (social) engineering yet.

4. I use the terms "critique" and "criticism" more or less interchangeably here, having in mind the German word "Kritik" under which both terms can be subsumed.

5. "Krino" is also the root of the word "crisis," which explains the close connection between the (semantical) appearance of a crisis and its critique. This correlation is illustrated in Koselleck's work (1959).

6. During that time its embodiment is of course the philosopher as the institutional critic per se – a critic, but not necessarily a social dissenter.

7. The sociology of knowledge, primarily and explicitly formulated by Karl Mannheim enlarges the Marxian conception of ideology by distinguishing between partial and total ideology, the latter being the necessary limitation of every judgment caused by the social position of the speaker. See Mannheim (1952).

8. For an account of Foucault's concept of critique see Foucault (1974, 1990, 1992).

9. Foucault's discussion of the Iranian revolution serves as a good example of the search for a theoretical "exit-option" that seeks the subversion of power in situational performance. See Foucault (1978). For an excellent analysis of Foucault's account of the Iranian revolution see Lemke (2002: 73ff.).

10. In this chapter, I am using both terms: social and socio-ecological movements. There is apparently no clear distinction. What is definitely interesting is the question of whether (mostly global) ecological or environmental movements are "socially exclusive" (see Forsyth 2007). Another question is what happens if locally based movements – which might have a particular understanding of the interaction between man and nature for example – enter a globalized discourse, which makes reference to different developmental ideas and rhetoric.

11. To bring the value of morality into play seems to be highly significant. Whilst on the one hand opponents of certain developmental projects are typically being discredited for arguing morally – as opposed to rational, and scientifically substantial – on the other hand morality is being evoked as a sort of "national value," an attribute of the "greater common good" that is been used as a defensive strategy against dissenting voices. For two of the more prominent examples see Guha (2000) and Verghese (1999) on Arundhati Roy's political essays on big dams (1999). See also the various letters to the editor that follow up on that discussion in *The Hindu* (2000).

12. An interesting comparison can be drawn here to Mannheim's concept of total ideology, namely the replacement of ideology as false consciousness through (social) perspective. See n. 7, this chapter.

13. Neera Chandhoke's contribution to that dilemma is quite enlightening, since it radicalizes the question of authenticity and representation and brings it back to the sphere of language: "[c]ertainly, activists have made the pain of the tribals their own, but this is not the point at all. For can the tribal be represented at all? The historian of the tribal after all can never be a tribal herself. She is condemned to being at the most a translator, but the control over translation, recollect, is hers and hers alone. Therefore, we have no way of knowing whether the tribal speaks in her own voice, or whether others speak for her. This, let me hasten to add, is not an adverse comment on the integrity of the social activist. It is a comment on the restricted languages of our civil society, languages that condemn large sections of our people to being spoken for, being written about, being represented by others who are, to put it bluntly, outsiders" (2001).

14. By "historical common goods" I mean ideological elements and methods of dissent – here: non-violence, passive non-cooperation, and so forth – that are being taken for granted with regard to the significance of their meaning. An ahistorical, decontextualized utilization of these concepts, however, easily reduces them to "empty signifiers" that neither do justice to the historical particularity of their deployment nor the actual situations in which they are used as a frame of reference.

15. It has to be critically asked, however, to what extent acts of translation are possible at all. See n. 13, this chapter.

16. "Knowledgeability," the ability to know something, refers to the (prior) background knowledge against which certain things are classified, connected to the preexisting environment, evaluated, and so forth. For the use of the term, see Lave (1993: 13ff.).

17. It is an integral idea of Foucault's conception of power that the subject develops within given social norms, through the reiteration of normative practices. The idea of resistance is interestingly located in the very same framework. The subversive potential lies in the possibility that given practices can be enacted, or repeated differently, i.e., "insufficiently" with regard to the hegemonic norms. Regulations are modified, strategies of the game are recognized as contingent and altered, and thus disobedience is shown towards hegemonic norms. The problem lies in the fact that within this process of subversion, the subject, through a violation or neglect of the same principles that form his identity, risks his status as subject itself. And the question remains what such an ethical stand point – ethical because it runs the risk of an ontological insecurity – ultimately means for the person who risks to take and defend it. See Butler (2000: 265).

18. See Goldsmith and Hildyard (1984) and McCully (1996) for two popular accounts.

References

Adorno, T. W. 1971. "Kritik," in *Kleine Schriften zur Gesellschaft*. Frankfurt and Main: Suhrkamp.

Arndt, H. W. 1987. *Economic Development: The History of an Idea*. Chicago and London: The University of Chicago Press.

Bormann, C. V. 1976. "Kritik," in J. Ritter and K. Gründer (eds), *Historisches Wörterbuch der Philosophie*, Band 4. Darmstadt: Wissenschaftliche Buchgesellschaft.

Butler, J. 2000. "Was ist Kritik? Ein Essay über Foucaults Tugend," *Deutsche Zeitschrift für Philosophie*, 50 (2): 249–65.

Chandhoke, N. 2001. "The Conceits of Representation," *The Hindu*, February 7. http://www.hindu.com/2001/02/07/stories/05072523.htm. As accessed on November 9, 2008.

Chatterjee, P. 2008. "Modernity and Indian Nationalism," in R. Jahanbegloo (ed.), *India Revisited: Conversations on Continuity and Change*. New Delhi: Oxford University Press.

———. 1997. *A Possible India: Essays in Political Criticism*. New Delhi: Oxford University Press.

Dharmadhikary, S., S. Sheshadri and Rehmat. 2005. *Unravelling Bhakra: Assessing the Temple of Resurgent India: Report of a Study*. Barwani: Manthan Adhyayan Kendra.

Dixit, K. M. 2007. "Big Dams in Southasia: The Dangers of Inevitability," *Himal*, 20 (9): 20–23.

Dogra, B. 1992. *Forests, Dams, and Survival in Tehri Garhwal*. New Delhi: Bharat Dogra.

Forsyth, T. 2007. "Are Environmental Social Movements Socially Exclu-sive? A Historical Study from Thailand," *World Development*, 35 (12): 2110–30.

Foucault, M. 1992. *Was ist Kritik?* Berlin: Merve.

———. 1990. "Was ist Aufklärung?" in E. Erdmann, R. Forst and A. Honneth (eds), *Ethos der Moderne: Foucaults Kritik der Aufklärung*. Frankfurt, Main and New York: Campus.

———. 1978. "A quoi rêvent les Iraniens?" *Le Nouvel Observateur*, 727: 48–49. October 16–22. http://1libertaire.free.fr/MFoucault143.html. As accessed on March 10, 2014.

———. 1974. "Nietzsche, die Genealogie, die Historie," *Von der Subversion des Wissens*. München: Fischer.

Geuss, R. 2000. "Kritik, Aufklärung, Genealogie," *Deutsche Zeitschrift für Philosophie*, 50 (2): 273–81.

Goldsmith, E. and N. Hildyard. 1984. *The Social and Environmental Effects of Large Dams*, vols 1 and 2. San Francisco: Sierra Club Books.

Guha, R. 2000. "The Arun Shourie of the Left," *The Hindu*, November 26. http://www.hindu.com/2000/11/26/stories/13260411.htm. As accessed on November 9, 2008.

————. 1989. *The Unquiet Woods: Ecological Change and Peasant Resistance in the Himalaya.* New Delhi: Oxford University Press.

Jahanbegloo, R. 2008. *India Revisited: Conversations on Continuity and Change.* New Delhi: Oxford University Press.

Jairath, V. 2010. "Writing Resistance, Revisiting Ruptures," *Economic and Political Weekly*, 45 (36): 75–77.

Kant, I. 1996[1783]. "Beantwortung der Frage: Was ist Aufklärung?" in E. Bahr (ed.), *Was ist Aufklärung? Thesen und Definitionen.* Stuttgart: Reclam.

Koselleck, R. 1979. *Vergangene Zukunft: Zur Semantik geschichtlicher Zeiten.* Frankfurt and Main: Suhrkamp.

————. 1959. *Kritik und Krise: Eine Studie zur Pathogenese der bürgerlichen Welt.* Freiburg and München: Karl Alber.

Lave, J. 1993. "The Practice of Learning," in J. Lave and S. Chaiklin (eds), *Understanding Practice: Perspectives on Activity and Context.* Cambridge: Cambridge University Press.

Lemke, T. 2002. "Die verrückteste Form der Revolte – Michel Foucault und die Iranische Revolution," *Zeitschrift für Sozialgeschichte des 20. und 21. Jahrhunderts*, 17 (2): 73–89.

Linkenbach, A. 1994. "Ecological Movements and the Critique of Development: Agents and Interpreters," *Thesis Eleven*, 39: 63–85.

Mannheim, K. 1952[1929]. *Ideologie und Utopie.* Frankfurt and Main: Schulte–Bulmke.

McCully, P. 1996. *Silenced Rivers: The Ecology and Politics of Large Dams.* London: Zed Books.

O'Neill, O. 2000. "Starke und schwache Gesellschaftskritik in einer globalisierten Welt," *Deutsche Zeitschrift für Philosophie*, 48 (5): 719–28.

Rangan, H. 2000. *Of Myths and Movements: Rewriting Chipko into Himalayan History.* London: Verso.

Röttgers, K. 1982. "Kritik," in O. Brunner, W. Conze and R. Koselleck (eds), *Geschichtliche Grundbegriffe*, Band 3. Stuttgart: Klett-Cotta.

————. 1975. *Kritik und Praxis: Zur Geschichte des Kritikbegriffs von Kant bis Marx.* Berlin and New York: De Gruyter.

Roy, A. 1999. "The Greater Common Good," *Friends of River Narmada*, April. http://www.narmada.org/gcg/gcg.html. As accessed on December 1, 2008.

Scott, J. C. 1998. *Seeing Like a State: How Certain Schemes to Improve the Human Condition Have Failed.* New Haven and London: Yale University Press.

Shiva, V. 1991. *Ecology and the Politics of Survival: Conflicts over Natural Resources in India.* New Delhi: Sage.

The Hindu. 2000. "The Arun Shourie of the Left: Letters to the Editor," December 17. http://www.hindu.com/2000/12/17/stories/1317061a. htm. As accessed on November 9, 2008.

Verghese, B. G. 1999. "A Poetic License," *Outlook Magazine,* July 5. http://www.outlookindia.com/article.aspx?207723. As accessed on December 1, 2008.

Walzer, M. 2000. "Mut, Mitleid und ein gutes Auge. Tugenden der Sozialkritik und der Nutzen von Gesellschaftstheorie," *Deutsche Zeitschrift für Philosophie,* 48 (5): 709–18.

World Commission on Dams (WCD). 2000. *Dams and Development: A New Framework for Decision-Making: The Report of the World Commission on Dams.* London and Sterling: Earth Scan. http://www.dams.org/report/contents. htm. As accessed on December 1, 2008.

Zachariah, B. 2005. *Developing India: An Intellectual and Social History.* New Delhi: Oxford University Press.

2

Chasing the Long Tail
of Climate Change

Matti Pohjonen

We can no longer have that reassuringly trivial conversation about the weather with someone on the street, as a way to break the ice or pass the time. The conversation either trails off into a disturbingly meaningful silence, or someone mentions global warming. The weather no longer exists as a neutral-seeming background against which events take place. When weather becomes climate – when it enters the realm of science and history – it can no longer be a stage set. You can't visualise climate. Mapping it requires a processing speed in terabytes a second (a terabyte is a thousand gigabytes) (Morton 2010b: 28).

It must have been the fake polar bear costume that got me thinking. Or perhaps it was the woman who followed the bear around like a shadow, exploiting all the media attention her furry friend was attracting: "if we don't cut carbon dioxide emissions by at least 30 percent by year 2020, the polar bears are going to . . . drown," she pleaded in an articulate yet warmly concerned voice to anybody and everybody interested. Around her tens of photographers took pictures, cameras flashing, each trying to capture the ultimate money shot of what climate change *really* means. This photo-op took place inside Bella Centre, a Lego-like fortress created in the outskirts of Copenhagen, Denmark, to safely digest the thousands of governmental delegates, business lobbyists and non-governmental organization (NGO) activists who had come to observe the 2009 United Nations climate change conference, commonly known as the COP 15 environmental summit.[1] The outcome of these negotiations, which commentators had speculated for months, was crucial not only for reducing carbon dioxide emissions globally but also perhaps for the very future of the planet.

Each of the thousands of participants who had gathered here had an urgent message to tell – and they were using increasingly sophisticated media tactics to get their messages heard across the fray.

I had come here to do research that looked at how such climate change negotiations were mediated by the mass media globally. Given the escalating controversies around how we define this "object"[2] of climate change today, I was especially interested in how its significance was articulated by the hundreds of participants who had gathered here. In particular, I wanted to know how the meaning of climate change was refracted through all these elaborately-designed posters, carefully-branded promotional messages, interactive multimedia screens and cutting-edge internet applications that were each trying to now capture my fleeting attention. What did the fake polar bear performance really have to do with rising levels of carbon dioxide in the atmosphere? Or the corporate lobbyists selling their latest green-washing service through expensive multimedia presentations? Or the school children singing in chorus to a row of TV cameras, pleading for the world leaders to save their future? What were all these people even referring to behind this well-rehearsed rhetoric? In other words, what was this mysterious thing called climate change that everybody had an opinion about but nobody seemed to be able to agree on? And for just an instant, all I could do was think of a quote by the one-time high priest of postmodernism, Jean Baudrillard:

> Abstraction today is no longer that of the map, the double, the mirror or the concept. Simulation is no longer that of a territory, a referential being or a substance. It is the generation by models of a real without origin or reality: a hyperreal. The territory no longer precedes the map, nor survives it. Henceforth, it is the map that precedes the territory – precession of simulacra – it is the map that engenders the territory and if we were to revive the fable today, it would be the territory whose shreds are slowly rotting across the map. It is the real, and not the map, whose vestiges subsist here and there, in the deserts which are no longer those of the Empire, but our own. The desert of the real itself (1994: 1).

That is, when faced with this circus of media representations around me, I suddenly had this uncanny feeling. For a moment, I felt that it was not only our climate that was in danger; it was also the very frameworks of knowledge that we use to understand it. It was as if this postmodern nightmare had suddenly come true: all that remained were these glitzy representations of climate change around me, each more seducing than the other, and behind these many screens – *the desert of the real*!

French philosopher Gilles Deleuze has argued that thinking should not be seen as an orderly rational process. Facts do not come ready-made for us to reflect on in a quiet manner. On the contrary, something in the world forces us to think, something disquieting, something unfamiliar – a shock from the outside. A research project or a new idea (or a book chapter, for that matter) rarely begins with a clearly-formulated question that one then meticulously and systematically pursues. Instead, it begins with a *heterogenesis* of a problem that inspires us, even compels us, to begin the difficult task of thinking about it. Deleuze has written:

> do not count upon thought to ensure the relative necessity of what it thinks. Rather count upon the contingency of an encounter with that which forces thought to raise up and educate the absolute necessity of an act of thought or a passion to think . . . *something in the world forces us to think. This something is an object not of recognition but a fundamental encounter* (1994: 139; emphasis in original).

Similarly, this chapter is the outcome of one particularly gruesome encounter with a fake polar bear. It looks at the work I have done since – both empirical and theoretical – in trying to understand better what this "object" of climate change is and how it becomes mediated by the changing technologies of communication around us. It describes, however tentatively, some of the problems that emerged out of this encounter: theoretical reflections that have led me to question the orthodoxies through which we understand climate change today and, as importantly, some of the reasons why I have begun to flirt with perhaps more unconventional ways of understanding this pressing problem. As such, it hopefully describes some of the changing contours of environmental activism in a globalized world.

Chasing the Long Tail of Climate Change

Environmental philosopher Timothy Morton argues that one of the biggest obstacles in environmental activism today is what he calls the "beautiful soul syndrome" (2007: 160–61). By this Morton refers to a kind of critical attitude that looks at the world from the safety of

distance and detachment, without ever compromising one's own ideological purity, without ever getting one's hands dirty.[3] He writes:

> a truly theoretical approach is not allowed to sit smugly outside the area
> it is examining. It must mix thoroughly with it. Adopting a position
> that forgoes all others would be all too easy, a naive negative criticism
> that is a disguised position all of its own . . . This is a political as well as
> intellectual position, one to which ecological thinking is prone . . .
> The "beautiful soul" washes his or her hands of the corrupt world,
> refusing to admit how in this very abstemiousness and distaste he or
> she participates in the corruption in the creation of that world. The
> world-weary soul holds all beliefs and ideas at a distance. *The only ethical
> option is to muck in* (2007: 12–13; emphasis added).

With this in mind, my own quest to better understand this "object"
of climate change led me to the remote mountains of Ethiopia . . . to
count trees. More specifically, it brought me to Ethiopia to work on a
pilot development project whose aim was to develop a new method
to calculate how much carbon dioxide is sequestered by the many
trees that dot the smallholder farms of this mountainous region. The
method we developed relied on the categories farmers themselves use
when describing the different sizes of trees that grow on their farms.
Categories such as *limich* (1 cm), *mager* (3 cm), *atana* (10 cm) and *zaf*
(18 cm) each indicate how thick the diameter of the tree is according
to its price on the local market. These usually are determined by the
different uses these trees have from house-building to construction-
scaffolding. We then took these categories and converted them with
the help of growth algorithms from environmental and forest science
into how much carbon dioxide is sequestered by each individual
tree, how much this potentially changes over time (carbon offset)
and how much this offset is valued on the international carbon offset
market. Take for instance, a farmer named Ato Minnehailu. He grows
Eucalyptus Globulus trees on his small farm close to Bahir Dar, in the
Amhara region of Ethiopia. When added together, these trees that line
his farm hold an estimated carbon amount of 5,465 tons. Compared
to similar measurements made a year ago, we can see that there has
been an aggregate growth of 520 tons of carbon that has been sequestered to the trees on his farm. This positive offset – that is, if valued
on the current carbon offset market – would be worth around 520
Ethiopian birr (around 20 euros).[4] This may be a small amount but it
would nonetheless provide a significant additional income in one of

the poorest areas of the world. And while Ato Minnehailu's farm is just one among millions of such farms in Ethiopia, when combined together, numbers start adding up. Such small-scale tree and plant-based carbon offsets play a significant role in sequestering carbon dioxide from the atmosphere.

My role in the project has been to investigate strategies for how new information and communication technologies (ICT) could help with these calculations. Towards this end, we developed a mobile-/ web-based prototype that allows farmers such as Ato Minnehailu (or the farmers' association project that he is a part of) to perform such calculations on his mobile phone.[5] This is a simple approach using technology that already exists in the area: the farmer sends a coded Short Message Service (SMS) message with the relevant measurements – that is, how many *limich*, how many *magers*, how many *atana* and how many *zaf* the farm in question has on a given date. Our application then receives this SMS message, parses it, sends it to a cloud-based web server that performs the necessary calculations and then finally sends the calculations back to the sender in the form of another SMS message. The data that accumulates during this process is then stored on a central database where geo-mapped information about tree growth patterns, carbon sequestration rates and their relationship to broader climate change patterns in countries such as Ethiopia can be better analyzed. As a *New York Times Green Inc.* blog article described this pilot:

> Small farmers near Bahir Dar, Ethiopia, are testing a carbon offset market facilitated by mobile phones. One of the most daunting hurdles for the trade in carbon offsets is the logistical challenge of connecting customers – typically carbon dioxide emitting companies based in America or Europe – with offset producers in places like South America, Asia, and Africa.
>
> . . . Under Mr. Pohjonen's system, small Ethiopian farmers, for example, would measure the diameters of trees on their land twice a year and put the information into a text message, which, along with each farmer's unique identification code, is then sent to the regional Watershed Users' Association office.
>
> Software computes the amount of carbon stored on each farm as well as the change from the previous measurement; any increase in stored carbon dioxide is converted into cash using the going rate of CO_2 on international markets, and farmers are paid by their local association (Marlow 2009).

Our work was inspired by two observations we had made about the relationship between ICT and climate change in rural Asia and Africa. The *first* observation was that – following the Kyoto Protocol (1997) – little progress had been achieved in including tree and plant biomass into the combat against climate change. This had been a result of the difficulties involved in calculating, monitoring and accounting for the "real" levels of carbon dioxide sequestration in especially the small farms in the developing world. As a consequence of such "high transactions costs" involved in these calculations, most of the projects under existing carbon offset schemes such as the Clean Development Mechanism (CDM)[6] or voluntary carbon offset schemes[7] had focused mostly on large-scale block tree plantations where such calculations could be done more cost-effectively. Such "small is expensive" mentality had therefore led to money being channeled away from the grassroots level to larger megaprojects in the developing world – to what some called a new form of "carbon colonialism."[8] Yet with the arrival of new digital technology such as mobile phones and mobile internet to even the remotest parts of rural Africa, Asia and South America, some of the problems involved with these high transaction costs could now be potentially avoided. The *second* observation followed from this. We had noticed that most of the existing digital technological solutions to climate change had so far focused on the industrial countries in the North. In other words, they had mostly focused on calculating the so-called "carbon footprint" of consumers and corporations based in the industrial north. Yet, if we look at the rural areas of the developing world where (almost) the majority of the world's population still lives, we realize that most of the people in the world are not consumers yet. They are producers. That is, they produce plants and trees for their livelihoods into which carbon dioxide becomes sequestered in complex and mostly yet unaccounted ways. *Their carbon footprint is more that of production than consumption.* And while such individual activity done by smallholder farmers only represents a small part of the overall carbon dioxide calculations globally, when combined together, numbers begin to add up. These tens, if not hundreds of millions of smallholder farmers across Africa, Asia and South America represent a significant force in our attempts to understand and reduce carbon dioxide emissions globally.

Given these dual developments, we asked: *how could we then best reach out to this long tail of climate change?* The concept "long tail" refers

here of course to a property of statistical analysis describing popu-
lations at the long end tail of probability distribution.[9] This concept
has been used commonly to understand new developments in digital
culture such as citizen journalism, crowd sourcing and peer-to-peer
networks, that is, situations where the many small actions by a large
number of people gain more significance than the big actions by
only a few people. For instance, according to some contemporary
theories of digital media, the radical potential of new communication technologies such as mobile phones derives from their ability
to reach out to this "long-tail" of users because of the many-to-many
structure of communication and low-cost of use made possible by
them (Anderson 2006; Shirky 2009).[10] So instead of dismissing people
such as Ato Minnehailu in Ethiopia as passive victims only to be
helped, we wanted to explore if we could come up with a method
that would support their already ongoing tree-planting efforts on their
farms. Could new emerging technologies of communication such
as the mobile phone help us reach out to this "long tail" of climate
change better? And most importantly perhaps – for the purposes of
this chapter – would such work taking place in an entirely different
context give me some new insights into understanding this "object"
of climate change better when removed from the hypermediated
debates in the urban North?

The Cultural Translation of Climate Change

One question I get commonly asked (as somebody with a background
in media anthropology and critical theory) is: "so . . . what do the farmers themselves think about climate change? Have you asked them?"
This question is often accompanied by a subtle smirk, as if to indicate
that by what ethical right do I, an elite university-trained researcher,
conduct such "experimental" research with farmers in one of the poorest areas of the world. In other words, the broader theoretical problem
underlying my attempt to understand this "object" of climate change
from a different perspective is the complicated power/knowledge
issues involved in defining climate change in those parts of the world
which have radically different cultural, political and social histories. As
critical anthropology and post-development theory has shown us, how
such projects articulate key concepts such as "climate change" should
never be seen as a neutral process. Instead, the practices through
which we produce knowledge are always already embedded in the

complicated politics of development aid materially as well as *epistemologically* (see Hobart 1993; Escobar 1994). So besides the obvious politics of development-aid funding, such expert knowledge is only made possible by neglecting local knowledge systems that have been in place for hundreds of years in other parts of the world. So when doing work, for instance, with developing mobile phone applications with farmers in Ethiopia, we have to rely on a dominant scientific-technological discourse that might not be compatible with the local reference-worlds of the farmers themselves. So how do we reconcile the many different perspectives to changes in weather patterns that are taking place? Do they mean the same thing to different people? As Talal Asad has warned us "such process of cultural translation is always invariably enmeshed in conditions of power – professional, national, international . . . given that this is so, the interesting question for enquiry is . . . how power enters into the process of 'cultural translation'" (1986: 163).

I have found the work of philosopher of science Bruno Latour useful when looking at this problem of cultural translation. Latour (2007) argues that when we look at any set of scientific facts, we should not desperately try to find the deeper underlying reality or "object" somewhere behind these facts. Instead, we should empirically focus on the different events – social and material – that have made the production of these facts possible in the first place. A set of material phenomena such as climate change can never be a simple "object" that underlies its many different representations. Rather, its *reference circulates.* What this means is that any set of scientific facts such as facts about climate change are constantly *translated* from one context to another. As Harman writes about such a model of knowledge:

> there is never an immediate visibility of the fact, but only a series of mediations, each of them translating a more complicated reality into something whose forces can more easily be passed down the line. Though a skeptic might claim that these mediators are mere utensils that can be tossed aside at the end, there is no such thing as transport without transformation. Truth is nothing but a chain of translation without resemblance from one actor to the next. To focus only on the end-points is to distort the meaning of truth . . . this is the meaning of 'circulating reference' (2009: x).

In other words, when looking at an "object" such as climate change (and how the media represents or mis-represents it), we should not focus too much on the "biases" on how this happens. Instead, we should look at the long chain of events through which the material world is abstracted into formal knowledge by different groups of people with different interests, motivations and world views. That is, instead of looking at climate change from a classical *correspondence* theory of knowledge where a statement refers to an underlying reality/object with varying degrees of accuracy, the "object" of climate change thus can be seen as composed of the myriad sets of practices through which the often muddled data about weather patterns becomes abstracted with one set of technological tools (measurement devices, sensors, computers, customized software performing weather calculations, algorithms from forestry science, mobile phones, etc.) and then communicated using another set of technological tools to convince others of its validity (verbal communication, rhetoric, email, journal articles, peer-review, book chapters, etc.). And each of these steps through which this happens is always a translation; such practices of translation are ubiquitous: "any relation is a mediation, never some pristine transmission of data across a noiseless vacuum" (Harman 2009: 77).

Similarly, when we look at cultural translation between, say, my experience at COP 15 and my work with farmers in Ethiopia, we can similarly trace out a long chain of events through which an abstract theoretical idea became practice.[11] In other words, how did an abstract idea around the "hyper-reality" of climate change then become translated into a pilot Information and Communication for Development (ICT4D) project experimenting with the use of mobile phones to calculate the carbon sequestration rates of trees? Before concluding with a preliminary definition of how I understand climate change today and its relationship to new technologies of communication – with a working definition acquired somewhere along this long chain of translations – I will first provide a brief account of how this relationship was made possible in the first place. That is, how a symbolic encounter with a fake polar bear led me to write about counting trees in Ethiopia for a book on environmental politics.

The Encounter

The initial problem was inspired by my experience at the COP 15 summit. This was influenced by my observations about the mediated nature of the summit but also by the many discussions I had with other activists, researchers and participants during the time I spent there. My background in media anthropology and critical theory as well as prior research with digital technologies in India had already provided me with the first set of filters that would allow me to focus on the different digital media tools through which climate change was being represented at the summit. I therefore quickly translated this experience – often chaotic, noisy and fragmented – into the language of media anthropology and critical theory I was already comfortable with, especially with issues around the politics of representation and the "hyper-reality" of contemporary mass media. Watching the fake polar bear performance gave me a good metaphor to structure some of the questions that I left the summit with.

First Translation: Theoretical Language

Being interested especially in the controversies around climate change debates, I next read extensively about environmental theory and eco-philosophy. These readings mixed with my already-existing background in media anthropology and critical theory to give rise to a set of problems that combined the two perspectives. That is, on the one hand, politics of climate change and on the other, the politics of media representation. In particular, I formulated these two overlapping sets of points into three preliminary questions that I wanted to explore:

(*a*) If digital technologies of communications are centrally implicated in the construction of climate change as a nodal point for contemporary environmental politics, how do we then understand *that which is being represented?* As we have seen, for instance, in the recent media scandals around the leaked climate change emails,[12] the public debate around climate change still seems to revolve around whether we can trust scientific data to represent reality accurately enough and who has the most accurate scientific data.

(*b*) Contemporary approaches in media anthropology and critical theory have usually bracketed away the possibility of knowing what such "objects" such as climate change are behind their mediated representations. In other words, when we look at something like climate change, a commonly held assumption is that we can never know what really exists behind these representations. All we ever have is access to the different articulations of how something is represented *as* something for different people and the complicated politics involved in this – what Foucault called the "politics of truth" (1980: 109–34). To talk about things as *they really are* is generally considered a naïve form of scientific realism.

(*c*) Herein, however, also perhaps lies the irony of the contemporary moment: when we most need to understand the reality around the threat of climate change, we have the least theoretical tools available to help us do this. If we can only access mediated representations but not the things in themselves, how do we understand the rapid changes in weather that are taking place in the world *despite* how we represent them? That is, in order to be able to effectively prepare for climate change, should we not be able to – at least speculatively or experimentally – postulate a method that would allow us to understand these changes more accurately and respond to them? How could we do this?

With these tentative questions in mind, I wanted to look at these problems from a perspective of a practice-based method I had used earlier in India with emerging digital technologies that combines such theoretical reflection and practical work (see Pohjonen and Paul 2011). That is, I wanted to further explore what kinds of experimental "practice-based" research into this subject would perhaps help me re-imagine the problem of climate change and media representation in new and interesting ways.

Second Translation: Practical Work

As I became involved in such practice-based research in Ethiopia (through another complicated chain of events involving personal history, friends and family ties), I wanted to look specifically at how new emerging ICTs and especially mobile phones could help us understand these tentative questions better (De Bruijn et al. 2009). As our team involved researchers, technologists and environmental scientists, the abstract theoretical language had to be translated into something more practical and usable. What started off as a rather abstract philosophical problem about the "hyper-reality" of climate change representations was therefore translated into a rather simple set of parameters that could be quantitatively approached: that is, what methods would best help us collect data about how much carbon dioxide is sequestered by trees; how we could communicate this data with an internet-based server via a mobile phone using available technology; and how we could use databases to calculate and structure this data that was collected. This abstract theoretical problem, through a sequence of events, was therefore transformed into a set of simple calculations into how much carbon dioxide was sequestered by trees in Ethiopia, as a possible way of understanding what climate change is. Would this help me understand climate change better?

Third Translation: Speculations on Theory and Practice

This practice-based research had to be, in turn, then translated back into theoretical language of contemporary digital theory that we were developing with our practice-based work (see Pohjonen and Paul 2010). In other words, what could such work tell us more broadly about the changing dynamics of how digital technology can be used to address real world problems such as climate change? As we know, the brief history of the internet has seen its transformation from the early military-scientific network (ARPANET) to the World Wide Web (WWW) and, more recently, from what is called Web 1.0 to Web 2.0 and the social media we talk about today.[13] However, if we look at some of the current trends in digital theory and technological development, we can see a new set of ideas emerging about the future of the internet. Indeed, one of the most recent of such developments is what is loosely called the Internet of Things. This refers to a network of objects connected through the Internet. In other words, what is envisioned to be one of the possible emerging stages of the internet will now take us beyond the internet as a network of interconnected computers (Web 1.0) and network of people (Web 2.0/social media) towards a new kind of network where everyday objects and places will also become connected (Internet of Things).

Similarly, when we look at some of the environmental applications that use latest digital technology, we see a similar trend in connecting data from the environment to the computational power of the internet. A number of services today already allow individuals, institutions and corporations to calculate their so-called carbon footprint and also provide suggestions on how to reduce it.[14] Other services allow users to map global carbon dioxide emissions based on data from real-world sensors. Projects such as *Breathingearth* combine scientific data and the internet by "integrating satellite mapping, airborne-laser technology and ground-based plot surveys" to provide "high-resolution maps of carbon locked up in tropical forest vegetation and emitted by land-use practices" (*Science Daily* 2010: 1). When experimenting with mobile phones in Ethiopia, we also wanted to see how we could combine real-world data about trees and plants with the internet using the available mobile phone. Similar to the idea behind the Internet of Things, we wanted to see – however experimentally – if such new emerging ICTs in rural Africa, Asia and South America could be used in creative ways to produce data about climate change from places where such information was scarce. In other words, if a large part of the world's population still grows biomass for a living, could we somehow make their actions more central in the battle against climate change? That is, could we extend this model of the Internet of Things to connect not only human-made objects to the internet but also the natural objects in the ecosystem such as trees and plants that people grow for their livelihoods? Could we thus experiment with creating something akin to the Internet of Things – an Internet of Nature perhaps – that would facilitate our understanding of how ecosystems react to changing levels of carbon dioxide in different parts of the world? And would this kind of a model perhaps provide a new approach to environmental activism in a globalized world – an open source platform for accessing and analyzing the data that is emitted by our ecosystems as a way of understanding the complex changes in weather and ecosystems that underlie this thing called climate change?

Final Translation: Writing a Chapter

In the end, all these questions, speculations and experimental ideas had to be translated into the constraints of a 6,000-word chapter, a set deadline and a simple argument. This written chapter is therefore the outcome of a working paper presented at the "Between Mainstream and the Fringe: Environmental Activism in a Globalized World" Conference in New Delhi,[15] shortened to fit the word limit and given a somewhat artificial structure and narrative in order to give an ongoing research project some temporary closure. Such experimental projects and ideas only tend to seem coherent when you temporarily freeze the action and, looking backwards, write self-reflexively about where you have arrived. As a consequence, this chapter has focused on the different steps and translations that have brought me here, finally, to a point where I can answer the question I began with. That is, inspired by my encounter with a fake polar bear and translated many times along the way to reach this point, I can now give a working definition of what I think this "object" of climate change is behind these hypermediated representations that I first observed at the COP 15 environmental summit.

Conclusion: From Hyperreality to the Hyperobject

In continental philosophy, an emerging body of work has begun to look at how we could understand theoretically what "objects" such as climate change are. A key idea behind this is that for a long time, philosophy has mostly focused on categories of language and representation as central to our understanding of the world around us. However, by focusing only on how our frameworks of knowledge represent and mediate the world, we have neglected the subterranean world of things and objects around us. We have not developed a vocabulary to talk about them. A new generation of philosophers therefore – united under the broader rubric of the "Speculative Realism" or "Object-Oriented Philosophy" – have tried to address this lack and have come up with a new set of conceptual tools that attempt to understand this reality *outside* and *beyond* our relationship to it (see Meillassoux 2008). A recent anthology introducing this work describes this growing body of philosophical research in the following way:

> it has long been commonplace within continental philosophy to focus on discourse, text, culture, consciousness, power, or ideas as what constitutes reality. But despite the vaunted anti-humanism of many of the thinkers identified with these trends . . . humanity remains at the centre of these works, and reality appears in philosophy only as the correlate of human thought. In this respect phenomenology, structuralism, post-structuralism, deconstruction, and postmodernism have all been perfect exemplars of the anti-realist trend in continental philosophy. Without deriding the significant contributions of these philosophies, something is clearly amiss in these trends. In the face of the looming ecological catastrophe, and the increasing infiltration of technology into the everyday world (including our own bodies), it is

not clear that the anti-realist position is equipped to face up to these developments. The danger is that the dominant anti-realist strain of continental philosophy has not only reached a point of decreasing returns, but that it now actively limits the capacities of philosophy in our time (Bryant et al. 2011: 2–3).

While these complex philosophical debates are of course beyond my chapter here, what is nonetheless interesting about these new ideas are the different ways they have speculated about what such "objects" are outside the human-centered frameworks of knowledge.[16] Applying ideas from object-oriented philosophy, Morton has come up with an entirely new category of objects he sees as unique to our current environmental crisis. He calls these "hyper-objects." Such hyper-objects are any kinds of objects that "stretch our ideas of time and space, since they far outlast most human time scales, or they're massively distributed in terrestrial space and so are unavailable to immediate experience" (Morton 2010a: 1). Objects such as plutonium can have a radiation half-life of tens of thousands of years: they will still be around when humans are not; they inhabit time scales that cannot be understood merely by our anthropocentric perspectives of the world. They force us to think big and far into the future.

This finally brings me to my question: what kind of an "object" is climate change? What is this "object" behind the hyper-reality of the fake polar bear I started off with? Climate change is also a hyper-object. And like other hyper-objects, it is so complex that we cannot understand it anymore with our classical methods of representation or common sense. Instead, even to conceptualize what climate change is we already need the help of supercomputers to calculate what the changes in weather patterns are and what their future predictions mean. We need massive amounts of data from environmental sensors to even imagine what the cumulative effect of changing carbon dioxide levels in the atmosphere will be to fragile ecosystems across the world. Most of what climate change will entail, we are not even able to predict yet. We do not know. Because of the sheer complexity that such climate change calculations involve, we need to rely on the technological power of computers even to think about it systematically. In other words, climate change can be understood only as a computational abstraction – a hyper-object – that is only made possible through these complicated calculations. It is not changes in weather or fluctuations in temperature. Instead, conceptualizing what the "object" of climate change is forces us to step outside our common-sense understanding of the world and experiment with new ways of combining research, technology and science in order to understand this reality that is upon us, however strange it may be. Perhaps this is one task for environmental activism of the future.

❄

Notes

1. See http://unfccc.int/meetings/copenhagen_dec_2009/meeting/6295.php. As accessed on February 1, 2014.
2. The specific use of "object" will be discussed later in the chapter.
3. I have argued similarly elsewhere that the best way to understand the changing significance of contemporary technologies of communication is to forgo a critical distance and to get closely involved in the changing practices of working with these technologies. Therefore, when I became interested in the more general philosophical problems behind what climate change is, I wanted to avoid this "beautiful soul syndrome" in trying to understand what it is. Instead, I wanted to adopt a method of "creative experimentation" and/or "practice-based" research in my work (Pohjonen and Paul 2011).
4. These calculations are from November 23, 2010, conducted on the farms in Ethiopia.
5. See http://mcarbonweb.a3ai.com/user_session/new. As accessed on April 1, 2011.
6. See http://unfccc.int/kyoto_protocol/mechanisms/clean_development_mechanism/items/2718.php. As accessed on February 1, 2014.
7. See http://www.ecosystemmarketplace.com/pages/dynamic/web.page.php?section=carbon_market&page_name=otc_market. As accessed on February 1, 2014.
8. See http://www.carbontradewatch.org/. As accessed on April 1, 2011.
9. See http://www.wired.com/wired/archive/12.10/tail.html. As accessed on February 1, 2014.
10. Of course work in the politics of digital technologies is much more complex than I have room for here. This, however, is not the main aim of the chapter here.
11. Since I have not done detailed anthropological research into local knowledge systems of climate change and weather patterns in Ethiopia (another fascinating topic), I will in this chapter focus only on the practices of translation in my own work. The broader work in Ethiopia still needs to be done (see Haakansson 2009).

12. See http://www.guardian.co.uk/environment/2009/nov/20/climate-sceptics-hackers-leaked-emails. As accessed on April 1, 2011.
13. This is perhaps most clearly exemplified by the enormous success of social network sites such as Facebook (500 million plus users) and Twitter (around 100 million users) as the new spaces that dominate activity on the internet.
14. See http://www.carbonfootprint.com/. As accessed on April 1, 2011.
15. See http://www.asia-europe.uni-heidelberg.de/en/news-events/events/event-view.html. As accessed on April 1, 2011.
16. For a good anthology of this work see Bryant et al. (2011).

References

Anderson, C. 2006. *The Long Tail: Why the Future of Business is Selling Less of More.* New York: Hyperion.
Asad, T. 1986. "The Concept of Cultural Translation," in James Clifford and George E. Marcus (eds), *Writing Culture: The Poetics and Politics of Ethnography.* Berkeley: University of California Press.
Baudrillard, J. 1994. *Simulacra and Simulation.* Ann Arbor: University of Michigan Press.
Bryant, L. R., G. Harman and N. Srnicek, eds. 2011. *The Speculative Turn: Continental Materialism and Realism.* Melbourne: Re-Press.
Science Newsline. 2010. "Carbon Mapping Breakthrough," September 6. http://www.sciencenewsline.com/nature/2010090612000007.html. As accessed on April 1, 2011.
De Bruijn, M., F. B. Nyamnjoh and I. Brinkman, eds. 2009. *Mobile Phones: The New Talking Drums of Everyday Africa.* Bamenda: Langaa Research and Publishing Common Initiative Group (RPCIG).
Deleuze, G. 1994. *Difference and Repetition.* New York: Columbia University Press.
Escobar, A. 1994. *Encountering Development: The Making and Unmaking of the Third World.* Princeton Studies in Culture, Power, History. Princeton: Princeton University Press.
Foucault, M. 1980. *Power/Knowledge: Selected Interviews and Other Writings, 1972–1977.* New York: Random House.
Haakansson, M. 2009. *When the Rains Fail: Ethiopia's Struggle Against Climate Change.* Copenhagen: Informations Forlag.
Harman, G. 2009. *Prince of Networks: Bruno Latour and Metaphysics.* Prahran: Re-Press.
Hobart, M. 1993. *An Anthropological Critique of Development: The Growth of Ignorance.* London: Routledge.
Latour, B. 2007. *Reassembling the Social: An Introduction to Actor-Network-Theory.* Oxford: Oxford University Press.

Marlow, J. 2009. "Selling Offsets by Mobile Phone in Ethiopia," *Green Inc. blog, The New York Times*, October 28. http://green.blogs.nytimes. com/2009/10/28/selling-offsets-by-mobile-phone-in-ethiopia/. As accessed on April 1, 2011.

Meillassoux, Q. 2008. *After Finitude: An Essay on the Necessity of Contingency.* Trans. Ray Brassier. London: Continuum.

Morton, T. 2010a. "Hyperobjects and the End of Commonsense," *The Contemporary Condition.* http://contemporarycondition.blogspot. com/2010/03/hyperobjects-and-end-of-common-sense.html. As accessed on April 1, 2011.

———. 2010b. *The Ecological Thought.* Boston: Harvard University Press.

———. 2007. *Ecology without Nature: Rethinking Environmental Aesthetics.* Boston: Harvard University Press.

Pohjonen, M. and S. Paul. 2011. "Theory and Practice in Emerging Digital Cultures in India," in S. Batabyal, A. Chowdhry, M. Gaur and M. Pohjonen (eds), *Indian Mass Media and the Politics of Change.* New Delhi: Routledge.

Shirky, C. 2009. *Here Comes Everybody: The Power of Organising Without Organisations.* New York: Penguin.

PART II

Media and Environmental Discourse in India

3

Greenathon

Organizing the Social-Conscience of Post-Liberalization Urban India

Smita Maitra

In 2009, India's leading news network New Delhi Television (NDTV) organized the first ever live fund-raiser for an environmental cause. The *Greenathon* – as it was called – has now become an annual event, and it is still the biggest environmental television event in India. It has passed into the general lexicon of environmental discourse in urban middle-class India and you can see the word being used by a wide range of people – from Bollywood idols to school teachers. It is used in various contexts, with varying meanings. In fact, the word "Greenathon" has detached itself from its original locale and become somewhat of a floating signifier for urban "elite" environmentalism.

But, when we at NDTV[1] came up with the idea of the *Greenathon*, our objective was much simpler. We wanted to do two things – (*a*) to create a television spectacle that would spread a basic environmental message to India's 200 million cable TV viewers and (*b*) to raise money for a specific environmental project. In some senses, it was a culmination of NDTV's dream of pushing the environmental issues into the mainstream news agenda. Till then, talking about the environment was considered to be the preserve of *jholawalas*[2] and non-governmental organizations (NGOs). NDTV had regularly covered environmental issues, but these failed to make it to the headlines. Environmental reporting and debates that revolved around radical activists and movements found few takers among NDTV's viewers, since much of the English news viewership today comprises the urban upper middle class with its conservative and consumerist orientation.

For the *Greenathon* team, this was a key concern. The viewer in India can choose between over a hundred channels at the press of a button, and with reducing attention spans, news television constantly fights to make the screen as engaging as possible to "hook" viewers. At its worst it degenerates into sensational tabloid TV,[3] but at its best it has created some world-class television. And, it will not be entirely inaccurate to say that NDTV has had a better record with quality television programming than others in the genre.[4]

The *Greenathon* needed to be interesting. It needed to get eyeballs. More so, because this was also going to be India's first telethon – a 24-hour fund-raiser live on TV.[5]

Variety show style entertainment is crucial to all telethons. If no one is watching, the entire purpose would be defeated – one would neither get the message across, nor raise the money meant for charity. There were two famous international models that we could emulate – the annual Jerry Lewis telethon which raised funds on Labor Day in the United States (US) and the British Broadcasting Corporation's (BBC's) *Red Nose Day*. Our sponsor Toyota also made us aware of a popular Japanese telethon called *Love Saves the Earth* organized by Nippon Television Network.

Although, we did find some elements in the Japanese telethon that we could borrow, we realized we would need an entirely different model to make it work for Indian viewers. Since the *Greenathon* was going to be telecast simultaneously on both our English and Hindi news channels it had to have a more heterogeneous appeal. Anyone who has watched both English and Hindi news television would realize the completely different tonality and aesthetics that the two languages inhabit, while ostensibly being in the same news business. While English news channels tend to emulate their counterparts in the US and United Kingdom (UK), Hindi news channels have developed their own idiom which is largely informed by indigenous story-telling traditions and the aesthetics of Bollywood. Therefore, we had the somewhat difficult task of catering to two very different demographics and finding a common programming ground for two different cultures.

In some senses, the choice for that common ground was obvious – Bollywood, India's massive film industry. Popular cinema, despite its growing gradations, has always been a great leveler in India, and we wanted to use it as the vehicle for spreading the green message. Our 24-hour telethon was going to be interspersed with Bollywood stars and popular singers and their performances. This was meant to be the "trap" to bring in the indifferent viewer who would otherwise not be interested in any cause. Once in, we expected them to get more involved in the environmental agenda and the fund-raising project. This was not a unique strategy. Using popular iconography to convey more serious messages has become a part and parcel of Indian news or social media, given the reducing attention spans of India's television-viewing audience. In other words, right from the beginning we knew for our green message to be consumed and digested, it first had to be packaged as entertainment.

The other part of the *Greenathon*, as a television event, was to make it participatory. This is yet another standard trope in live television across the globe. A television event seems to attract more eyeballs when it is interactive – where the audience feels they have agency in the way in which the event will unfold. Therefore, the *Greenathon* had elements of public participation woven into it – school children cleaning the Yamuna or a Mumbai beachfront, people running a marathon along with model-athlete Milind Soman, green quiz competition in Chennai among others.

Involving schools was a crucial part of the strategy as well. Children are the most receptive to new messages, especially when they are counter-intuitive and counter-experiential. Changing over to an environmentally-sensitive lifestyle requires a certain disruption in everyday lived practices and received rituals of daily living. Children, especially younger ones, are the most receptive to new messages because even existing family practices are new to them, which they acquire through years of training and emulating. Schools are a crucial part of this complex process of training.

Critical theory would see this as the process of "normalization," of turning a child into a social subject and marking it with the power relations immanent in the institutions and practices of "modern" society. Within that theoretical space, schools are seen as the most organized institutions that act as the conduit between the state and the family. Schools are the sites where an individual gets disciplined into a subject and gets embedded in the power/knowledge continuum. While critical theory admits that there is no space that escapes power-knowledge, it lends itself to a politics that is anti-institutional and critical of the very act of "disciplining." [6]

There is no doubt that critical theory would see *Greenathon* as a similar disciplinary project, which fits in easily within mainstream "statutory" discourses and does not question existing power structures. I have no intention of disputing that. On the contrary, I intend to defend the *Greenathon* as an event, which attempts to effect changes in mainstream everyday practices, which are desirable in an absolute sense, irrespective of their cultural contexts. I submit that commitment to protecting the environment and adopting "green" practices are universal, absolute values, which do not require politico-cultural justification or legitimacy. In that sense, it is simply a lifestyle choice such as quitting smoking or taking regular exercise. The *Greenathon*'s legitimacy – and desirability – lay in that specific ahistorical, apolitical sense of changing lifestyles and making people more aware about the fallout of environmentally harmful life choices.

As we proceeded, however, this largely "bourgeois" project got "complicated" by traces of older, socialist tropes, which brought the *Greenathon* straight back to its specifically Indian moorings. Those familiar with the *Greenathon* would know that it raised funds for a project run by The Energy Research Institute (TERI) called Light a Billion Lives (LaBL). LaBL aims to provide solar lanterns to villages in India that are not electrified. Solar lanterns, designed by TERI are provided to each family in the village and TERI also sets up solar charging stations. Each family can get its lanterns recharged for a nominal fee, which is enough to financially sustain the charging station. While TERI's model is mainly entrepreneurial [depending to a certain extent on Corporate Social Responsibility (CSR) initiatives of the private sector], in popular imagination LaBL has a certain "socialist" aura since it is aimed at the rural poor who operate outside the market system and the formal institutions of capitalism.

Even the government agrees now that India's two-decade-old experiment with structural adjustments and neo-classical-style economic liberalization has largely benefited the urban middle class. Despite high growth, inequities have increased and the rate of decline of poverty has actually dropped in the post-liberalization years. It is commonplace to assert that this has created a schism in India's socio-political fabric – the affluent are now largely disconnected from the poor, even where they live cheek-by-jowl next to each other. However, this is a simplistic statement of a complex social process. As our experience with the *Greenathon* shows, India's middle class still believes that giving to the poor makes for good "optics" – it makes one appear socially-conscious and responsible. On the other hand, standard green practices – recycling, shunning plastics, planting trees, etc. – are often perceived to be embedded in elite practices and their respective iconographies. Environmentalists are often dismissed as being pretentious and elitist and, at times, even being anti-people ("they care more for trees than people"). The *Greenathon* provided a bridge between these two discourses, marrying the middle-class concerns of environmentalism with the wider inclusive activism of lighting up the homes of the rural poor.

However, as I said earlier, the *Greenathon* was meant to be a straightforward environmental fundraiser. In fact, NDTV had been planning to do a telethon for many years, and its initial plan was to plant a million trees across India. Of course, a telethon is not an ordinary fundraiser. It is more an awareness builder than an efficient way to raise money for a cause. Organizing a 24-hour telethon costs big money and it was beyond NDTV's individual financial scope to do it alone. In 2008, Toyota walked in with a proposal to organize a telethon on the lines of Nippon Television's *Love Saves the Earth* event. It tied in perfectly with NDTV's own plans and Toyota was also going to provide crucial funds to put the show up.

At the outset, our team was told by the top management that this would not be a commercial project. NDTV would not make any money out of the *Greenathon.* Instead, the network would spend its own funds and incur the opportunity cost of handing over airtime to spread the green message. It wasn't just pious posturing – NDTV wanted to be remembered as the pioneer in bringing environmental-ism from the margins onto the mainstream broadcast platform. In fact, we realized very quickly, that the event itself would cost more than the money it was likely to raise. After all, this was the first of its kind social campaign. Our own team was kept small to manage costs and NDTV's own internal expenses were kept to the bare minimum.

In post-liberalization India even fundraisers have to be entrepre-neurial ventures. Our aims might have been non-commercial, but our decision to use Bollywood celebrities for the actual *Greenathon* event was bound to be costly. The Mumbai entertainment industry – actors, entertainers, event managers – does not understand the idea of non-commercial events. Each and every performer who appeared on the *Greenathon* had to be paid for their performances. For us at NDTV, this was a necessary evil. We needed the celebrities and stars to grab eyeballs and engage viewers, and the celebrities had no intention of doing it for free. (However, it is important to mention that several Bollywood stars – including India's biggest movie star Shahrukh Khan – donated significant sums during the *Greenathon* fundraiser.)

I feel almost maternal towards the project because it took about nine months to put the show together. It was our baby. NDTV and Toyota Motor Corporation came together in April 2008 and this was when the idea of the *Greenathon* was conceived. Before we even knew what the event would be like precisely, we had to get the word out and establish that NDTV was doing something like this so that we could claim the space even before we occupied it.

The first thing to do was choose a campaign ambassador. This was a very carefully thought-out decision. We needed a popular face and at the same time someone who was articulate and appealed to both the "masses and the classes." After some thinking we closed in on the popular Bollywood actress Preity Zinta. She seemed popular with all age groups, had a liberal image and did not have too many scandals attached to her back then. Zinta had done a few crossover films, had even played a journalist once and didn't hide her opinions about the world.[7] That made her perfect for us, as she gelled well with NDTV's news-based branding. Several meetings, negotiations and Delhi–Mumbai trips later she was on board for a certain sum. It was decided that she would appear in a music video, print and television spots, press conferences and even co-anchor the show with an NDTV anchor.

The *Greenathon*'s objective was to popularize environmentalism among the Indian urban middle class – that was the cause. But, we also needed a project for which we would raise funds. It had to be environmentally friendly, and it also had to make a concrete difference to people's lives. Finding the project turned out to be relatively easy. NDTV already had a rapport with TERI and their LaBL struck a chord with everyone.

Six out of ten villages in India plunge into complete darkness after the sun sets. These unlit villages use dung cakes and other primitive forms of lighting to see after dark. These indigenous forms of lighting were not meant to cater to the time-discipline of modern institutions, not even those which appear mundane to us, such as homework. The project would provide solar lanterns to each household in the chosen villages and also encourage entrepreneurship amongst women by putting them in charge of the lantern-charging stations where villagers could charge their lanterns for ₹2 every day.

Left to themselves, these villages were not scheduled to have electricity for another decade. By speeding the clock by 10 years, we were doing something radically meaningful. This meant that as a donor the viewer would be donating something concrete. ₹3,000 would mean one lantern and ₹300,000 would mean an entire village. It was not something intangible like "your money will help save the environment" or "your money will go to the poor." The viewer would know exactly where the money was going and they could contribute as little or as much as they wanted.

We tied up with newspapers, magazines and radio stations and an air of anticipation was built up – the *Greenathon* was coming soon. Over the next few months NDTV telecast a daily green report from across the country. We did stories on green crusaders, ordinary people like you and me doing something for the environment in their own small way. For example, the case of "Poly Baba" who made cloth bags and distributed them around his area in exchange for plastic bags, or the man in Allahabad who cleans the water coming in through a rivulet using his own home-made technology. There were also classroom-format programs explaining the science behind environmentalism and climate change. There were daily tips on how to make small changes in one's lifestyle to live a more green-friendly life.

We also produced a music video to target the young, especially school-going children. The song was written by Gulzar and the music composed by the Bollywood team of Shankar Mahadevan, Ehsaan Noorani and Loy Mendonsa. It was a catchy song and it became our first vehicle of making the project interactive for our viewers. School children all over the country were invited to send us video clippings of themselves singing the *Greenathon* anthem, which was then aired on NDTV's channels.

The next task was to develop a mechanism to accept donations live during the 24 hours that the show would be broadcast. It was decided that the money collected would be deposited directly to an existing TERI fund. So a system was set up whereby all online donations were routed via NDTV's own green website to TERI's portal. This was relatively easy. The difficult part was setting up more interactive and immediate modes of donation. Checks, demand drafts, etc. were fine but would not translate into immediate money on air. We needed Short Message Service (SMS) donations and phone donations. SMS donations were more difficult to set up than we thought. Telecom companies wanted their cut and we had to have several negotiations to make them understand that they could not make money off a charitable event. Commissions were kept to a bare minimum. A miniature call centre was set up within the NDTV office. NDTV teamed up with a call centre team who gave us the know-how while we gave them the content. They were trained for every possible question that the donor might have. And to encourage people to give larger sums, all donations were made tax exempt.

Quite frankly, we were not even sure we would raise even a hundred thousand rupees from this event and so we decided to raise some money prior to the actual telethon from corporate donations. I personally went to several corporate houses and marketed the event to them asking for donations for a cause I myself had started to feel strongly about. Several companies turned us down, especially as this was the beginning of the downturn of 2008, but a lot of them were positive as well. We raised a good bit of money through this route and in turn gave the corporates a few minutes' time during the *Greenathon* to talk about their company's green plans.[8]

The main event itself was to be a gala entertainment show interspersed heavily with the environment message. Every performer was taken aside for a chat on what environmentalism means to them and how we can do our bit. The production team's job was to weave together disparate elements into a single green fabric. The irreverent comedian Cyrus Broacha was brought in to anchor the show for 24 hours with Preity Zinta and senior NDTV journalist-anchor Vikram Chandra. Cyrus was meant to add a bit of fun in case things got boring, and to keep us from taking ourselves too seriously.

Each celebrity, actor, performer was to sign a solar lantern and all these were to be auctioned off later to raise more money for the LaBL project. We chose to do the event in Mumbai because our show depended heavily on Bollywood. Delhi would mean flying everyone and their entourage down first class and putting them up in fancy hotels, a cost we could not afford to incur. We booked a famous studio in Mumbai for the event. But, as NDTV people our expertise lay in producing news-related events. Working with Bollywood was uncharted waters for us. That's why we hired an event management company, with a lot of experience with organizing Bollywood-based shows to help us with key logistics. Of course, we had the expertise in covering cross-country live events (such as general elections) and NDTV's award winning engineering team was at its best and we pulled off the technical complexities of the fund-raiser effortlessly.

We felt that for the *Greenathon* to be successful we would need nationwide participation. We planned events in several Indian cities which would be open to the public. In Delhi we organized a "clean the Yamuna" drive in collaboration with an NGO called *Swecchha*, which does this every year. People turned up in hordes including several well-known people from the then Chief Minister of Delhi Sheila Dikshit to eminent artists (e.g., Anjolie Ela Menon) and popular rock bands. The river-cleaning went on for 24 hours and the garbage that came out of the river was transformed into an installation art by a sculptor and Menon did an impromptu painting which was later auctioned for the cause.

Several events were simultaneously held in other cities as well. In Mumbai, celebrities went to one of the city's dirty beaches and worked round the clock with local residents to clean it. Residents carried this further by cleaning their own localities. We sent our reporters out to cover as many of these events as we could. Model-athlete Milind Soman ran non-stop for 24 hours and raised money for every kilometer that he ran. He did not take any money for himself. Trees were planted around the country for 24 hours and we had live reports from across the country on everything – big or small – that people were doing to be part of the *Greenathon.*

We teamed up with Nokia to set up e-waste disposal boxes across the country and collected electronic waste, such as old cellphones and chargers. For every kilo of waste collected, Nokia planted a cor-responding number of trees. The show had something for everyone – a green fashion show, an organic cookery show, a green quiz, a green gadgets show. Some of India's best known classical musicians performed live, while Bollywood actors, singers and performers entertained viewers. The response was stupendous.

The word spread beyond India. Money came in from different parts of the world through SMS-checks and online donations. Famous people walked in to our studio on their own, without being part of the main program. It was a sign that the *Greenathon* had become a brand within just a few hours and celebrities wanted some of its shine to rub-off on them. In the end we had to increase the duration of the program by a couple of hours to accommodate donors. We raised nearly half a million dollars to light up 80 villages. In its own way, the *Greenathon* did manage to change the way India's urban middle class thought about environmentalism.

Our work didn't end with the show. Money kept trickling in for a long time after and every penny had to be accounted for. Tax exemption certificates needed to be sent out and we kept carrying out reports on activities that people continued to do for months after the event. In fact NDTV decided to keep the green stories alive through the year and not just around the time of the *Greenathon*. The campaign was initially a three-year campaign out of which two subsequent *Greenathons* have already been done.

Its biggest success is that the term "Greenathon" has entered popular lexicon in India's metros. This is especially true for schools and educational institutions. I was pleasantly surprised to see the word used in class displays in three prominent Delhi schools where I had gone for my daughter's nursery admissions. Interestingly, the word was used in random contexts for anything deemed environmentally friendly. In schools, "Greenathon" is being used for specific days that are declared as green or environmental days; the word itself has become a sort of "floating signifier" which is adapted to denote rudimentary environmentalism.

Environmentalist activism is not necessarily radical. In the US "reform environmentalism" has increasingly taken over ground from more confrontationist environmentalist groups, thanks to access to vast amounts of corporate funding (Barker 2010). The objective of reform environmentalism is to be:

> cautious reformers, challenge specific violators, take the worst of them to court, lobby for environmental regulations, educate the public, but don't rock (or knock) the industrial boat if you intend to rely on significant foundation funding (Dowie 2001: 94).

That should not be a surprise for a country which had been described as a plutonomy by a confidential Citigroup report to its clients in 2005. Citigroup analysts argued that the US is not a democracy, but rather a country where "economic growth is powered by and largely consumed by the wealthy few" (Kapoor et al. 2005: 1). Plutonomies can only exist where the government is "friendly and cooperative" to the interests of the super-rich. The Citigroup report also hints that real electoral democracy is a threat to the survival of plutonomies:

> Perhaps one reason that societies allow plutonomy, is because enough of the electorate believe they have a chance of becoming a

Plutoparticipant. Why kill it off, if you can join it? In a sense this is the embodiment of the "American Dream". But if voters feel they cannot participate, they are more likely to divide the wealth, rather than aspire to be rich (ibid.: 24–25).

I would argue that this "American Dream" is a meta-discourse in the US, which pervades many "local" discourses including mainstream or reform environmentalism. The effect of such discourses is to deflect public conscience away from environment-destroying corporate action and to perceive the reformist agenda of corporate-funded NGOs as true environmentalism. In other words, environmentalism has got reduced to "middle-class" urban practices of saving water, recycling paper and turning off the electric switch. This is a clear dilution of and in distinction to the more radical environmentalist activism, which attacks the very foundations of the industrial system, and in effect questions the economic and ethical rationale of capitalism.

I will use this as an entry point to explain "why" NDTV's *Greenathon* needed to be "popular" and "reformist" in its basic structure. To establish that, I will take the liberty of a detour into the cultural-discursive space of post-liberalization India. Some would argue that India today is also a plutonomy of sorts, where income and resources are concentrated in the hands of a very small minority.[9] The argument goes that government policy since the 1990s has been oriented towards enriching the rich further and public culture has sanctified that by giving it a garb of "good economics." This growing economic and cultural chasm between the rich and the poor, even where they share the same physical space, has many symptomatic expressions. Bollywood is one of them. It has moved away from the "socialist" narratives of the 1980s where Amitabh Bachchan[10] could be a coolie or a trade unionist, through the "nationalist/vigilante" narratives of the 1990s where a Dharmendra or Sunny Deol[11] took on the entire corrupt firmament of the state, to the current multiplex-oriented films that cater to upper-middle class and Non-Resident Indian (NRI) concerns.[12]

Television reproduces this cultural space of a very small part of India and turns it into a kind of aspirational device. Daily soaps try to bridge the gap between a Shahrukh Khan-starring NRI romance and the reality of everyday middle-class consumerism. Reality or talent shows represent a worm-hole to the wider viewer, where you enter as a marginalized aspirant and emerge miraculously "made-over" into someone who has arrived in the brash new world of high-growth India. News television, in turn, gives the theoretical/philosophical grounding for this consumerist ideology and its concurrent politics.

The iconography of middle-class discourse has undergone a tectonic shift since the market reforms of the 1990s. Austerity and self-denial were key to the basic socialistic iconography of pre-liberalization India, whereas the post-liberalization era is character-ized by the core thematic of consumption as a social and individual desideratum. The ideology of consumption pervades every aspect of middle-class existence and structures middle-class discourses.

The shift from state socialism to market economy and austerity to consumerism founds its corollary in the decline of the role of activ-ists and the intelligentsia. Much of this shift has been facilitated by a collaborative mainstream media, which has been an enthusiastic sup-porter of the all-pervasive role of the market. I submit that the decline in the social status and prestige of the activist has gone hand-in-hand with this marketization of middle-class existence. And this, in some ways, restricts the scope of any middle-class activism, including the middle class's ability to negotiate the politics of environmentalism.

This "handicap" defined the programming choices for NDTV as well, when we started planning the *Greenathon*. It will be an overstate-ment to say that our team was "aware" of the discursive basis of our choices – much of it is now de-rigueur. Yet, we knew that we had to make "populist" programming decisions to make the *Greenathon* a success and to attract people to the fund-raiser. Otherwise, the entire purpose of the show would have been defeated.

Our decision to privilege Bollywood over activists was clearly driven by this acute awareness that middle-class discourse is defined by consumption – it "consumes" news, politics and current-affairs as "entertainment." Therefore, we made the decision that the program-ming would be interspersed with Bollywood dance numbers and performances by playback singers from the Hindi film world. We did show a "serious" environmental film – Al Gore's *An Inconvenient Truth* (2006) – but it was tucked away late at night, where we did not expect much viewership or viewer participation. Prime time was occupied by performances and endorsements by Bollywood stars.

An analysis of our ratings and the "live" experience of the ebbs and flows in the fund-raiser clearly proved that our strategy of combining activism and entertainment was a major success. The *Greenathon* ran for 26 straight hours and despite its subject it matched the ratings of the most successful prime time shows of NDTV's flagship English language news channel – NDTV 24×7. It was broadcast simultaneously on three other NDTV channels – NDTV India (Hindi news channel), NDTV Profit (business news channel) and NDTV Good Times (Lifestyle channel). The *Greenathon* outperformed the average ratings of both NDTV Profit and NDTV Good Times.[13]

From everything that I have written till now, the *Greenathon* appears to fit into the typical descriptor of a corporate-sponsored, market-friendly environmentalist event whose effect is to distract from the "real" radical agenda of environmentalist activism and reduce it to a reformist middle-class hobby. Critics would argue that environmentalism of the *Greenathon* type that does not challenge the power-structures that *cause* environmental degradation end up supporting those power-structures.

This would be especially true if someone with a critical-theoretical lens looked at the way the *Greenathon* targeted, and was appropriated by, public schools. For a critical theorist the school is the primary site of "disciplining" a child into a modern subject who embodies the power-knowledge relations of our society. Schools push reformist environmentalism aggressively and even train children to take the elements of this environmentalism into their family space. Young students are encouraged to tell their parents how virtuous it is to "recycle and reduce." In fact, many schools actively believe that by training children in this kind of *reformist* environmentalism, they are making a *radical* contribution to the future of the environment.

On the face of it, the *Greenathon* falls squarely within this category of reformist environmentalism. Yet, I would argue, the real process was much more complex, and this complexity unconsciously determined our own choice of who would be the beneficiary of the funds that the *Greenathon* raised. As I have written earlier, we believed that for the fundraiser to be successful donors needed something concrete and tangible that could be identified as a beneficiary. This is partly because television works best when it is structured around a concrete narrative which can be broken down into experientially tangible elements. Thus, television newswriting often works on the "P to G" format that begins with the personal (P) and then goes to the general (G). That is why we needed our fundraiser to have the same personal/concrete character. Raising money for the environment at large, or even for a large environmental project (e.g., recycling paper), would have been too general and abstract for viewers to identify with.

The other reason why we needed a concrete project as the beneficiary of our funds was because viewers are increasingly suspicious about fundraising drives. An abstract objective that could not be monitored was likely to be seen with a degree of skepticism, despite the NDTV name, which commands a high level of credibility among India's urban viewership. It would not be wrong to say that the post-liberalization Indian thinks twice before parting with their money, and that they require a very good reason to donate money in a non-market transaction, which does not bring anything in return.

Of course, one has to discount for the fact that environmentalism is now considered to be something fashionable by the urban Indian middle class. Reformist environmentalism is seen as a "safe" way to show a conscience and at the same time its appropriation by the elite makes it a good ideological vehicle for upward mobility. Therefore, we could always expect a certain degree of participation, especially from organized ideological institutions like schools and colleges. One could also count on participation from celebrities, since everyone wants to be considered an environmentally-conscious person nowadays. Yet, as our experience showed, espousing the green cause was not considered a "charitable" function in India. While celebrities were easily accessible, those who performed during the event did charge their standard fee. It is true however that a part of that fee was returned as donation to the LaBL project.

There seems to have been a virtual mental compartmentalization, wherein a performer sub-consciously distinguished between the overall green cause and the immediate reason for which funds were being raised. It was easy to find people to speak for the environment, but it wasn't easy for us to get them to do it for free. On the other hand, money poured in for the LaBL project, not only during the 26 hours that we were on air, but also after that. The *Greenathon* cost a lot of money to organize and present, because unlike NDTV, every other participant – event managers, studios, celebrities – treated the event itself as a business transaction. However, lighting the lives of marginalized villagers was seen as a worthy objective and the very same participants ended up donating money to it.

I would argue that this internal dichotomy that was characterized by the distinction between the cause (green awareness) and the donation target (LaBL) mirrors India's middle-class conscience today. My argument will take me into uncharted territory, which some might dismiss as pure speculation. Nevertheless, I will hazard an attempt to explain what I faced experientially as being part of the *Greenathon* team.

Environmentalism or green activism is not new to the Indian experience and neither is it restricted to the elite. In fact, as the legendary *Chipko Andolan*[14] showed, some of India's most successful green movements have had entirely indigenous origins and emerged from rural settings. Yet, in dominant public discourse, environmentalism has often been branded as "elite" activism. Even the mainstream left, which in other countries has provided political sustenance to environmentalism, has been skeptical about environmental activism in India. Ironically, this tag of "elitism" brands both the fashion designer who uses recycled plastic to create the latest couture line and the Medha Patkars or Arundhati Roys who go on hunger strikes or court the ire of the judiciary to fight the battle of the dispossessed.

It is this "elitist" branding that worked as an inherent handicap for the *Greenathon* as well, and made it difficult for us to get celebrities to contribute their services as a kind of "activism." I doubt if anyone would have charged us performance-fees if the cause was the eradication of child malnutrition.[15] I would submit that poverty is still the key thematic that moves India's urban middle class to donate selflessly.[16] It is a continuation of the socialist rhetoric of the pre-liberalization Indian state which centered around/on the tropes of giving and sharing. This was a *positive* rhetoric that fashioned an identity. Market reforms introduced by the Rao–Manmohan duo in the 1990s displaced this socialist rhetoric, calling it utopian and branding it as "bad economics." Yet, unlike other market-driven nations, which have their own "positive" identities that have been developed over decades of gradual transformation, the post-liberalization urban Indian was left with only *negative* identities. It was negative because it *negated* the past and defined itself in contradistinction to a history that was seen as obsolete. Attempts to propagate a positive identity of "India Shining" failed miserably in the 2004 general elections and it forced India's urban middle class to take another look at the "India Invisible."[17]

It is this failure of developing a positive market-based ideology that allowed the traces of the old socialist rhetoric to continue within the post-liberalization urban Indian discourse. These traces show up in the social value associated with "giving" to the poor and the marginalized. This could be termed the ideology of "donor-socialism." In everyday practice, the poor function within the power dynamics of the market place as sellers of labor and services – "we pay them what the market decides, so they better work, in sickness and in health." Yet, the same person can become a beneficiary of a donation when he or she is perceived as being in need. In our daily urban experience, we let the market operate through an act of "forgetting" where the structural nature of poverty appears only in and as a market relation that "discovers" a market price for all goods and services. Despite that, there is a real experience of poverty and destitution all around us. That experience is treated as marginal, or even external, to the ideal functioning of the market, where everyone is supposed to get remunerated for the quality and value of the goods or services they provide. For the middle class, therefore, "giving" to the poor becomes a marginal/external experience that is meant to iron out the kinks in the system.

I believe this dual existence – within and outside the market – defines India's middle-class discourse. When it appropriates an "elite" ideology like reformist environmentalism, the middle class operates within the market place, albeit within the sphere of ideas. Environmentalism of this kind is seen as an aspirational idea, which provides opportunities for cultural mobility. It is an idea that is "cool" and "with it." It is an idea that is to be *consumed,* just as cultural trends are consumed by the middle class to mark out its own identity and separate social space.

On the other hand, "donor-socialism" is an expression of the collective guilt of the urban middle class, which realizes that the gains of liberalization have not been universal. In fact, as I have argued earlier, there is clear evidence that inequities have increased in post-liberalization India and the pathology of this growing inequality shows up as so many symptoms within the social body. It is like a niggling pain that one ignores lest its investigation leads to a more serious diagnosis.

One can argue that the choice of LaBL as the final beneficiary of the fundraiser was itself unconsciously driven by our own proclivities towards donor-socialism. At the end of the day, the money being raised was literally for the poorest of the poor – people who live in the remotest villages that still don't get electricity. Of course, the LaBL project is environmentally sensitive since it seeks to popularize solar energy, but its appeal to the average viewer lay not so much in its commitment to green energy, but in its ability to light the lives of poor villagers.

The *Greenathon* provided a bridge between the two levels at which middle-class activism can work. On the one hand, there is reformist environmentalism, which is an aspirational and fashionable ideology. On the other, there was the quasi-socialist activity of giving to the poor. In bridging these two different – but connected – discourses, the *Greenathon* organized the collective conscience of the urban middle class in post-liberalization India.

It is easy to dismiss this kind of activism. It is easy to deride as being simplistic and wrong-headed. Yet, I would argue, one can make a case for the desirability of reformist environmentalism as an absolute value. No one can doubt that it is better to recycle than continue to manufacture more products that are non-biodegradable. Similarly, it is better to switch off the light and turn off the tap than waste resources. Yes, none of these actions will make any radical difference to the systemic degradation of the environment. But, surely it is better to make a limited effort than be entirely indifferent and ignorant about environmental issues. As mentioned earlier, a green lifestyle is a value in itself, irrespective of the political context in which it appears. In that sense, it can be compared to the desirability of universal humanitarian values that are irreducible to their cultural-ideological contexts.

It is in this sense that I would like to claim a valid cultural discursive space for the *Greenathon* and all its future avatars. It has brought a dry subject like the environment into urban drawing rooms. It has imparted a glamorous sheen to practices which were perceived to be the preserve of faddists. And for me personally, it has given me every reason to be proud of being part of a pioneering effort to make television meaningful again.

❄

Notes

1. The author was part of the core team that produced the first *Greenathon* in 2009. She was an employee of NDTV at that time. However, the views and opinions expressed in this chapter are entirely her own and have not been authorized by NDTV.
2. The term *jholawala* is used to denote the left intellectual who literally dresses the part by carrying a trademark *jhola* (shabby cloth bag) as a marker of her/his politics.

3. Much of the Hindi news space is dominated by tabloid television, which focuses on things like gossip about movie stars, bizarre events, astrology and superstition. The leader in this tabloid genre is the Hindi news channel India TV, which recently broadcast a show claiming the slain Pakistani leader Benazir Bhutto's ghost had entered their television studio!

4. NDTV or New Delhi Television is a news network run by one of India's most respected broadcasters, Prannoy Roy. It is widely recognized as one of India's most credible news platforms.

5. *The New Oxford Dictionary of English* defines a telethon as "a very long television programme broadcast, typically one broadcast to raise money for a charity" (1906).

6. I am obviously referring here to the works of Michel Foucault (especially Foucault, 1991). I would also like to acknowledge the influence of Foucault's one-time teacher Louis Althusser (especially Althusser, 1971).

7. Preity Zinta had earned public respect when she became the only Indian actor who agreed to become a witness against underworld don Chhota Shakeel in court, while most of her colleagues were too scared to appear in the case.

8. One could argue that this essentially gave a free platform to corporates and NDTV ended up giving them legitimacy. However, it would be utopian to expect that companies will do anything without a direct or indirect profit motive. Our stand was that it makes no difference to the ultimate beneficiaries of the fundraiser if the donor gets a branding spin-off from the exercise.

9. The Gini coefficient for India has increased from 0.325 in 1999–2000 to 0.44 in 2004–05.

10. Amitabh Bachchan is arguably India's most popular movie star of all times. He was voted the "Greatest Star of the Stage or Screen of the Millennium" in a BBC online poll held in 1999, beating Lawrence Olivier who ranked a distant second.

11. Dharmendra and his son Sunny Deol are two Bollywood stars known for playing vigilante characters in extremely violent Hindi films of the 1980s and early 1990s.

12. The NRI-oriented films were pioneered by Aditya Chopra [*Dilwale Dulhaniya Le Jayenge* (1995)] and his cousin Karan Johar [*Kuchh Kuchh Hota Hai* (1998), *Kabhi Alvida Na Kehna* (2006)]. Their films are typified by their grand scale, high production quality, advertisement-film style colors, and urban middle-class themes.

13. Interestingly, despite the heavy dose of Bollywood, the show flopped on NDTV India. Does that mean that the agenda of reformist environmentalism is still a concern of the English-speaking elite?

14. It was a movement started by peasant women in the Chamoli district in Uttarakhand, where they stopped timber merchants from cutting trees by hugging them, or figuratively "sticking" (*chipko*) to the trees.

15. The experience of the Give India Foundation, which collects anything and everything for the needy, shows that even the busiest of celebrities are willing to donate their time for causes related to poverty.

16. Of course, I am excluding religious donations, which some would say are like business transactions – offerings made to God in exchange for divine blessings.

17. In 2004, the ruling National Democratic Alliance (NDA) built its campaign around the concept of "India Shining" which focused on the supposed gains made by the average Indian citizen during NDA's rule. The NDA's defeat surprised many – including the media – who had started to believe the mythologies of market reforms that they themselves had helped to create.

References

Althusser, L. 1971. "Ideology and Ideological State Apparatuses: Notes towards an Investigation," in *Lenin and Philosophy and Other Essays*. London: Verso.

Barker, M. 2010. "Co-Opting the Green Movement," *The New Left Project*, August 1. http://www.newleftproject.org/index.php/site/article_comments/co-opting_greens_the_environmental_foundations_of_capitalism. As accessed on August 5, 2010.

Dowie, M. 2001. *American Foundations: An Investigative History*. Massachusetts: MIT Press.

Foucault, M. 1991. *Discipline and Punish: The Birth of the Prison*. London: Penguin.

Kapoor, A., N. Macleod and N. Singh. 2005. "Plutonomy: Buying Luxury, Explaining Global Imbalances," *Citigroup Industry Note*, October 16. https://docs.google.com/file/d/0B-5-JeCa2Z7hNWQyN2I1YjYtZTJjNy00ZWU3LWEwNDEtMGVhZDDVjNzEwZDZm/edit?hl=en_US&pli=1. As accessed on October 16, 2005.

The New Oxford Dictionary of English. 1998. Oxford: Oxford University Press.

4

New Delhi's *Times*

Creating a Myth for a City

Somnath Batabyal

It was while I was answering the queries of a prospective landlord in south Delhi's Panchsheel Enclave that some of the idiosyncrasies of the city's class struggles became clear. The interview had been going well so far. The usual boxes had been ticked, educational status, foreign-based job, etc. Now it came down to the nitty-gritty – how loud a party could I throw, were there any restrictions on friends (read women)? It was about then that the good doctor (an implantologist) mentioned that he had four cars. I nodded appreciatively enough despite thinking "why the hell do you and your wife require so many?" He then said that I could park my car (what do I drive?) nearer to the market. I smiled reassuringly and told him not to worry: I would take the bus. It was here that the mood of the interview changed perceptively. Husband and wife exchanged glances, moments of uncomfortable quiet ensued and then I was asked to show my salary slip.

One does not, of course, stay in the posh colonies of south Delhi and take the bus, not unless you are a menial worker, cleaning its streets and houses, tending the well-kept lawns and wives. I had chosen the location however, precisely because the Bus Rapid Transport (BRT) corridor was situated round the corner. The BRT, simply put, is a dedicated bus corridor that allows for faster movement of public transport thus incentivizing its use. In Delhi, however, it has meant that car owners have felt deprived of what they feel is their birthright to use every inch of motorable space and then some more. The BRT, therefore, is perhaps the largest symbolic manifestation of the class struggles of Delhi in the first decade of the 21st century; fought in the city's media and streets, amongst opinion makers and the voters. Unwittingly, I had stumbled on to a war zone.

An Ex-Journalist Tries to Remap His City

My academic qualifications still feel new, and it was in the garb of a journalist that I had known Delhi for nearly a decade. It was to this profession that I turned as I sought to understand what I felt was an epistemic shift in Delhi's urban politics, its sudden and utter rejection of the poorer classes, "the politics of forgetting" the economically disadvantaged (Fernandes 2004: 2415). I went about meeting ex colleagues and bosses whom I had worked with and the younger, rising stars of television in an effort to understand what had changed.

The *change* I refer to must be understood in a context as the very word that presupposes a history. One of India's foremost historians, Ramachandra Guha, comparing environmental movements in India and the US, has stated that unlike the post-materialist discourse in the States, there has been an "environmentalism of the poor" (Guha and Martinez-Alier 1998: 70), which has included social movements like the *Chipko Andolan* and the *Narmada Bachao Andolan* – movements which have "pitted rich against poor: logging companies against hill villagers, dam builders against forest tribal communities, multinationals deploying trawlers against traditional fisherfolk in small boats" (ibid.: 3). Most of these movements are well documented in both national and regional media which have reflected a strong support for the under-privileged.

As somebody who has been a city reporter in the 1990s in Delhi, I, however, had a different hunch. I started sifting through scores of newspaper clippings focusing on two media-led environmental campaigns – the clean air drive of the mid-1990s and the campaign against the BRT in 2008. I also interviewed several journalists and non-governmental organization (NGO) activists. What I found was that from the 1990s onwards – the post-liberalization era – an inherently middle-class media has actively worked with other actors, including NGOs and courts, to shift the environmental politics from its "red" leanings to richer hues. I realized that as long as the environmental concerns had remained "out there," the national media – a sector of which I was a part too – was happy to be looked upon as "pro poor." However, the moment the focus of environmental activism and awareness shifted to the cities (here Delhi), an essentially middle-class media shrugged off its pro-poor pretensions to reveal a new kind of *bourgeois environmentalism* which privileged middle-class concerns above anything else.

The Mid-1990s: Gasping for Breath

In 1995, I was just out of college and working as a crime reporter in one of the leading broadsheets, scouring the city's streets for stories on a motorbike, a handkerchief tied across my face. Delhi was unliveable. Black, acrid smoke hung in the air, buses and trucks belched out poisonous fumes, diesel cars were fast becoming the rage and clean air was confined to the concept of the idyllic countryside which was captured in pictures and hung above the mantelpiece. The environment was not really a city beat and no one reported much on it, nor did we know anyone who did. The government launched the Pollution Under Control (PUC) drive, which involved the checking of the exhaust of cars at petrol pumps and it was the duty of the crime reporter to check for evasions. We knew things were bad but we did not know whom to hold responsible, how to write the story. In a medium which prefers simplicity above all else, the subject matter was rather complicated. Thus we continued.

Somewhere around the end of 1997, a full-page advertisement was carried out in *The Times of India* by one of Delhi's leading environmental NGOs, the Centre for Science and Environment (CSE).[1] The advert screamed "51,779 dead by breathing" (CSE 1998: 5). The press community got interested. Headlines followed "Air pollution in Delhi has claimed more victims than the terrorists' guns in India" (ibid.: 5). Another pointed out that there was one pollution-related death per hour in India's capital. A simple narrative which linked air pollution to sickness and death and managed to bypass the complicated mathematics of harmful particulate matters in the air, its relationship to the petroleum and auto industries, the nexus between politicians and the transport lobby and so on, was picked up by the journalists. Reporters understood through experience of being out on the streets that bad air was harming us. The story easily became personal.

The Centre for Science and Environment (CSE) Campaign for Clean Air

The CSE campaign, as their late director Anil Aggarwal put it, "began without any premeditated design" (CSE 2006: 5). It was in the summer of 1995, while waiting to get the tail pipe of his car checked for pollution at a petrol pump that Aggarwal felt vehicle owners were being unnecessarily penalized for a problem that did not start with them. CSE launched an investigation into air pollution in our cities which was published in the public domain as "Slow Murder" in November 1996. It brought to light not only the wide-ranging factors which had contributed to the "pollution mud pie" but also the politician/auto industry nexus which turned a blind eye to the problem (ibid.: 3).

Just after the publication of "Slow Murder" on November 18, 1996, the Supreme Court of India joined hands with the activists and issued a *suo motto* notice to the Delhi Government to submit an action plan to control air pollution in the city in November, 1996, merging the notice with a public interest litigation (PIL) filed by a lawyer, M. C. Mehta way back in 1986 and on which little action had been taken till now. To put pressure on the government to take action, CSE also decided to launch a public interest campaign called the "Right to Clean Air" around the same time. Through advertisements in newspapers and lobbying journalists who were only too eager to comply, a forceful campaign was built up. Anumita Roychowdhury, who heads the CSE's Air Pollution division, told me in an interview:

> It was the Clean Air Campaign which marked a definite shift in the CSE policy. We became an advocacy group, a lobbying force for change. We understood how to use the media to pressurise the state through this campaign. Our later campaigns were shaped through this understanding (New Delhi, January 9, 2010).

The Union Ministry of Environment and Forest, forced into action, formed the Environment Pollution (Prevention and Control) Authority (EPCA) in January 1998 which would be responsible for the National Capital Region (NCR). It was headed by senior bureaucrat Bhure Lal, environmental activist Anil Aggarwal, the then Transport Commissioner of Delhi, Kiran Dhingra and Jagdish Khattar, former Executive Director (marketing and sales), Maruti Udyog Ltd, who represented the automobile industry. The EPCA, therefore, saw for the first time the coming together of the state, activists and the corporate sector to give a definite shape to Delhi's physical environments.

Based on the recommendations of the EPCA, a comprehensive court order was issued in July 1998 that included the elimination of leaded petrol, the replacement of old autorickshaws (motorized three-wheel passenger vehicles) and taxis, the augmentation of the bus fleet in the city to 10,000 from 6,600 and, most strikingly, the conversion of all buses, autorickshaws, and taxis from diesel and petrol to compressed natural gas (CNG). After some back and forth on the CNG issue, the final phase-out period for diesel buses was from April to November 2002. Furthermore, new emission standards for private vehicles (Bharat-I and Bharat-II based on the euro standards) were introduced, and the driving of (diesel) trucks was banned during daytime in the NCT (Veron 2006: 2099).

The court order was one thing, getting it implemented another. "The orders could only be implemented if there was political will; unfortunately there was none. Politicians were not convinced about the problem" (CSE 2006: 7). However, the struggle to implement the court's orders, given the government's prevarication, was dealt with severely by the media. When the then Health Minister Harsh Vardhan claimed that air pollution was not a serious health problem, the media hounded him and forced him to retract. The Lieutenant Governor's remark that the Delhi pollution was simply dust particles, sparked off a huge media outcry (CSE 1998: 7). Public opinion, moulded by the press and an activist judiciary, forced the Delhi government's hand and by mid-2003 the Clean Air Campaign launched by CSE had achieved most of its objectives. The air quality improved visibly and even today, when the burgeoning affluent population adds a thousand cars a day to the city, Delhi is spared the noxious diesel and petrol fumes from ancient buses and trucks.

However, along with the air quality of Delhi, a few other things also changed, which perhaps CSE had not bargained for. The campaign definitely helped in making urban environmental issues a legitimate concern in the city's mainstream media. But in attempting to push environment from the fringes to the center of political discourse via the media, it probably did not envisage that essentially middle-class journalists writing for a largely middle-class audience would throw aside the earlier "pro-poor" concerns of India's environmental movement. As studies show, the poor had other more immediate things to worry about than air pollution. While the media placed priority on clean air and beautification drives, it was "water supply and sanitation [that] formed the greatest environmental priorities for Delhi's poor inhabitants" (Veron 2006: 2101). In a comprehensive study done on Delhi's slums, inadequate and insufficient sanitation were found to be the most severe deficiency while noise and air pollution were mentioned as merely "adding to the extremely poor conditions of environment" (Ali 2003: 2). These concerns were however not the media's priority for Delhi, nor of the new kind of environmental awareness which was emerging in urban India. The "environmentalism of the poor" vanished into the dustbins of history as an elite media and its readership sought to etch a *bourgeois environmentalism* that privileged the concerns of the burgeoning middle class over any other.[2]

In this context, the next section will look at the campaign against the BRT corridor.

The Anti-BRT Media Campaign

Unlike the CNG, the BRT's public profile was doomed from the start. A residential colony of the city's influential journalists was situated close by and a host of them who made their way towards central Delhi for work every morning were inconvenienced. A senior editor in one of the city's biggest newspapers told me that as his car was stuck in traffic one morning, he decided to run a campaign against the corridor. Like the CNG campaign, it was also personal. But in a different way. Other newspapers and television channels, especially in the English language, unequivocally panned the project. Even at its trial period in May 2008 (the height of summer is probably a bad time to start anything), the press coverage was unsparingly scathing. The project did not stand a chance.

"What the press missed," said the genial Sam Miller of the British Broadcasting Corporation (BBC), pausing from his evening run near the Siri Fort to have a chat with me, "was that it was *supposed* to inconvenience cars. That was the whole point." In contrast to the Metro, which started in the poorer parts of the capital, Sam pointed out that the BRT suffered from being situated in the heart of the affluent south Delhi. "The Metro came up quietly. People got to know about it, then they wanted to have a day out on it. They got used to it. The BRT inconvenienced the powerful," he said (New Delhi, February 2010).

In another interview, Siddharth Pandey, a senior journalist in NDTV who covers environment-related issues, started laughing when I asked him if he had ever taken a bus on the BRT corridor. "Are you joking? I am just trying to get to my office in the morning. The bosses will lynch me if I try a stunt like that and say I am taking the bus." I asked him how he knew, in that case, that the BRT was a disaster. "Well you should look at the cars stuck in the morning traffic. It is a long queue. I mean they (the government) should have tried something else" (New Delhi, February 22, 2010).[3] Like what? No clear answer emerges.

In *Down to Earth*, Sunita Narain, Director of CSE, writes: "BRT is about equity on the road." She states that the logic of a bus corridor is irrefutable:

> The bus moves more than 50 per cent of the city but does not get proportionate space. In the first stretch of the Delhi BRT corridor, over this last year, buses have doubled to 3,000 – they now commute roughly 200,000 people each day (2010: 1).

As Narain points out, the BRT "meant taking from a few and giving to many" (ibid.). But amongst these *few* were the powerful articulators of our reality, the journalists and their audience. Together they created a public opinion against the BRT that was so strong that the then Chief Minister Sheila Dixit was worried that her re-election in 2009 was doomed. The Bharatiya Janata Party's (BJP's) chief ministerial candidate, Vijay Kumar Malhotra, taking advantage of the media outcry, promised to make the BRT an "election issue."[4] A close aide in Sheila Dixit's office who monitors the press told me in an interview that after much thought it was decided that the "song and dance" about the BRT was being created by an elite media which did not represent a vast section of the people. "The poor people who actually voted in the elections use buses. We decided to ignore the media's doom and gloom predictions," he said (New Delhi, February 18, 2010). The predictions turned out to be false and Sheila Dixit won a thumping victory. A media, divorced from ground realities, had egg on its face.

How did an urban media manage to convert an environmentalism which had emerged primarily out of social concerns in India to its new *bourgeois avatar?* This monumental shift must be understood in the context of the larger political economy of the country and the changing media ecology.

A Changing Delhi and its Journalists

The liberalization process of the mid-1990s was, whichever side of the fence one sits on, a watershed moment, both for the economy and the wider socio-political sphere. Nowhere was this more marked than in the country's media – staid old Doordarshan gave way to Star's *Bold and Beautiful*. Newspaper wars were just hotting up as *The Times of India* and the *Hindustan Times* launched their one-up-manship campaigns to achieve dominance in the capital. But more importantly, the journalists – their aims, ambitions and desires for themselves – were changing. The particularities of the profession require a certain skill level which in India, as also in most other countries, is equated with the middle and more affluent classes. Media scholar J. V. Ginneken writes: "Most journalists are middle-class in social background, social position and social aspirations" (1998: 71). In an interview with me, Debashish Mukerji, Senior Associate Editor of the *Hindustan Times* put it succinctly:

> We suddenly had journalists who were travelling regularly, some on meaningless junkets, some on stories. Closer to home destinations like Singapore and Hong Kong were getting to be a regular fare. These journalists, dazzled by what they saw, started imagining the same for their city. Judges travelled, petty officials travelled and the glamour of the West was brought home. Now they wanted the same in their city (New Delhi, March 8, 2010).

The "same in our city" zeal metamorphosed into several "cleanliness" drives. Just a couple of years before the Clean Air Campaign was launched, noted academic Amita Baviskar wrote:

> through a series of judicial orders, the Supreme Court of India has initiated the closure of all polluting and nonconforming industries in the city, throwing out of work an estimated 2 million people employed in and around 98,000 industrial units. At the same time, the Delhi High Court has ordered the removal and relocation of all jhuggi squatter settlements on public lands, an order that will demolish the homes of more than 3 million people. In a city of 12 million people, the enormity of these changes is mind-boggling (2003: 90).

What Baviskar perceives to be mind-boggling was nothing compared to what was to come:

Between 1990 and 2003, 51,461 houses were demolished in Delhi under "slum clearance" schemes. Between 2004 and 2007 alone, however, at least 45,000 homes were demolished, and since the beginning of 2007, eviction notices have been served on at least three other large settlements (Bhan 2009: 127).

The fourth estate, with minor exceptions, has been largely supportive of the drive. K. S. Sachidananda Murthy, Resident Editor of the Malayala Manorama Group in Delhi said in an interview with me:

> Of course the press is middle class with a middle class vision. We are so middle class that we are also anti- super rich. We are happy when, say Delhi Development Authority, goes out to acquire land (DDA) or the Noida Development Authority does so. We think we can get housing under their schemes, our readers can. But come SEZs we turn against even the top corporate houses indiscriminately, be it an Indian company like Reliance or a foreign entity like the Salim group in Nandigram. But yes, it is the middle class interest we have in our hearts and that is very closely linked to our reader profile. One must keep that in mind (New Delhi, January 21, 2010).

Murthy's link between the social status of the journalist and that of his/her reader is extremely important. He is saying that middle-class journalists write for a middle-class audience, the rest of the world be damned. A few years back, researching the politics of television news production in India, I had a long interview with the Vice President of Human Resources of Star News, Sanju Saha, who said:

> Of late we realise that even within our top target audiences or target consumers, there is a certain niche. There are a lot of English speaking people who watch news; hence what is relevant to them requires a little change in the sort of profiling of our editorial people. We need journalists who are able to understand lifestyle, who are able to understand big city issues, big city stories, and stories which are of interest to a different mass (Mumbai, August 2006).

Saha takes Murthy's observations a step further by wanting to profile journalists as per their socio-economic background so that a direct match-making can be made between viewers and news producers.

But why is this worrying? Why should a conversation between middle-class producers of news and their consumers bother us? Let me provide an illustration of what can go horribly wrong when a singular vision is pursued at the annihilation of all others. In 2006, during a research stint in Kolkata, I was closely following the news on the recently launched first 24-hour Bengali news channel, Star Ananda. One of the most followed stories was that of an Indonesian businessman who was coming to the Haldia district of West Bengal, proposing to invest millions of dollars in opening a petro-chemical hub there. This naturally involved the acquisition of thousands of acres of farmlands from villagers. In one of the live updates, while the businessman was visiting the land soon to be acquired, a studio anchor asked the reporter present at the spot whether the villagers felt unhappy about being dispossessed from their lands. The reporter replied quite to the contrary, saying that the villagers had realized that such investments were for their own good and they were happily giving up their lands. A year later, in the series of incidents now referred to as "Nandigram massacre," hundreds of villagers died in clashes with the state. A middle-class reporter on Star News had articulated his own, and his perceived audience's desire for foreign investment and job opportunities. It contradicted other desires, but these were left silenced by the coverage. Nandigram must by no means be seen as an exception. The BJP's much publicized "India Shining" election campaign of 2003 also failed without the middle-class media noticing. They had bought into the BJP's IT and software dream for themselves and their audiences. The India that voted had other desires.

What is noteworthy in both the media-led environmental campaigns is the silencing of dissident voices that could contest the dominant rhetoric in the press. Sure, during the campaign for CNG, the media would pay lip service to the story of the disgruntled auto-rickshaw driver who was forced to switch from petrol to cleaner fuel and thus invest a sum of money which he had not anticipated. But these were bracketed as "human interest" stories of people "out there," not germane to the main concern of a pollution-free city. It was never personalized. The anti-BRT campaign, by contrast, was personal. The journalist and his/her audience were on the same footing; they were both affected. The condemnation was utter and complete. The national media as one voice almost universally panned the project. All other possible constructions were silenced or marginalized.

Conclusion

The Clean Air Campaign and the BRT corridor have at their heart a core similarity; both wanted to reduce vehicular pollution, the former by the use of clean fuel, the latter by encouraging public transport. But while the media took excitedly to the first, the more recent one was rejected. Behind this acceptance of one and rejection of the other lies the crux of *bourgeois environmentalism* whereby the middle and affluent classes demand a clean, beautiful city for themselves, but without having to pay a price for it. The poor, therefore, must bear the brunt of a middle-class imagination that has very little in it for them. This imagined city is dreamt up in our films, books, foreign visits and now, increasingly in our media. Outside the world of this discourse lies the war zone, the BRT corridor, a reminder of a battle that we have lost, if temporarily. Here, despite the haggard-looking traffic minders in their blue uniforms, we succeed in imposing our own order. We drive our cars into the bus corridors. Our scooters and motorbikes (sometimes cars) speed on the bicycle lanes, honking the pedestrians and cyclists out of the way. What the state has taken away from us, we reclaim in our everyday protests. The chaos that ensues is blamed on the BRT corridor.

Bourgeois environmentalism as opposed to the "environmentalism of the poor" describes the politics of our times. "While state socialist ideologies tended to depict workers or rural villagers as the archetypical citizens and objects of development in the early decades in post-colonial India, mainstream national political discourses increasingly depict the middle classes as the representative citizens of liberalizing India" (Fernandes 2004: 2416). In an increasingly urbanized India, we have little time to hear of the travails of the landless peasant, of the tribal driven out of his home, of forests being denuded, of illegal mining contracts that ravage our hills. But even as we refuse to talk about them, they do not go away. When violence erupts, like the Naxal movements in several parts of the country, we throw in the state might against them. The violence is still out there. If the mainstream media continues to misrepresent the majority, the discontent in cities may express itself in newer ways, and closer to home than expected.

❊

Notes

1. CSE is an environmental NGO based in Delhi. It advertizes itself as a "public interest research and advocacy organisation." Amongst its more famous campaigns, the finding of high levels of pesticides in Coke and Pepsi bottles captured media imagination in the early 2000s.
2. On January 19, 2010, the Delhi High Court pulled up Delhi government for spending "blindly" on beautification drives at the cost of the poor.
3. An opinion poll carried out by NDTV on May 1, 2008 reveals the class bias of the opposition to the project. While 65 per cent of car drivers said that the BRT corridor made driving difficult, 75 per cent of bus drivers disagreed.
4. *Indian Express*, October 16, 2008.

References

Ali, S. 2003. *Environmental Situation of Slums in India*. New Delhi: Uppal Publishing House.

Baviskar, A. 2003. "Between Violence and Desire: Space, Power and Identity in the Making of Metropolitan Delhi," *International Social Science Journal*, 55 (175): 89–98.

Bhan, G. 2009. "'This is No Longer the City I Once Knew': Evictions, the Urban Poor and the Right to the City in Millennial Delhi," *Environment and Urbanization*, 21 (1): 127–42.

Centre For Science and Environment (CSE). 2006. *The Leap Frog Factor: Clearing the Air in Asian Cities*. New Delhi: CSE.

———. 1998. "The Delhi Story." New Delhi: CSE.

Fernandes, L. 2004. "The Politics of Forgetting: Class Politics, State Power and the Restructuring of Urban Space in India," *Urban Studies*, 41 (12): 2415–30.

Ginneken, J. V. 1998. *Understanding Global News: A Critical Introduction*. London: Thousand Oaks.

Guha, R. and J. Martinez-Alier. 1998. *Varieties of Environmentalism: Essays North and South*. Delhi: Oxford University Press.

Narain, S. 2010. In *Down to Earth*, March 1–15.

Veron, R. 2006. "Remaking Urban Environments: The Political Ecology of Air Pollution in Delhi," *Environment and Planning A*, 38 (11): 2093–2109.

5

Banishing the Hyphen

The Rural-Urban Divide and Mainstream Television in India

Pratap Pandey

Any consideration of mainstream media in India today must dwell on a compelling trope or signpost: the rural-urban divide. If, arguably, a feature of the mainstream media in India today is its stake in an on-going, larger debate on the country's development trajectory and its relation to the state of India's environment, then the question of how the media deals with and/or represents the "the rural-urban divide" is one that must be unpacked.

The uses of "the rural-urban divide" are incredibly many. It is a point of entry as well as a point of departure in development–environment debates. It can exacerbate or incite discourse on environment–development, rendering the debate completely open-ended, thus incapacitating resolution. It can also quickly clarify the debate, leading to seamless closure. It can signify lack as well as potential. It provokes the socio-political imagination and is also a culturally imagined complex: a "real issue" as well as an internally consistent image-repertoire, a "matter of grave concern" and the stuff of much computer-generated imagery. Such over-determination is precisely what makes this trope compelling/compulsive.

This chapter will look at the representation of "the rural-urban divide" in television in India today. It will seek to locate this trope and its many manifestations/expressions within the necessity Indian television today has of transmitting/beaming/disseminating an arguably neo-Malthusian approach to the environment-development debate. Whether or not such a divide actually exists in India today, the chapter will argue, is completely immaterial to television. Television needn't understand it. Yet it is compelled to present an understanding of it. To that extent, "the rural-urban divide" is necessary to what is broadcast, to the very "content" of television.

Scarcity resides in nature; natural limits exist. To say this is to ignore/elide (a) that "scarcity" is socially produced and that (b) "limits" are a social relation with nature. But are such questions ignored/elided? Can they be? What happens in what is broadcast and seen on the (plasma) screen?

The rural-urban divide is a metaphor that captures and seeks to communicate a condition of economic and social iniquity and policy short-circuit. Many believe that this condition is intrinsic to India. Others say that it is an unchanging characteristic in how this nation has developed since its independence in 1947. Development economists aver that it is a central feature of development planning in India; others feel that it was made into a central feature of development planning by these very development economists. Nobody doubts that it underpins India's growth story. It is a brute reality, activists will tell you; it has always been so, and since 1991 – since the liberalization of the Indian economy – it has been getting decidedly brutish. It is a schizophrenic experience, India-expert literature reveals (see for instance Mishra 2013). It is a black hole, a white paper, a purple patch, a red zone. It is a pure challenge, an immense opportunity. Its potential is endless, with serious ramifications for all and sundry.

But why does this metaphor exist? So far as this chapter is concerned, it exists because a hyphen has been inserted between "rural" and "urban," yoking them. This hyphen is quite a ruse, actually. As we shall see, it can be argued that it is completely possible to not take this hyphen seriously. That is to say, its presence is so taken for granted that it has always been relied upon, as a punctuating mark, only to be layered under or papered over.

In this respect, mainstream television in India today has gone a step ahead.[1] It has really attempted to refuse this ruse. It inherited the hyphen as well as attempts to banish it from other domains of thought, writing and representation. TV too has been doing its best to banish the hyphen from representation, writing and thought, for it is a puncturing mark, a conspiracy that runs counter to what TV stands for, the world TV projects and the future anterior as per TV.

AD BREAK

Thunder, as in 1940s' and 1950s' Indian film industry mythologies. The sky rents. Fully-manufactured tyres drop out, falling on godless ground – parched, stark, treeless, and perilous. They bounce and begin to roll, in perfect military parade formation. There is no doubt the terrain is dangerous, as the very bad brass band crescendos that comprise the background music attempt to convince. The fully-manufactured tyres roll uphill, avoiding non-existent escarpments and badly-designed pitfalls, such as the leafless stem of some plant that sticks out of the cracked earth the fully-manufactured tyres are rolling on.

Crescendo, cheap production-value music, like a regiment band's music recorded on mono and dunked in here. But at least now the fully-manufactured tyres have reached the end of the uphill incline and are now rolling down, in perfect military parade formation.

From below the horizon, left-of-screen, emerges a glorious monument. It is immediately clear that the fully-manufactured tyres are racing towards this monument. But it isn't clear what monument they are racing towards. It could be the India Gate, which is in Mumbai. Or it could be the War Memorial, which is in Delhi. It doesn't matter; it's a monument that is nationalistic, that stands for nationalism.

Towards this monument, roll the fully-manufactured tyres, which now can only be called nationalistic fully-manufactured tyres. The nationalistic fully-manufactured tyres rolling in perfect military parade formation reach the monument and stand before it in all humility, duty, glory, respect and honor.

As they do that, the seriously-cheap production-value military-regimental-brass-band-background music reaches its last crescendo, with strains or overtures of the national anthem now.

AD BREAK OVER

TV channels that broadcast in English in India ostensibly broadcast a terrific amount of content. News, features, interviews, sports. American soaps and talk shows broadcast nowadays in India – if the promos are to be believed – the same day as they are broadcast in the United States (US). What an achievement. There's also fashion, lifestyle, travel, history Americanized, weaponology, the science of the universe, the wild world of hyenas, orangutans and lions, food, hotels, millionaire houses, music old and new, concerts, mega-engineering, mega-buildings, new inventions as well as movies, old and new, mainstream Hollywood and alternative award-won or award-nominated global cinema.

But none of this is the true content of TV. The true content of TV in India today is the advertisement. I suggest that an ad is not an ad but the space where, today, a fresh attempt is on to banish the hyphen visibly. It is not an agonistic space. Far from it: it is a non-contested, non-contestable space. This attempt is very serious, and very different.

From here, it is but one step to the central preoccupation of this chapter: the exploits of my favorite television character – the GAI, acronym for "global aeducated indian." It appears as the protagonist in what is called a "break." It appears between overs when a cricket match is on, or as soon as a wicket falls. A train falls off a bridge, killing 225; next, it appears. Hitler's about to be assassinated; wait, it appears. Aishwarya Rai has a cold; there, it appears. News anchor Arnab Goswami is hectoring three politicians, one economist and other nonplussed experts on a matter of extreme national importance; still, it appears.

In short, although the GAI is a fictional representation that appears in a multitude of 10-, 15- or 30-second stories, please do not take it lightly. I take it much more seriously than what appears as "content" in a "program" in television. The program is just an excuse. If you are a true TV watcher, as I am, I request you to re-align your priorities: consciously watch the adventures of the GAI.

Here's why. The GAI is omnipresent: merely switch channels and you will know what I mean. The GAI is omnipotent: its adventures are always about winning, about proactive action leading to a positive outcome. The GAI always snatches victory from the jaws of defeat – even during a cricket match. But it is not omniscient.

Who is?

Put differently, the GAI is the only universal in this medium, and therefore the support of its truest content – the "program" – is just an empty form. This persona transcends the generic barriers of news, entertainment, history, science, lifestyle, timeout and timepass. It transcends gender, being male and female. It transcends race; its physiognomy is contextless. It transcends caste, simply because the fictional world it lives in is a casteless world. But it doesn't transcend class.

Who has? Anywhere? And especially in India today?

AD BREAK

Blue filter. Notes played on an electric guitar, sounds routed through the flanger pedal. It is a riff that announces an epic situation. As the notes are played, a paddle comes into the picture. The camera zooms out. The situation becomes clearer. The paddle is in the hands of a beautiful woman, who can only be called a GAI. This lissome GAI beauty, it transpires as the camera zooms out, is marooned in the middle of a wide, fast-flowing mountain river. The backstory becomes clear: lissome GAI has been river-rafting, the rapids overwhelmed her, she is on this pebbly sandbank in the middle of the river. It's also clear she is distraught. She's wet, is wearing a wetsuit, and flicks her hair from side to side, possibly in alarm. The scene unfolds in slow motion and is seen through blue filter. The story is at a tantalizing point: now what?

The riff changes to rock chords, flanger to reverb. As the new sound belts out, the filter lifts even as the camera zooms out further. Where lissome GAI is standing, an SUV appears, literally out of nowhere, matching the 4-by-4 rhythm of the music, possibly propelled by it. More backstory is revealed. Someone, driving on the road on the mountain through which this river snakes, has spotted lissome GAI in peril. The vehicle has jumped into the river, has steadily driven through the fast-flowing water and has now stopped right in front of lissome GAI.

It's a situation in overdrive. This isn't a normal, everyday rescue. It is an act of supreme civility extended to lissome GAI. Gallantly, as the SUV reaches her, the driver reaches over and opens the front passenger seat door. As we have learnt and understood from countless Hollywood road movies as well as non-road movies, it is a clear gesture of offering her a lift. Again, the story reaches a tantalizing cross-road. Will she take up the offer?

A young, handsome, male is the driver of the SUV. It is quite clear he is also the owner of the vehicle, for no one paid to drive that SUV – no paid driver or hired SUV-taxi driver – would or could take such a radical decision as plunging the vehicle into a fast-moving mountain river in order to rescue lissome GAI.

Hunk GAI – for that is what we have to call him given the situation, his looks and his response to the situation – maneuvers the vehicle to right where she is standing. Generic rock music is heard. Very generic; squeals, messianic peals. He is gallant, she is willing.

With lissome GAI beside him, hunk GAI rides the river again. He drives towards the river-bank, across this fast-flowing mountain river, and in a flourish rides beyond the water. The SUV propels out of the river, water scattering. It rides the steepish bank and vanishes.

A little boy, sitting on that bank, has been watching the entire episode. As the SUV zooms out of the river and beyond, raising dust on the bank, the little boy doffs his cap, evidently in admiration. The cap is a Himachali cap, so at least the boy is identifiable as a Himachali, a resident of Himachal Pradesh. The SUV zooms off and the boy claps, completely mesmerized by the performance which can only be called a GAI performance, given the sheer bravado of it, and the coolness with which the rescue has been done.

AD BREAK OVER

Consider a film called *Tarzan Goes to India* (1962). Of 89 films with "Tarzan" in the title made between 1918 and 2008, *Tarzan Goes to India* is one of only two films where Tarzan moves out of Africa. I didn't know this when, on a Sunday evening in late December 2010, while trying to figure out whether the Chelsea–Manchester United match was snowed over or not, I flipped channels to HBO at the very moment the film was about to be broadcast.

Indian princess Kamara (a very young Simi Garewal) has invited Tarzan over to her country/palace. They know each other – doubtless, they must have met in England, at a do thrown by the socially eccentric recluse John Clayton, Lord Greystroke (the other identity of Tarzan). The princess has called him over because she believes only he can solve a problem that is vexing her badly. A dam is being built. Its reservoir will submerge a tract of forest where a huge herd of 300 elephants wander. Can Tarzan rescue the herd from imminent death, thereby assuaging the princess's troubled conscience? Of course he can. He battles a non-Indian senior engineer/ivory poacher, an Englishman. He overcomes the obstacles placed by the chief engineer, also non-Indian and decidedly American. Tarzan leads the herd through a pass in the mountains to the other side, to life and the freedom to roam. In the process, he wrestles with an emaciated leopard and transforms the developmental mind-set of Raju – a young, efficient, idealistic, caring Indian junior engineer (a very young Feroz Khan).

I enjoyed the film, not only because I am a Tarzan fan and so the film was good to consume, but also because I found it was good to think about.

Consider, for starters, the way the dam site is shown swarming with peasants-turned-laborers – you know they are peasants by the clothes they wear: white turban, kurta and dhoti – working at a frenetic pace. You have seen a different, but related version of it in the title song of *Jis Desh Main Ganga Behti Hain* (1960). The resemblance is uncanny. Now throw in an ethical, Caucasian ape-man/English aristocrat, the product of the imagination of Edgar Rice Burroughs, who lived in Oak Park, Illinois, in a town that forbade non-whites from living in it. Add the strong conservationist ethic the princess embodies in a film made way back in 1962, and the pot verily boileth.

Equally uncanny is the context for the film's action: dam-building. It is – along with the idealistic engineer – a staple motif in Hindi films till as late as *Satyam Shivam Sunderam* (1978). Moreover, it is a staple feature of India's economic/developmental history. In April 1948, Prime Minister Jawaharlal Nehru laid the first batch of concrete for the Hirakud dam in Orissa. In November 1955, he poured the first bucket of concrete into the foundation of the Bhakra Nangal dam. In December 1955, he inaugurated the Nagarjuna Sagar dam project in Andhra Pradesh. In April 1961, Nehru laid the foundation stone for the Sardar Sarovar dam in Gujarat. Independent India's first large dam, the Maithon dam over the river Damodar, was completed in 1953. As in *Tarzan Goes to India*, this dam was designed by an American, V. L. Wood.

The year of the film's release, 1962, is even more piquant. Today, economists agree this was the year the graph of development planning in India hiccuped for the first time. The Second Five-Year Plan had just ended. P. C. Mahalonobis's strategy of import, substitution and industrialization hadn't delivered in its entirety: India was staring at a balance-of-payments crisis.

Moreover, coinciding with the Cuban missile crisis, India and China faced off across two fronts. It was a bad war for India. Three years later, India fought a war with Pakistan. The Multilateral Aid Consortium (AIC) suspended aid to both India and Pakistan. In 1966, it agreed to resume aid, but with conditions. The AIC demanded, and got, a substantial devaluation of the Indian rupee (57.5 per cent), partial dismantling of the export incentive system and considerable liberalization of imports. Then Prime Minister Indira Gandhi accepted the conditions, only to abandon liberalization within two years, and not only to return to pre-crisis controls but to intensify them. The justification was that the World Bank had reneged on its promised non-project assistance of nearly US $700 million to ease the adjustment to liberalization.

In *Tarzan Goes to India*, Tarzan is played by Jock Mahoney, an American actor of French, Irish and Cherokee descent. A World War II-pilot-turned-stuntman who had done daring stunts for actors such as Gregory Peck, Errol Flynn and John Wayne, Mahoney replaced the iconic Johnny Weismuller. Three years later, Mahoney acted in a sequel set in Thailand. *Tarzan's Three Challenges* (1963) is the only other Tarzan film where he goes outside Africa. Plagued by dysentery and dengue during film-making, Mahoney lost his physique and was never considered for another Tarzan film.

AD BREAK

Twilight. Praise the lord, no music. We are at what looks like a water-hole. It's a small patch of water amidst tall, green grass. Centre-of-screen, from out the tall green grass, pokes the head of a magnificent tiger. How do we know it's magnificent? It's a tiger. The striped, iconic, magnificent, endangered beast bends its head down, and with its tongue begins to slop the water. The scene is so captivating that one can entirely ignore the tropical species of grass that surrounds the little pool from which the head has poked out. Although tigers in India usually live in dry deciduous forests so that tall green grass around a waterhole is a sheer impossibility, those facts should be ignored. It is a captivating, unique moment, for it is that rarest of events: a tiger sighting.

The tropical green grass on the other side of the pool, the side opposite to where the tiger has poked its head out of, roils. It roils and parts as, on to the scene, there bursts into full view a fully-manufactured vehicle obviously in the throes of dementia. Simultaneously, total burst of generic rock music.

At the helm of this stupendous disturbance, behind the wheel of an obviously mind-blowing jeep – it's obviously mind-blowing because its power is immediately apparent, and there's not a speck of dust on it – is a young, handsome, athletic, broad-shouldered male. Yes, hunk GAI. This hunk GAI is a little different though, from the jumping-into-the-river-to-rescue-lissome-GAI. He's a hunter, as is made clear by the headgear he is sporting. It is eerily similar to the headgear Richard Chamberlain, as protagonist of the cult African romp-adventure film *King Solomon's Mines* (1985) (in which, it is irresistible to add, also stars a very young Sharon Stone) sports. It is equally similar to the head-gear Robert Redford sports in the cult adaptation *Out of Africa* (1985). Remember, too, the cult American adventure film *Safari* (1940). It is similar to the headgear countless white, athletic, broad-shouldered male hunters, some of them villains, sport in Tarzan comics. A floppy hat, with a leopard-skin band. A hunter's hat.

But this hunk GAI is a different kind of hunter. There is difference brewing under that hat, it transpires, as he bursts on to the idyllic scene, rendering it completely non-idyllic. In his hand, he carries not a rifle such as a .357 Magnum, a staple elephant- or lion-hunting rifle, but a camera. Bursting upon the scene, Hunk GAI manages not only to control the – dare I say? – magnificent vehicle, but also to be ready to shoot with his camera. It is a remarkable feat, but natural for hunk GAI. His intensity and nonchalance are not at odds.

Not at odds because as he bursts on to the idyllic, unique, tiger-sighted moment, the backstory becomes clear. He is an old hand at this. He has a passion. It could be a weekend hobby too. Hunk GAI's passion or hobby or both is to eternally race, at high speed, through core areas of national parks in forests in India to reach a waterhole with tropical high green grass around it, to catch the magnificent animal drinking and take a photograph of it.

Startled, the tiger pulls in its tongue and races away. Hunk GAI, just about to fulfil his hobby/passion, is baulked. But the magnificent setback – of not being able to shoot the tiger – does not daunt hunk GAI at all. The tiger races away. Hunk GAI races after it. Tiger's racing, vehicle's racing. The still-thirsty tiger, iconic animal also endangered, startled, baulked and now chased, leaps across the forest floor, bounding away now absolutely scared out of its wits. Hunk GAI, at one with magnificent vehicle – or hunk vehicle, at one with magnificent GAI – also leaps across the forest floor. Both leap, tearing through the wild, overgrown, tall, tropical green grass, which has obviously sprouted on immensely bumpy ground. Driving, hunk GAI shoots.

Even as the generic rock music reaches an orchestral crescendo, a musical drift or direction or tactic unheard of in the annals of rock music, and the superiority of the hardy vehicle is extolled, some questions emerge. How did hunk GAI manage to drive and shoot such clear pictures (of seriously bolting tiger leaping over undergrowth) on such bumpy terrain at such speed from the driving seat of a self-driven vehicle, however magnificent?

Moreover, given the Wildlife (Protection) Act 1972, which forbids human entry into the core zone of protected areas – the only spaces where, in India, tigers roam or take a drink from a waterhole in twilight – how has hunk GAI managed to race up to that waterhole and then chase the tiger? Until it was first amended in 1981, this piece of legislation was bad in law: it could be and was used to declare forest areas as protected without settling the rights of people who lived in that patch or area. It is still in force and it is still illegal for humans to enter core areas. So, is (isn't) hunk GAI bad in law too? How could he, chasing his hobby or passion or both, flout the law of the land so drastically? Is this a law that must be flouted? Is it a law only hunk GAIs can flout, and be forgiven for, for obviously he's not arrested or harassed, by the forest department? Has he bribed the forest department?

All such questions are non sequitur. The vehicle has proved its vehicality. Hunk GAI has indulged in, and fulfilled, his passion or hobby, or both. Adrenaline win-win.

AD BREAK OVER

Tarzan Goes to India is not only a film, but a phenomenon. It needs unpacking. To do so, let's minimally take recourse to Eric Thorbecke's essay "The Evolution of the Development Doctrine, 1950–2005."

Writing about development strategy in the 1950s, Thorbecke says:

> Economic growth became the main policy objective in the newly independent less developed countries. It was widely believed that through economic growth and modernisation *per se*, dualism and associated income and social inequalities which reflected it, would be eliminated. Other economic and social objectives were thought to be complementary to – if not resulting from – GNP growth. Clearly, the adoption of GNP growth as both the objective and yardstick of development was directly related to the conceptual state of the art in the fifties. The major theoretical contributions which guided the development community during that decade were conceived within a one-sector, aggregate framework and emphasised the role of investment in modern activities. The development economists' tool kit in the fifties contained such theories and concepts as the "big push" (Rosenstein-Rodan 1943), "balanced growth" (Nurkse 1953), "take-off into sustained growth" (Rostow 1956) and "critical minimum effort thesis" (Leibenstein 1957).
>
> The one-sector, one-input nature of these models precluded any estimation of the sectoral production effects of alternative investment allocations and of different combinations of factors since it was implicitly assumed that factors could only be combined in fixed proportions with investment. In a one-sector world, GNP is maximised by pushing the investment-ratio (share of investment in GNP) as high as is consistent with balance-of-payments equilibrium. In the absence of either theoretical constructs or empirical information on the determinants of agricultural output, the tendency was to equate the modern sector with high productivity of investment and thus, direct the bulk of investment to the modern sector and to the formation of social overhead capital – usually benefiting the former.
>
> Industrialisation was conceived as the engine of growth which would pull the rest of the economy along behind it. The industrial sector was assigned the dynamic role in contrast to the agricultural which was, typically, looked at as a passive sector to be "squeezed" and discriminated against. More specifically, it was felt that industry, as a leading sector, would offer alternative employment opportunities to the agricultural population, would provide a growing demand for foodstuffs and raw materials, and would begin to supply industrial inputs to agriculture. The industrial sector was equated with high productivity of investment – in contrast with agriculture – and, therefore, the bulk of investment was directed to industrial activities and social overhead projects. To a large extent the necessary capital resources to fuel industrial growth had to be extracted from traditional agriculture (2006: 3–5).

Human beings, too, as in swarming at dam sites or in factories. In sum, first, the hyphen is placed between "rural" and "urban": rural-urban. Immediately, the hyphen is sought to be banished: rural→urban.

AD BREAK

Soft music. A gorgeous GAI female, played by the Bollywood film actress Katrina Kaif, twirls. The skirt of her dress also twirls. Gossamer dress, gossamer GAI.

The "aamsutra," breaks in an unintrusive voice-over, is all about waiting for the right moment of pleasure to arrive. Anticipation, the up-swell of desire . . . all must be finely calibrated into an aesthetics and practice of delay. Wait, wait. Hold.

While this wisdom, that can only be translated as the "Art of Mango-ing," is relayed, gorgeous GAI is seen dancing in a landscape with only one mango tree. The tree is never shown, but can be presumed from the way this story unfolds. From this one tree hangs one perfectly pear-shaped mango. It is an unripe mango. Cut to close up. Gorgeous GAI – who can now, without being sexist, be called Mango Baby GAI – leans forward to almost kiss the green mango. Almost, but not quite.

It immediately becomes clear that Mango Baby GAI is waiting for the mango to ripen. Music, swirl of time. The mango is ripening. Wait . . . it is ripening.

Still, Mango Baby GAI postpones her pleasure, which presumably is to consume that single mango. We see her twirling, waiting. She has beautiful hair and is exceptionally fair. The perfection of her body is not unlike the blemishless mango, which is still ripening.

Now the mango is fully ripe, green turned to mellow yellow. It is a truly gorgeous mango. Still she waits. Then the mango disappears. We do not know where it goes. We can only wait, along with Mango Baby GAI, for its return. For the fulfillment of her desire, it is clearer, is linked to this one mango.

The wait is over! The moment when mango fulfills Mango Baby GAI is an exquisite close-up. Mango Baby GAI parts her lips, and a drop of fully processed mango juice falls on her lower lip, wets it. Soft music ends in an unobtrusive crescendo.

The powerful mystery that propels this story is not where the mango disappeared, or that Mango Baby GAI's pleasure is solipsistically focused on a mango. It is that she will simply not consume a mango, i.e., consummate her desire, until it has been re-sent to her as fully processed juice.

AD BREAK OVER

Indian economist Jayati Ghosh's 2002 essay "Social Policy in Indian Development" is written from a political economy perspective, for a United Nations Research Institute for Social Development (UNRISD) project on "Social Policy in a Development Context." "In this paper," she writes at the very beginning:

> an attempt is made to analyse the nature of social policy in the recent Indian development experience, ask why it has taken these specific forms and patterns, consider its achievements and limitations, and probe how it can be transformed into a more effective instrument for equitable and sustainable development (2002: 1).

From a political economy perspective, tracking how social policy has been embedded in the development process in India up until the moment of writing (2002), Ghosh finds a "less than satisfactory performance during the decade of economic liberalization" (ibid.: 9). This, she has written, "was not just the result of the nature of integration with the global economy" (ibid.). It also reflected – and we are approaching what is pertinent to this paper – "continuing contradictions in Indian political economy that have been so crucial in inhibiting economic growth and reducing the wider spread of its benefits across all the citizenry, over most of the second half of the 20th century" (ibid.).

According to Ghosh, there were "at least four such mutually reinforcing and interrelated political economy contradictions" (ibid.). Although only the fourth is most pertinent to this paper, it is worth mentioning all four. They, too, seem pertinent. They explain a lot about what mainstream TV has inherited, about the inherited lifeworld of the GAI. Hence I have chosen to quote from this essay in some detail.

First, then:

> The state has had to simultaneously fulfil two different roles that have turned out to be incompatible in the long run. On the one hand it has had to maintain growing expenditure, in particular investment expenditure, in order to keep the domestic market expanding. At the same time, however, the state exchequer has been the medium through which large-scale transfers have been made to the capitalist and proto-capitalist groups, so that the state effectively became the most important instrument for primary accumulation by the domestic bourgeoisie in its various manifestations (ibid.).

The second, she states, is:

the inability of the state to impose a minimum measure of "discipline" and "respect for law" among the capitalists, without which no capitalist system anywhere can be tenable. Disregard for the laws of the land, including especially those relating to taxes and also other laws which affected the economic functioning of the system, was an important component of capitalist primary accumulation in the post Independence Indian case (Ghosh 2002: 9).

As we have already seen, this tendency is a feature of GAI behavior. The third contradiction, she says:

had its roots in the social and cultural ambience of a developing country like India. Metropolitan capitalism, which is characterised by continuous product innovation, has experienced the phenomenon of newer goods constantly entering the market and even creating new lifestyles, whereas most developing countries have not only less dynamic innovative capacity because of less resources devoted to such innovation, but also more narrow markets which cannot benefit from economies of scale to the same degree. This creates an imbalance between the possibilities of domestic production and the patterns of demand emanating from the relatively affluent sections of society who account for much of the growth of potential demand for consumer goods (ibid.: 10).

About the fourth, she explains:

[it] reflected the political economy configurations in India throughout this period, which implied a high level of social tolerance for high and growing asset inequality, persistent poverty and low levels of human development among a vast section of the population, especially in the rural areas (ibid.).

Further, she writes:

Two striking features of this pattern of development, even in the more dynamic phases, have been the growing rural-urban divide in terms of per capita incomes, and the inadequacy of productive employment generation relative to the expansion in population. The same sociopolitical forces which allowed such features to persist and become accentuated, also meant that social policy which ensured the provision of basic needs to the entire population was never a priority, nor were provisions which focused on improved work conditions in most workplaces (ibid.).

AD BREAK

Moon and stars, made of cardboard cutouts wrapped in gold and silver paper, hang in the foreground. Very young GAIs – little-kid GAIs – can be seen behind and between these hangings. Obviously, these kid GAIs are on a stage, it is a little drama that they are staging.

As part of their performance, they sing a nursery rhyme. The tune of the rhyme resembles "Jack and Jill." But the lyrics are different. The lyrics are about lowering air-conditioner AC bills. Use a particular AC, that has the in-built technological innovation of using less electricity, "and the bills come tumbling after."

In another version, the little GAIs appear with a façade of a castle. They sing a nursery rhyme whose tune resembles "Humpty Dumpty." Here, Humpty Dumpty's savings "had a great fall," because of electricity bills related to AC use.

Serially, then, a performance by kid GAIs shows how, even at a tender age today, GAIs are product- and spending-sensitive. They possess the art of nursery-rhyming consumerism. An ethic of thrift is sought to be recycled as intelligent and sustainable energy-use. Don't be fooled. The use of an AC is not questioned at all; an AC is intrinsic to the existence of these young GAIs.

AD BREAK OVER

AD BREAK

It is evening. 7 o'clock in the evening, to be precise. Young GAI has returned home, presumably after play. His stomach is rumbling. GAI son wants to eat.

Enter GAI mum. Young, petite, in a sari. Not as gorgeous as Mango Baby GAI, but beautiful. Also, unlike Mango Baby GAI, she is a serious problem-solver.

What is the problem? The problem is that GAI son has a growling tummy, but it is too early to eat, as per mummy.

What is the solution? Fully-processed soup. Ready in a jiffy. GAI son is sated; for GAI mum, a crisis abated. Moreover, since the fully-processed soup makes her child happy, and is a health boon, GAI mum has killed two imperatives with one aluminium-lined satchet. That's the way to go.

AD BREAK OVER

I just enjoy the fairy-tale exploits of the GAI. After a swig of a drink, he can batter a ram on the head, or drive a car off the cliff to win a rally – breaking all rally rules, but that is a non-sequitor – or fly above a bird that has crapped on it to pee upon it in sheer revenge. She can chase a boy down, racing through a railway station and catapulting over traffic, for a dollop of sauce.

He is very fond of deodorizing himself. Walking about in a mallish landscape, a landscape of glass and steel, a sudden impulse takes over. He unbuttons his shirt and squirts himself gregariously with deodorant. Or, walking beside a swimming pool, he suddenly bathes himself in deodorant. The action has amazing consequences: water from the swimming pool evaporates; in the other scenario a gaggle of blondes and brunettes cleave to him, like staple pins to bond paper.

She is very fond of combing her hair. She analyzes her hair all the time, identifying problems, seeking solutions.

Of course, the GAI's actions are often confusing. He buys a watch and, for no reason, gets so obsessed with it he must see a shrink. For no reason, she rips off a rail using her hair like a rope. He test-drives a vehicle and gets so captivated by that experience that he seems to become increasingly nervous, unhappy, visibly traumatized by the fact that he is on a test-drive and must return the vehicle. She, advised by a doctor, keeps buying soap. She/he creams herself/himself all the time. He defoliates, she exfoliates, vice-versa *ad nauseum.* The hair color and style keep changing. Both are anti-age themselves and are completely paranoid about germs, stipples, wrinkles, being dark and the tropical sun.

She is hardly seen at work. He is a winner in the office. If married, they live in impossibly big flats, coochie-koo with air-conditioners and refrigerators, and always have very expensive wooden furniture and two children: a boy and a girl. He zooms only on empty roads, posing on a cliff-top with his vehicle; she is still washing the shirt, making it whiter.

These actions are confusing, but they are not inexplicable.

AD BREAK

Hunk GAI at the back of a big car, a sedan. He is being driven through a port. His vehicle passes through the docks, where loads of containers are piled. Where is he going?

It transpires he is attending a meeting. When he walks into the room, everybody defers to him. Quick shots of the meeting show he is a hard and persuasive bargainer. Very quickly, he settles all the issues. There are smiles and handshakes. Hunk GAI sits, aloof. He opens a tin of chewing tobacco and pops a spoonful into his mouth.

Meeting over. Hunk GAI is being driven away. It then becomes clear that the conference room he had been to was in a building owned by his company. The name of the company? The English East India Company.

Punchline: *Muh mein rajnigandha, kadmon mein duniya.* (Rajnigandha [chewing tobacco] in your mouth, the world at your feet).

In another version, hunk GAI owner of the English East India Company is at an auction. A number of people are gathered at what transpires to be an old hotel, the object of the auction.

The bids do not fly thick and fast. Hunk GAI makes an offer – 400 million – that nobody can refuse, or match. Auction over. The other bidders gather around him, obviously marveling at him. A Japanese bidder asks him: "Why did you pay such a high price?"

English East India Company-owning Hunk GAI turns to look at him. He walks over to an old, bent man who is now suddenly visible standing at the corner of the room. The old man is wearing a liveried uniform. Hunk GAI put his arm around him.

Now we understand: the old man is his father, and he used to work in that hotel. But no longer. Verily, hunk GAI is the Prodigal Son. Cheap music crescendo. Choral refrain: *Muh mein rajnigandha, kadmon mein duniya.*

AD BREAK OVER

One clarification of the GAI's actions is available in the classic *An Essay on the Principle of Population.* "A man who is born into a world already possessed," wrote John Robert Malthus in this timeless classic:

> if he cannot get subsistence from his parents on whom he has a just demand, and if the society do not want his labour, has no claim of *right* to the smallest portion of food, and, in fact, has no business to be where he is.
>
> At nature's mighty feast there is no vacant cover for him. She tells him to be gone, and will quickly execute her own orders, if he does not work upon the compassion of some of her guests. If these guests get up and make room for him, other intruders immediately appear demanding the same favour . . . The order and harmony of the feast is disturbed, the plenty that before reigned is turned into scarcity.
>
> . . . The guests learn too late their error, in counteracting those strict orders to all intruders, issued by the great mistress of the feast, who, wishing that all her guests should have plenty, and knowing that she could not provide for unlimited numbers, humanely refused to admit fresh comers when her table was already full (1803: 531).

Malthus' greatest fear was that if population growth and notions of equality were not contained, "the middle classes of society . . . would be blended with the poor" (Malthus 1803: 531). As the great man put it, "[t]he principal argument of this Essay only goes to prove the necessity of a class of proprietors, and a class of labourers" (ibid.).

AD BREAK

Hunk GAI, wearing a hard hat, stands in front of a tiled, one-storied house. Lo! It changes to a glass-and-steel swanky villa.

Swelling music accompanies a song that clarifies we are looking at hard-hat GAI's vision of the world.

What would happen if this vision changed to an absolutely empty landscape? A flyover comes up, around it huge skyscrapers. The empty landscape, bereft of people or trees, turns in a computer-generated imagery (CGI) jiffy into a metropolis.

The song enunciates the logic of the vision: village to city, city to country, country to world. Utter transformation. Absolute change.

AD BREAK OVER

Although this chapter is strictly restricted to the GAI as it appears in ads, this section begs your indulgence, for it seems the GAI has spilled over from ads and now appears in a thousand different guises.

Some gems from "knowledge" channels: these are names of programs. "Jesse vs Al Capone." "Persian Immortals vs Celts." "Rajput vs Knight." "Atilla vs Alexander." "Apache vs Gladiator." "Predator vs Prey." "The Dark Side of Hippos." "Nat Geo Wild: The Dark Side of Elephants." "I, videogame." "Predation! Predators at War." "International Terrorism Since 1945." "Predation: Scavengers of the Savannah." "Untamed and Uncut: Teeth, Talons, Terror." "Untamed and Uncut: Heroes and Horror." "Dangerous Encounters: Monster Bite." "Fight Science: Super Cops."

From "entertainment" channels: "Adam vs Eve." "Emotional Atyaachar" (emotional repression), the Indian version of "Cheaters". "Indian Idol," the Indian version of "American Idol".

Okay, enough. If all TV programs broadcast in India today, in whichever language, were to be distilled into a single word, that word would be: "versus."

I'll quote now from Pierre Bourdieu's essay "The Essence of Neoliberalism," published in the December 1998 issue of *Le Monde Diplomatique*. Reading the essay, you would think he's got the GAI in mind. He's pin-pointed what makes the GAI tick. But privately-owned Indian television did not really take off until 2002, or thereabouts. The GAI did not exist, therefore, in 1998.

Or, did it?

The movement toward the neoliberal utopia of a pure and perfect market is made possible by the politics of financial deregulation. And it is achieved through the transformative and, it must be said, *destructive* action of all of the political measures (of which the most recent is the Multilateral Agreement on Investment (MAI), designed to protect foreign corporations and their investments from national states) that aim to *call into question any and all collective structures* that could serve as an obstacle to the logic of the pure market: the nation, whose space to manoeuvre continually decreases; work groups, for example through the individualisation of salaries and of careers as a function of individual competences, with the consequent atomisation of workers; collectives for the defence of the rights of workers, unions, associations, cooperatives; even the family, which loses part of its control over consumption through the constitution of markets by age groups (Bourdieu 1998).

Thus the absolute reign of flexibility is established, with employees being hired on fixed-term contracts or on a temporary basis and repeated corporate restructurings and, within the firm itself, competition among autonomous divisions as well as among teams forced to perform multiple functions.

Finally, this competition is extended to individuals themselves, through the individualisation of the wage relationship: establishment of individual performance objectives, individual performance evaluations, permanent evaluation, individual salary increases or granting of bonuses as a function of competence and of individual merit; individualised career paths; strategies of "delegating responsibility" tending to ensure the self-exploitation of staff who, simple wage labourers in relations of strong hierarchical dependence, are at the same time held responsible for their sales, their products, their branch, their store, etc. as though they were independent contractors. This pressure toward "self-control" extends workers' "involvement" according to the techniques of "participative management" considerably beyond management level. All of these are techniques of rational domination that impose over-involvement in work (and not only among management) and work under emergency or high-stress conditions. And they converge to weaken or abolish collective standards or solidarities.

In this way, a Darwinian world emerges – it is the struggle of all against all at all levels of the hierarchy, which finds support through everyone clinging to their job and organisation under conditions of insecurity, suffering, and stress (Bourdieu 1998).

AD BREAK

At a table in a dusty roadside tea-shop. The tea-shop owner addresses a young man: "Hey, now that you have finished your education, isn't it time for you to move to the city?" The young man, who is poring over a large sheet of paper, folds the sheet and looks at the tea-shop owner. He smiles, shakes his head.

The young man places the sheet on the table. It is a blueprint. Pointing to the other side of the road, the young man, who can now be called homeboy GAI-with-a-blueprint, proudly says: "Kaka, my call-center will come up here!"

In a CGI trice, the call-center comes up. Not only that; the sleepy, dusty small town changes into a bustling metropolis-like space, malls and all.

Nothing better symbolizes the change in fortune that the call-center has brought to the sleepy, dusty hometown than the change in fortune of the tea-shop owner. He now owns a fast-food joint. On a table outside this modern café he now owns, the former tea-shop owner himself serves homeboy GAI-with-a-blueprint, the one who has single-handedly fashioned the change. Homeboy GAI-with-a-blueprint explains to "kaka," or "elder": "The road that leads from the small town to the city, kaka, is also the road that leads from the city to here."

Like hard-hat GAI's actions, homeboy GAI's actions too can be explained only with a neologism: he is a transmorpher.

AD BREAK OVER

AD BREAK

Total rock music, bordering on very amateurish heavy metal. A hunk GAI, being played by the Bollywood actor Hrithik Roshan, walks through a variety of swanky vehicles towards what looks like a hangar. Among a helicopter, an SUV and a car that bears family resemblance to a Ferrari or a Lamborghini, walks hunk GAI. It is clear these machines belong to him.

Above, storm clouds gather. Out of nowhere, a twister dervishes its way in and in a trice picks at his baseball cap. The twister roils in and, skittishly, mischievously, flicks hunk GAI's baseball cap from him. It then flees.

Other ordinary human beings would have been blown away by this storm, but it is clear that hunk GAI is no ordinary human being. Instead of racing for cover or shelter, hunk GAI smiles.

In the background, amateurish heavy metal music with unintelligible lyrics. The male singer is yowling. In the foreground appears a two-wheeler. Hunk GAI walks towards this two-wheeler and guns the machine to life. "Hello Hri . . ." flashes on the illuminated speedometer.

But this is no time for greeting. Quickly turning the machine, hunk GAI begins to chase the twister. The twister has thrashed its way ahead into what looks like the sea, churning the water. As hunk GAI, who can now be called hunk storm-chaser GAI, and his machine go after the twister, bolts of lightning fall. It seems all the elements are conspiring against hunk storm-chaser GAI and his mission. But hunk storm-chaser GAI is unstoppable. Deftly swerving away from the lightning bolt, he rides after the twister.

Now we see the twister has so churned the sea up that a huge tsunami-like wave-front has formed. Under the curve of this about-to-crash-into-land wave, rides the hunk storm-chaser GAI, who now can also be called hunk storm-chaser-surfer GAI, straight into the whirling maelstrom of the twister.

Throughout this ride, as background, we hear the shriek of the singer, accompanied by amateurish heavy metal music. Maniacally, the singer shrieks: "I am coming out!" "I am coming out!"

We are now inside the twister. Riding the churn, hunk storm-chaser-surfer GAI reaches up and plucks the baseball cap from out the maelstrom.

Immediately, the twister vanishes. The wave subsides into oblivion. The clouds part. Hunk storm-chaser-surfer GAI, retrieved-baseball-cap firmly back on, poses with his machine on a rocky slope, silhouetted by the light of sunset.

AD BREAK OVER

In the years 2010–20, I wager that India will eradicate poverty. Yes, it is a wager and not a scam. No, I have not lost my onions.

The decade just gone by (2000–10) has been a decade of consumer euphoria for India, peaking in 2010. The automobile industry grew 31 per cent just this year: launches of 30 new models/variants are expected in 2011. Although crude oil prices just hit a 26-month high in December 2010, the Telecom Regulatory Authority of India data shows the number of mobile phone subscribers to be 706.68 million in October this year (Pandey 2010). On the go, the Indian consumer can now use an instant hand sanitizer that provides 99.99 per cent protection from germs, or a mouth freshener that makes him kiss-ready. Comment strings, seeding and cloud computing are passé. The GAI should be re-christened Apps-Person; this adept – at Estimated Monthly Installment (EMIs), Kindle and iPad, and lifestyle-tracking tools such as Bedpost, Love Vibes, Ego App and Meditation Timer – is living a fully-loaded life. It promises to get better. Bookings for the Super Low and Iron 883 models of the iconic Harley-Davidson bike open in India on Saturday, January 1, 2011.

It has also been a decade of financial euphoria. Government of India (GoI) this year raised ₹221.44 billion by disinvesting in just six central public sector enterprises – Sutlej Jal Vidyut Nigam Ltd, Engineers India Ltd, Power Grid Corporation of India, Manganese Ore India Ltd, Shipping Corporation of India Ltd and Coal India Ltd (its IPO raised a whopping ₹151.99 billion alone). The ecstasy goes further back. The asset class called the stock market has emerged a clear winner, appreciating 1,346.1 per cent since mid-1991. The commercial property market in cities, merely emergent in the early 1990s, has grown 455.5 per cent (Chennai) to 1,417 per cent (Bengaluru) since then. It is moot, as John Kenneth Galbraith writes:

> built into the speculative episode is the euphoria, the mass escape from reality, that excludes any serious contemplation of the true nature of what is taking place . . . All financial innovation involves, in one form or another, the creation of debt secured in greater or lesser adequacy by real assets (1993).

The future is completely transparent: Swiss authorities will provide information to India on the alleged ₹62,000 billion Indians have hoarded in its banks from Saturday, January 1, 2011.

All this has been made possible by the State's exponential growth, along with freight corridors, flyovers, underpasses and Special Economic Zones (SEZs) which have re-landscaped India. Now, apart from returning to the United Nations Security Council as a non-permanent member in 2011, after a gap of 19 years, all India has to do is channelize its new-found pizzaz towards poverty alleviation.

There is no doubt it will. India's targeted anti-poverty drive took real shape on March 31, 1952, when an institution called the Community Projects Administration was created under the Planning Commission. It took off on October 2, 1952, with the inauguration of the community development program. Handled by different ministries, the drive sharpened in March 1974, when a Department of Rural Development was set up under the aegis of the agriculture ministry. This department was upgraded to a Ministry of Rural Reconstruction in 1979, and was renamed the "Ministry of Rural Development" on January 23, 1982. The ministry was downgraded to a department in 1985 – under the aegis of a newly-formed Ministry of Agriculture and Rural Development – and again upgraded on July 5, 1991. Today, it remains a full-fledged ministry headed by a minister of cabinet rank.

In short, India's really been at it. Nothing proves its doggedness better than its performance through the years 1952–2002 [2002 was the last time a Below Poverty Line (BPL) survey was done].

Richard Mahapatra of the Centre for Science and Environment, Delhi, has crunched numbers for this period. He has considered the money spent in more than 2,000 rural development programs undertaken in this period. According to Mahapatra (2007), if all this money spent on all these programs is added up, we see:

- the State has spent ₹350 billion per year for poverty alleviation every year;
- it has spent ₹270 billion per year on food subsidy;
- ₹80 billion per year on irrigation;
- ₹2,270 billion per year to maintain the rural development bureaucracy.

The challenge has been a very difficult one, matched by the depth of its endeavor: today, it takes ₹3.65 to transfer ₹1 of program-money to the poor.

But India has not given up. Committed to meet its Millennium Development Goal of halving poverty/hunger by 2015, India has developed a new strategy of poverty eradication. Much thought has gone into it, for it has taken 11 years to formulate this strategy. Its target is to pay every household of five members ₹22,000 per year. Cash doles apart, there will be wage programs and self-employment programs. GoI has estimated that to achieve success via this strategy over the period 2008–16, it will need an investment of ₹3,960 billion.

What could be more euphoric? What an adventure to embark upon! I take up this wager because I know I will win. This is not a speculation.

AD BRAKE

Urban-rural. Rural → urban. TV today in India has gone far, far ahead. It has announced what it wants: Urban → rural. And so to Urban → ~~rural~~. And so to Urban → urban.

There will no longer be two domains, divided. There will be no division, or diversities. This movement will not stop until "urban" banishes "rural." The hyphen will be put to rest, no longer required, for whatever purpose. The rural should have been visible only in a mural.

Thus the true content of TV in India today can only be called: "militainment."

AD BRAKE OVER

❀

Note

1. "Mainstream TV" here means "TV channels that broadcast in English."

References

Books and Articles:

Bourdieu, Pierre. 1998. "The Essence of Neoliberalism," *Le Monde Diplomatique*, December. http://mondediplo.com/1998/12/08bourdieu. As accessed on March 24, 2014.

Galbraith, J. K. 1993. *A Short History of Financial Euphoria*. New York: Whittle Books in association with Viking

Ghosh, J. 2002. "Social Policy in Indian Development," United Nations Research Institute for Social Development, November. http://www.unrisd.org/80256B3C005BCCF9/(httpAuxPages)/7EE221555523155DC1256C77003CFAED/$file/ghoslong.pdf. As accessed on March 18, 2014.

Mahapatra, R. 2007. "Ecology for Economy," May 2. For details see http://www.slideshare.net/bmbks321/ecology-for-economy-by-richard-mahapatra. As accessed on April 30, 2014.

Malthus, T. R. 1803. *An Essay on the Principle of Population*. London: J. Johnson.

Mishra, P. 2013. "Which India Matters?" The New York Review of Books, November 21. http://www.nybooks.com/articles/archives/2013/nov/21/which-india-matters/. As accessed on March 18, 2014.

Pandey, P. 2010. "Wager of the Decade," *The Bengal Post*, December 30.

Thorbecke, E. 2006. "The Evolution of the Development Doctrine, 1950–2005," WIDER Research Paper 2006/155, December. UNU-WIDER. http://www.wider.unu.edu/publications/working-papers/research-papers/2006/en_GB/rp2006-155/. As accessed on March 18, 2014.

Films:

Day, R. 1963. *Tarzan's Three Challenges*. Banner Productions, Metro-Goldwyn-Mayer (MGM).
Griffith, E. H. 1940. *Safari*. Paramount Pictures.
Guillermin, J. 1962. *Tarzan Goes to India*. Allfin A. G., Metro-Goldwyn-Mayer (MGM).
Kapoor, R. 1978. *Satyam Shivam Sunderam*. R. K. Films Ltd.
Karmakar, R. 1960. *Jis Desh Main Ganga Behti Hain*. R. K. Films Ltd.
Pollack. S. 1985. *Out of Africa*. Mirage Enterprises, Universal Pictures.
Thompson, J. L. 1985. *King Solomon's Mines*. Cannon Group.

6

Politics of Body Spectacle

Old Movements Creating New(s) Stories

Shalini Sharma

The Bhopal gas tragedy – the world's worst industrial disaster – is as much a story of human resilience and unflinching determination for justice as it is of corporate greed and its power to influence. On the midnight of December 2–3, 1984, the city of Bhopal, situated on the edge of two lakes, was rendered helpless by a cloud of highly poisonous gases spewing from the Union Carbide Pesticide Plant. The next morning is imprinted in our collective memory through the haunting images taken by photographers – of a dead child with eyes open, half covered in dirt, of blinded victims, of roads and lanes littered with the dead bodies of human beings and animals, of bodies burning in open fields, of hospitals crammed not only with the bodies of the dead but also those who were desperately sick. These continue to remind us of the horror that "that night" was.

Thirty years later the disaster is far from over. On the one hand, children born to gas-exposed parents are also observed to be affected (Ranjan et al. 2003). On the other, the chemicals that Carbide abandoned in and around their Bhopal factory have contaminated the groundwater with toxics which are potentially carcinogenic and mutagenic,[1] and which are affecting more than 25,000 people in 18 communities (Moyna 2012; CSE 2009).

The first opposition against this gross injustice came in the form of spontaneous protests in the city soon after the disaster. It took some time for people to organize themselves into a struggle. What then started in the form of the Zahreeli Gas Kaand Sangharsh Morcha as a united front, soon found itself splintered into multiple groups due to clashes which were both ideological and personality-driven. It is in this context that the International Campaign for Justice in Bhopal (ICJB), a coalition of four survivors' organizations and several national and international groups came together in the late 1990s.[2] Ever since, ICJB has been demanding a complete remediation of the site and the provision of safe drinking water to people in the surrounding slums, and has been upholding the "Polluter Pays" principle by making Dow pay for clean-up. Essentially, the demands can be clubbed as "Justice for Bhopal" and "No more Bhopals." To emphasize its commitment towards a safer and just world continues to be the prime message of the campaign. It is noteworthy that the formation of ICJB coincided with the emergence of the worldwide Global Justice Movement. This also coincided with the entry of liberalization in India and the growing influence of market forces on the Indian media. With time, the details of any particular disaster begin to fade away in the memory of the people. To keep the memory of the gas disaster fresh and to keep the debate for accountability alive are some of the key aims of the Bhopal survivors' movement for justice. Because media and movement act as "interacting systems" (Gamson and Wolfsfeld 1993) consistent media work for informing public opinion becomes a strategic necessity for the movement actors.

Media-Saturated World and Challenges for the Activists

Bhopal happened before the entry of 24-hour news channels in India. In fact, the 1980s was the time when television had just started making its inroads into the households in India. Hence, much of the initial coverage on Bhopal was through newspapers, photographs and documentaries. However, media emergence in the 1990s saw some major changes. By then not only had India's newspaper revolution already taken place but the arrival of the satellite channels in the country had also been announced to the world through the entry of Cable News Network (CNN) in 1991(Jeffrey 2000). Thus began the period marked by the rise of the Indian media industry, ruled by market logics (Kohli 2003), and witnessing all the gimmickry that a rating-seeking television deploys. By 1998, India had the first of its 24-hour news channels on air waves and by 2007, around 54 out of 106 satellite channels that broadcasted news were 24-hour news channels (Mehta 2008). At the same time, both journalistic practice and news reflected the changes in the media industry:

> Subjectivity, inaccuracy, misquote; marketing men as editorial heads; sexing it up, dumbing it down, sting operations with methods and morals mixed up; 'breaking news' a dozen times a day on TV; TV studios as courtrooms; SMS voting on serious human rights issues; the PR industry as source; selling of editorial space (Vasudev 2005, quoted in Thussu 2007: 600).

Though these changes were not unique, increasing commodification of news posed new challenges for the activists to get their message out. Thus, while the disaster itself was reported in a period dominated by newspapers and radio, the struggle for justice emerged in a period when television ruled as a broadcasting media. Visuals became more and more important. Very little has been said about the consistent effort by the activists in keeping the issue alive on the mediascape, both nationally and internationally. This is the focal point of my research inquiry. And for the purpose of this chapter I concentrate on ICJB alone even though there are more than one survivors-led organizations operating in Bhopal. This is primarily because first and foremost, in contrast to other Bhopal survivors' organizations, ICJB has made international solidarity alliances linking the Bhopal struggle with other similar movements and affected communities. Second, it focuses on both national and international media in addition to adopting internet in its media repertoire. And third, having worked with ICJB between 2006 and 2009, I had the opportunity to observe its media practice from within. Now while examining the same through the academic lens, my inquiry is informed by my experience both as an insider as well as an outsider, critically engaging with a scheme of things that come to influence the activists' media strategy. The central point here is to see how protesters attempt to garner media attention in a neo-liberal media era and while this is strategically done in many ways, for the purpose of this chapter, I would use the example of ICJB to argue that the activist uses "protesting bodies" as a strategic choice for news-making. For this purpose, I will examine some of the key actions organized by ICJB between 2000 and 2010 and weave my argument around them.

Bhopalis and Their Story

But before we look at how the Bhopal activists do that, we need to know the story that Bhopalis aim to communicate to the world – the story of a toxic leak, of systems that failed, of corporate greed that put profit over peoples' lives, of a State that failed to provide adequate relief and rehabilitation, of a world that continues to run on the double standards. It is also a story of the global public that needs the media to know the facts of the story and to make connections with similar incidences in other parts of the world.

The story is powerful, compelling, morally appealing and with almost all the elements that make for a good copy. Yet, some of the key challenges that activists constantly faced were – how to communicate an ongoing disaster, how to counter the state and corporate narrative that limits the disaster to "that night" and how to in turn produce and effectively communicate a counter narrative of the "ongoing disaster." In ways more than one, Bhopal survivors stand both as "victims" and "witnesses" to this ongoing disaster that is multidimensional. Their bodies function as a kind of "counter logic" to both the State and the corporate argument that prioritizes profit over people. These same scarred, diseased, weak and frail bodies are also the "evidence" for the chemical trespass that the struggle sought to challenge both in the legal sphere as well as the public sphere. Their bodies carry both the knowledge of a system that went wrong as well as the message for this neo-liberal globalized world that situates Bhopal as a stand-alone case, to remember journalist George Bradford's early warning that "We All Live In Bhopal" (1985). At the same time, these bodies also act as an "alert" for the corporations, warning them that the struggle is far from over.

The unique aspect of the Bhopal story and its message lies in the specificity of the event and the specificity of the people who were victims of this event. These were people who were mostly poor, illiterate, living on the periphery of the city and who were taken unawares by the massive gas leak due to failure of safety systems by an American multinational. While the Union Carbide Company (UCC) refused to divulge the details of Methyl Iso-cyanate (MIC) Poisoning and its possible antidote, Bhopal gas victims piled up as sick or dead bodies in the hospitals. Dow, current owner of UCC, continues to refuse any liability. Bhopalis continue to be victims of toxic poisons, their health suffering, their children being born with severe physical and mental effects, and their water being contaminated by UCC's reckless dumping of toxic wastes in the surrounding grounds. As the disaster continues, the struggle for justice also continues. The notions of justice and accountability underline the story of Bhopal and its demands. Bhopal activists have attempted to tell this story through the bodies of the survivors, demanding their protest to be heard. The aim is to communicate their story to the world, to the Indian State, and to corporates in general and Dow-UCC in particular.

Protesting Bodies Communicating the Story

In 2002 Bhopal women survivors launched the "Jhadoo Maro Dow Ko" (Beat Dow with the broom) campaign. The campaign was launched marking the 18th anniversary of the Bhopal disaster and targeting Dow Chemicals. Used *jhadoo*s (broomsticks) were collected from all over India in response to the activists' call. Some were delivered to the activists and some were collected by visiting the colonies near the Bhopal factory site where women and children handed them over with a grin. Children in the gas-affected *bastis* (slums) came up with the slogan that came to symbolize the campaign. It said, *Idhar se maro, udhar se maro, jhadoo maro Dow ko!* ("Hit them from this side, hit them from that side, and beat Dow with a broom!").

Rashida Bi, a survivor herself and leader of the Bhopal Gas Peedit Mahila Stationary Karamchari Sangh (Bhopal Gas-Affected Women Stationary Workers Union) says while explaining their message:

> If Dow refuses to take responsibility for the disaster in Bhopal, then we are going to sweep them off the face of the earth. You all might know what a "jhadoo" (broom) is, but you may not understand its significance. A jhadoo is something that you use to clean up the house. And when a woman gets upset, the first thing that she reaches for is her jhadoo. She reaches for her jhadoo when she is dealing with domestic violence or other kinds of oppression. So the women picked up their brooms to deal with Dow Chemical and their mess. We were saying to them, "either take responsibility for what happened in Bhopal, or we will sweep you up like so much rubbish. We won't let you do business anywhere." And this, you know, is the kind of "clean up" that can only be done with a jhadoo (Bi 2004a).

And so on December 2, 2002, hundreds of women survivors marched to Dow's Mumbai headquarters. They brought with them contaminated soil and water from the abandoned pesticide factory site, more than 4,000 jhadoos and with it the message: "Dow clean up your mess." Dow's response to the Mumbai protest was to file a lawsuit against the survivors. Prior to this, Anabond Essex – a part-owned Dow subsidiary in Pondicherry was presented with brooms in mid-November, 2002. Protesters called upon the government to confiscate its property. Even though most bystanders were Tamil-speaking, they reportedly had no trouble understanding the message and power of women with brooms. The action was replicated in Europe where small teams of survivors and activists took the jhadoo to Dow executives. The supporters of the movement delivered jhadoos to Dow's offices on different occasions in various parts of the world.

The message that Rashida articulates was delivered effectively through the bodies of the women protesters – holding jhadoos with the determination to correct the wrong – who were among the worst-hit sections of the gas victims.

The Spectacle of Protesting Bodies

I wondered whether these protesting bodies are used to create a spectacle for the media. However, being a member of the campaign, I saw that while the decisions around the protest design inevitably included a consideration for what will work with the media, it is not the end in itself. The message needs to be communicated through this spectacle. And it seemed natural that in order to communicate the story of Bhopalis, their bodies were used as the most effective medium. For instance, on several occasions Bhopal survivors had to sit on hunger strike in New Delhi. Sometimes Bhopalis just arrived in the Capital and staged a fast. On other occasions hunger strike came as the last and desperate measure to get the government's attention. On two separate occasions, in 2006 and 2008, Bhopal survivors set on an 800-km march on foot from Bhopal to New Delhi. On both occasions the group included men, women and children. On their way they distributed pamphlets, sang songs, organized public meetings and informed people about why they have to walk on foot to meet their own Prime Minister. The foot march, bearing a characteristic resemblance to Gandhi's "Dandi March"[3] for Salt Satyagraha, demonstrated their rejection of the Government that had largely been apathetic to the needs of the survivors. It also demonstrated their faith in the Constitution and the Central government in their way of appealing to the Prime Minister. And it demonstrated the purpose and determination of their struggle. The Campaign received overwhelming support both nationally as well as internationally. In 2006, after a 21-day-long sit-in action at New Delhi and a six-day-long hunger strike, the Prime Minister agreed to their demands and suggested setting up a coordination committee to oversee implementation of rehabilitation schemes and environmental remediation. Two years later, Bhopalis launched the "Walk Your Talk" campaign targeting the Prime Minister, urging him to keep the promises he had made in 2006. This entailed a 500-mile-walk by some 50 survivors for over 38 days, a 73-day-*dharna* (sit-in protest) in Delhi and a 60-day worldwide relay hunger strike that was joined by more than 800 people around the world. On both these occasions media coverage was consistent and generous. But on both occasions it was pushed for by the activists through strategic planning and lobbying. This involved actions with strategic deployment of protesting bodies. The Bhopal movement has remained committed to the non-violent forms of direct action. So when a hunger strike is organized with demands that are moral and logical, when it comes as a last resort, when the ones who sit on fast are those who are seeking attention to crucial discourse of justice by seeking attention to themselves, it becomes their quest for truth or justice. In fact during its worldwide relay hunger strike organized to protest at Dow's Annual Shareholder meeting in Midland Nityanand Jayaraman, a member of ICJB noted, "[t]he hunger strike is a demonstration of how firmly we believe our version of the truth" (quoted in Vosters 2003).

What distinguishes their hunger strike from the others is the irony embedded in this non-violent action – the victims of chemical trespass willfully release toxics in their bodies to demand a life with dignity and justice. This gives enormous value to the truth of the poor and the powerless. This propensity of their claims increases further when the hunger strikers are also the ones who walked on foot from Bhopal, the site of the disaster, to the capital. Thus, the spectacle was not created by protesting bodies; rather, it was created by situating them in the context where this spectacle told their story to the media. The moral argument of this frame is hard to reject. The media reports:

> They have walked 800 km twice over with their demands of justice and water – just a measure of the distance that India has to travel before it declares itself as modern responsible industrial nation (Nanda 2008a).

Protesting Bodies Pushing the Boundaries

Hunger strikes alone cannot capture media imagination for long. The media is constantly looking out for new events and new issues. In such circumstances, so as to not lose public interest, ways have to be planned to get the media to report their protest and their demands. While demands and more intricate details of the subject could be communicated through press release and media briefings, an interesting direct action usually becomes the means to get media attention. This is the reason why Bhopal activists usually include some shock tactics in long protest campaigns, often pushing the boundaries. For instance, during the six-month-long "Walk Your Talk" campaign in New Delhi in 2008, there was a point when it seemed that media interest was fading, that there was nothing appearing in the media, no news was coming from the political corridors. It was then that the Bhopal survivors, who sat braving the heat of the Delhi summers on the roadside at Jantar Mantar, took to more radical protest forms than mere sit-ins. One morning a group of them chained themselves to the Prime Minister's residence, a high security zone, taking police and the officials at the Prime Minister's house by surprise. While security breach by victims of a chemical trespass as a desperate measure to get the Prime Minister's attention was an interesting news peg, the Bhopal victims holding on to their chained bodies, both in protest and solidarity, and telling the world through the media that they will not leave until their demands are heard provided the drama, the tension and the novelty that electronic media usually seeks. This was evident by the number of electronic media that was present at the location to cover the protest action. This included almost all major national and international channels, and the story dominated the day's coverage. For example, a story reported by a prominent Indian news channel asserted that this protest was "a serious breach of security and a desperate attempt to grab Prime Minister Manmohan Singh's attention" (Nanda 2008b).

Besides chain-in action there were other direct actions. For instance, men, women and children staging a "die in" at the Prime Minister's office, or mothers of second-generation-affected children leaving the latter at the doorsteps of the Prime Minister's house in New Delhi. Both the Prime Minister's house and office are high-alert areas and consequently, protesters always run a risk of police action. However, the breach of security by protesting victims became an interesting story for the media to cover where the protesting bodies pushed their own boundaries to take a leap often unimagined. The moral and legal appeal of the campaign was so powerful that it received consistent support not only from the civil society but also from the media and several Members of Parliament. On August 8, 2008, Ram Vilas Paswan, Union Minister, Fertilizers and Petrochemicals, came to the dharna site on behalf of the Prime Minister and declared agreement with the survivors' demands including that of an Empowered Commission on Bhopal and legal action against Dow, Warren Anderson and other Carbide's officials.

Protesting Bodies Playing Satire

While actions like *padyatra* (journey on foot) and hunger strikes often come as direct protests, there are other events or actions that are being planned to highlight the demands of the campaign in the media and public. On August 11, 2007, ICJB gave away "Mir Zafar Awards" for treachery above and beyond the call of duty to 12 eminent people.[4] In their press release ICJB claimed that the awards were being given to the selected bureaucrats, politicians, senior lawyers, corporate heads and others for their efforts to let Dow off the hook and pave the way for its business in India (ICJB 2007). Naming the awards after Mir Zafar, ICJB was successful in making a direct link between the betrayals of the past and the present, the modern-day Mir Zafars being the bureaucrats, politicians and others whom the campaign exposed earlier in the same year as working strenuously to help Dow expand its business in India and bury its Bhopal responsibilities. Betrayal and corruption have been the key factors in the manner in which the Bhopal gas disaster unfolded. These are also the themes that activists strategically communicated through the protesting bodies of the victims. Significantly, besides the Bhopal survivors, these awards were also given away by the residents of Singur and Nandigram. Just like Bhopal represented the worst face of corporate greed, both Singur and Nandigram in India were the sites of massive and often violent people's struggle against land acquisition for corporate gains.[5] It was a satirical ceremony where the awards were received by movement supporters wearing masks of the winning eminent people. The event was opened by Suhasini Muley, a noted Hindi-film actress, with the unfolding of a multinational flag that carried logos of prominent companies on it.

In a similar vein comes the "Jhooth Bole Kaua Kate" (Crow bites the liar) campaign, launched on the 25th anniversary of the disaster in 2009 to highlight the government's lies (ICJB 2009). By using the central figure of a crow which keeps a close watch on politicians and experts who, Bhopal survivors claim, are acting hands-in-glove with Dow Chemicals, and by organizing the buffet party outside the factory site using semi-processed toxic wastes, activists created a spectacular drama for the media without compromising on the point which they wanted to be known to the authorities – that the waste remains toxic even if they manipulate the studies, that by ignoring their invitation to the buffet they only confirm this and finally, that the victims as well as the public are not fools. The underlying message was that the lies and deceit will become known and the guilty will be punished, reinforcing the campaign's slogan that the "crow will bite all the liars!" As part of this campaign they also organized a "Benign Buffet" on November 28, 2009 at which the members of the state cabinet, the bureaucrats and members of government-research bodies, whom Bhopalis accused of foul play, were invited. The buffet included "delicacies" as "Semi-Processed Pesticide on Watercress" and "Lime Sludge Mousse." The event saw huge public and media presence.

Protesting Bodies and Change in Protest Forms

While rallies and effigy burning have been organized from the very beginning, the post-liberalization phase also saw some changes in the nature of the protests. Effigies were no more simply Dow and Carbide or Anderson. Instead, they were modeled on the "hall of shame" bringing-characters that the gas survivors believed had been manipulating their situation. Now, the protesting bodies also had certain accessories on them – protesters now wore head bandannas with slogans or held placards with messages in English and Hindi. There was certainly more emphasis on visuals and how to make these visuals striking. By a combined effect of protesting bodies and certain selected accessories, the aim was to create a spectacle through the use of the soft power of images, stories, and actions that capture media attention, especially that of television and garner public support without mitigating the political demands. This change in protest forms was the result of both a need to get media attention as well as that of an influence of international groups and associations. Greenpeace, which was an active member of ICJB in the 1990s, is known for its media-friendly protest tactics. It usually made use of a limited number of protesters in an often novel direct action where the protesters also wore head bands, bright clothes and banners or other such props to communicate their message. These actions are usually staged or choreographed actions for visual media with an implicit understanding of the medium. However whether it was Greenpeace alone that influenced the kind of protest forms being staged by ICJB remains debatable. ICJB has gained inspiration for its protest forms and its art of communicating its message both from its international allies and their experience, and from an understanding of global issues and how media operates through its constituent members. The campaign has, among its members, a number of people who come with experience in working with the media and with prior experience in participating or observing similar protest actions elsewhere. For example, prior to the Bhopalis' Mir Zafar Award ceremony, mock award ceremonies or hall of shame awards have been organized by many other people at different places. For instance, the Rogers Award in New Zealand started in 1997 (Richards 2004). Dow itself was awarded the first Public Eye Hall of Shame Award in 2005 (*The Public Eye Awards* 2005a and 2005b). Similarly, "Die-in"s emerged as a popular protest action to oppose invasion on Iraq in 2003 but for Bhopal its history dates back to 1989 when they staged a die-in at the Consulate in United States (US). The "Die in" action where Bhopal survivors lay down on the ground covering themselves in shrouds – either a plain white sheet or one with a picture of the iconic Bhopal child, at once brought to memory the scene of the morning of December 3, 1984. It highlighted the continued casualties owing to the lack of proper medical treatment, second generation effects and groundwater contamination. At the same time, these actions presented both the disaster as well as the struggle emerging from it; as demonstrated in the slogans used in these protests, for instance, one of the most common slogans used over years – "Mourn for the Dead, Fight for the Living" where the movement pays tribute to victims of the gas disaster and calls on survivors for vigilance. The unique thing in such instances is not the novelty of the action alone but also the issue of who is communicating the message through this action. Who are the participants and how are they saying what they are saying? The protesting bodies of victims and survivors in this case come across as a strategic choice to speak to the media and communicate their message to the public. Speaking bodies of those who are living through the aftermath of the gas leak and its effects, as well as the symbolic reference to the worst outcomes of the disaster, form the core of ICJB's protest tactics. These inevitably cause discomfort to their political targets. Thus, these protesting, revolting, speaking bodies also become the symbols that are waiting to be read by the media, and through media representations by the political corridors.

This communication is a gendered discourse and planned accordingly. Through my experience of participating in Bhopal protests, I have come to note that pictures of women and children communicate better than male protesters, a point which Bhopal activists and journalists have confirmed. Confirming the strategic centrality of women's bodies in protest and its outcome (Sasson-Levy and Rapoport 2003) and highlighting the importance of women-led action, Rashida Bi, winner of the 2004 Goldman Environment Prize, noted:

> Women are the worst affected from any kind of violence – be it domestic, development-related or that caused by corporate polluters like Union Carbide. It is up to us, the women, to join hands across the world and keep the fight for justice and against violence alive and unwavering (Bi 2004b).

Similarly, the "Jhadoo Maro Dow Ko" campaign, in which Bhopali women – who were among the worst-hit by the disaster – or their women supporters symbolically hit Dow by presenting its executives with Indian broomsticks, became a resistance against powerful patriarchy and at the same time, transformed a corporate entity into a human figure – one that commits mistakes but one that can also be disciplined. This captures the optimism within the struggle in the way in which it is able to pose a challenge to the mighty and the powerful.

Women and children remain in the forefront of most of the ICJB-led actions. By doing so, each protest is not only represented by two generations of the people affected by the gas leak and brings their plight to center stage but also represents the two generations that have been leading the struggle. Thus, the ones rendered most vulnerable by the disaster become the torchbearers or spokespersons of the struggle, "giving them the upper hand as authors of their own story and guardians of a more just humanity" (Erler 2010: 42). Their vulnerability adds to the ethical angst of their protesting bodies. I would notice journalists seeking out in particular old and burka-clad women for a sound bite and photographers competing to get their best close-up.

The Bhopalis on their part would strategically line children holding the banner in the first row and women would march together in a rally.

The action plan involves decisions about what kind of protesting bodies would take the center stage during the action, *what* they would say and *how*. First and foremost, the action has to cater to the goals of the movement. Therefore the frame of the demands and the political vision of the movement have to reflect in the framework of the protest action.

The campaign also counters the "routinization" that comes to mark annual rituals like anniversary events. Ever since 1984, anniversary actions are organized in Bhopal by the survivors' organizations in the first week of December. This is one occasion that marks both public as well as the media calendars. ICJB has used the anniversary to nail down the state–corporate nexus in several ways. It has invested in utilizing effigies and using local artists to take its message to people as well as politicians through the anniversary march. Effigies are mostly either in the form of a government or a company official or in that of the "Corporate," the "Government" and the "Corruption," thereby humanizing the very power that survivors seek to contest. Every year effigies vary and so does the immediate message although year after year the central theme of "Justice" continues to be the same. For instance, while the effigy of Dow Company was the main attraction in the 20th anniversary to stress corporate accountability, in the 25th anniversary, effigies of Dow and Indian Government officials were used prominently to demonstrate the nexus between them. One of the constant figures in such protests has been the effigy of Warren Anderson, who was the Chief Executive Officer (CEO) of UCC at the time of the disaster and a declared fugitive from Indian courts. In the end of each march the effigy is burnt and beaten with sticks by the public. On the one hand, this has mythological reference to the Hindu epic *Ramayana* where Lord Rama burnt Ravana, the king who had abducted his wife, with an arrow suggesting the victory of "good" over "evil" or "truth" over "deceit." In fact to be selected to light the fire is considered a great honor (Fortun 2001). The protesting bodies then not only remain the vehicle of this knowledge but become the messages themselves which embody the spirit of the struggle.

On the other hand, the ritual beating of the effigies also moves beyond being a "performance" and indicates an "interaction" between the participating protesters and the audience, where the audience is not passive and the "sole targets of the rhetorical strategies" but also "active interpreters, critics and respondents" (Brenneis 1987: 237). In this manner, these events no longer remain a spectacle signifying the politics of representation; they also signify the politics of confrontation. The event site becomes the site for bringing the oppressed and their oppressors on the same platform even as opportunities for a direct confrontation with political authorities are far and few in real terms. The event site becomes the stage where victims and supporters get the power to pronounce their own judgment on government officials and the company symbolically.

While some protests like padyatra were designed to "appeal" to political authorities for justice, in others the oppressed demonstrated the power to deliver justice themselves like in the case of women giving broomsticks to Dow executives, or that of victims and protesters from Singur and Nandigram giving away awards for treachery to powerful politicians, or even that of Bhopal survivors bringing Warren Anderson and other UCC-Dow officials to their own trial during the anniversary. The "absence" of the state or corporate officials at whom the protest was targeted as well as their symbolic presence in form of effigies carries the movement's message powerfully to the media and public. As a national newspaper reports:

> Sitting with a huge dummy crow and plates of "delicacies" made out of hazardous chemical waste, they awaited Chief Minister Shivraj Singh Chauhan, Gas Relief Minister Babulal Gaur, State Chief Secretary Rakesh Sahni and other bureaucrats to join them for the "benign buffet" . . . The invitees, of course, did not seem to have an appetite for "semi-processed pesticide on watercress" and "lime-sludge mousse" and failed to show up. The survivors, however, had a lot to say. Facing standard questions from media, they reeled out their tales of misery (Singh 2009).

Where the protest or action would take place and *when* have been careful decisions as well. These aspects figure not only as strategic decisions in order to have a successful action in terms of targeting the political authorities or their office but also to generate a renewed sense of awareness among the public and media. Gas victims chaining themselves to the Prime Minister's house, a die-in at India Gate or a satirical spectacle unfolding in a hall right opposite the Federation of Indian Chambers of Commerce and Industry (FICCI) auditorium are all carefully selected locations. The locations then in effect embody the protest with all its elements – protesting bodies (protesters), voices (slogans) and props (banners, pamphlets, etc.). By situating the protest and protesters in a certain specific locale, the message embodied could be delivered more effectively irrespective of the slogans or banners used as part of the action. This also provided the media with both words and visuals so that it could give the complete story to its users. How locations add new elements to the story are evident from some of these news stories:

> A group of Bhopal gas tragedy survivors staged a demonstration in front of North Block office of Home Ministry where the meeting of Group of Ministers on the issue were taking place . . . The demonstration . . . before the Home Ministry where any kind of protest or demonstration is banned (*The Hindu* 2010).

> Covering themselves with shrouds and lying inside coffins, the Bhopal gas leak survivors put up a protest in the capital on Thursday to commemorate the 25th anniversary of the disaster and highlight the government's apathy towards them . . . 'Die in Action', as the protest was called, sent a simple message – that the survivors will continue their fight for justice until the end (*IANS* 2009).

The message embodied in the effigies, victims and their supporters becomes clearly visible to bystanders and the spectator becomes a part of the spectacle designed by ICJB to counter what Debord calls the "integrated spectacle" of State and market economy (1990:11). The spectacle, the drama it provides and the politics it represents are enthusiastically accepted by the media both nationally as well as internationally.

Interestingly, these actions are not designed as media "gimmicks" but rather inspired by the socio-political situation and the movement's response to the political authorities. However, by doing so, the protesting bodies, whether in the form of effigies or human protesters, are able to engage media more directly in the reality they are trying to contest. For example, the die-in action of the Bhopal victims was an enactment of the disaster indicating possibilities of similar incidences if "lessons from Bhopal" are not learnt. The focus on "protesting bodies" and the media attention paid to them are also evident in other social movements in India such as the *Narmada Bachao Andolan* and the *Chipko Andolan*. Such actions then not only cater to the media's need for a sensational or dramatic spectacle that evokes human interest (readership) but also, more importantly, educate the media in the logic or argument of the protest. Thus, the use of protesting bodies as a strategy to drive a point home is not something unique to Bhopal or India alone. It is well-used in protests across the world though cultural elements in these actions might vary. For the resource-poor movements in India, "protesting bodies" become a very conscious counter-propaganda strategy targeting the media as well as the public. However, the protest does not emerge from the need to create a media spectacle; it is an emphatic move to inform, educate and engage the media.

The manner in which the Bhopal struggle engaged the media through its consistent actions to keep the issue alive and contemporary, building each of its actions on the lessons from the earlier ones and making connections between different complicated realities, also reflects in the way in which media knowledge on their decade-long struggle evolved even as the movement's own self-definition and priorities were evolving. Bhopal is remembered in many different ways; for some it stands for an industrial disaster, while others consider it a gross environmental contamination. Those affected by the gas leak have also witnessed a shift in their identities. One important factor contributing to this shift is the development of ICJB in the 1990s which was constantly making linkages with international groups and organizations and in so doing, was also constantly defining the Bhopal story in new ways which the media was quick to grasp. For instance from "victims" in 1980s to "survivors" in 1990s; from "gas victims" to "water victims" and later to "victims of Dow-UCC poisons" from 2000 onwards; Bhopal protesters have embodied many different identities and with each identity a new issue has been raised. This reflects both in the campaign's press releases as well as media stories. Bhopal then does not make its appearance only as environment news or health news or a human interest story. At the same time, the movement draws on the "body" to articulate a politics of representation that contests the politics of the state.

Conclusion

By using protesting bodies strategically – to shock and surprise, to break the routine of actions, to employ irony and humor in demonstrating the interplay between the powerful and the powerless, the haves and the have-nots, the native and the foreigner, truth and lie, good and evil, and interweaving drama and spectacle to bring out passion and emotion, conflict and threat – the Bhopal movement demonstrates awareness of the aspects in which the mass media is generally interested and the issues which target the middle class which in turn forms a large chunk of the audience and the media fraternity. It becomes a political commentary of resistance that the activist believes can fit into many of the news beat, fight media malaise and give scope to the journalist to find the appropriate vocabulary for a resistance that has become both mediated and embodied. The movement's protest-repertoire demonstrates the strategic centrality of protesting bodies where the ethical angst of the survivors' three-decade-old movement finds opportunities for new(er) stories.

❋

Notes

1. See Greenpeace (Labunska et al. 1999). A 1997 study conducted by Arthur D. Little, and commissioned by UCC, warned that pollution of the underground aquifer could be happening at a rate far faster than imagined and that in a worst case scenario, it could take as little as two years to contaminate the aquifer.
2. For more details on the International Campaign for Justice in Bhopal, see ICJB's official website at http://www.bhopal.net. As accessed on March 5, 2014.
3. Gandhi launched the Dandi March from Sabarmati Ashram in Ahmedabad to the sea coast near the village Dandi as part of The Salt Satyagraha on March 12, 1930 against the British salt tax in colonial India. This 390-km march took 24 days and saw huge participation from Indians. Finally on reaching Dandi, Gandhi broke the salt laws on April 6, 1930. This in turn triggered the wider Civil Disobedience Movement.
4. Mir Zafar was the eighth Nawab of Bengal who came to be known as a traitor after he made a secret pact with Robert Clive in his greed to remain the Nawab, thus surrendering his army and losing the battle of Plassey without fighting. This led to the foundation of British rule in India. For ICJB's position on organizing the Mir Zafar Awards ceremony see ICJB 2007.
5. In December 2006, Singur and Nandigram in West Bengal became national news and concern with people's resistance surfaced strongly against the issue of forced land acquisition for corporate projects. In Singur, Tata Motors was to set up an automobile factory while in Nandigram a chemical hub was to be established by Dow Chemicals. In 2007 RTI Documents exposed by Bhopal activists revealed that Mr Ratan Tata, the

then CEO of Tata group of companies who also chaired the Indo–US CEO forum, taking cue from Dow Chemicals, proposed a "clean up" of toxic wastes in Bhopal. Activists claimed that this was an effort to let Dow escape the Bhopal liabilities.

References

Bi, R. 2004a. "We Want Real Justice for Bhopal," interview of Rashida Bi and Champa Devi Shukla with Socialist Worker, June 28. http://socialistworker.org/2004-2/504/504_08_Bhopal.shtml. As accessed on May 20, 2010.

———. 2004b. Quote from Rashida Bi made available at official website of campaign group *Students for Bhopal.* http://old.studentsforbhopal.org/Quotes.htm. As accessed on May 20, 2010.

Bradford, G. 1985. "We All Live in Bhopal," *Fifth Estate*, Winter Issue. http://www.eco-action.org/dt/bhopal.html. As accessed on February 20, 2014.

Brenneis, D. 1987. "Performing Passions: Aesthetics and Politics in an Occasionally Egalitarian Community," *American Ethnologist*, 14 (2): 236–50.

Centre for Science and Environment (CSE). 2009. *Contamination of Soil and Water Inside and Outside the Union Carbide India Limited, Bhopal.* Report by S. Johnson, R. Sahu, N. Jadan and C. Duca. New Delhi: CSE.

Debord, G. 1990. *Comments on the Society of the Spectacle.* London: Verso.

Erler, C. 2010. "Memory and Erasure: Applying Visual Narrative Power Analysis to the Image War Between Dow Chemical and the Women of the International Campaign for Justice in Bhopal." Paper presented at '2010 ART&DESIGN for Social Justice Symposium & 15th Anniversary, Kids' Guernica Peace Mural Project,' Florida State University, January 15–18.

Fortun, K. 2001. *Advocacy after Bhopal: Environmentalism, Disaster, New Global Orders.* Chicago: The University of Chicago Press.

Gamson, W. A. and G. Wolfsfeld. 1993. "Movements and Media as Interacting Systems," *Annals of the American Academy of Political and Social Science*, 526: 114–27.

IANS. 2009. "Bhopal Tragedy Survivors Lie in Coffins to Protest," December 3. http://twocircles.net/2009dec03/bhopal_tragedy_survivors_lie_coffins_protest.html. As accessed on May 5, 2010.

International Campaign for Justice in Bhopal (ICJB). 2009. Press release dated November 26. http://www.studentsforbhopal.org/node/292. As accessed on May 20, 2010.

International Campaign for Justice in Bhopal (ICJB). 2007. "PM, Tata Win Mir Zafar Awards for Treachery Above and Beyond the Call of Duty,"

August 11. http://news.bhopal.net/2007/08/11/bhopalis-give-pm-tata-spoof-awards-for-treachery/. As accessed on May 20, 2010.

Jeffrey, R. 2000. *India's Newspaper Revolution: Capitalism, Politics and the Indian-Language Press 1977–1999.* New Delhi: Oxford University Press.

Kohli, V. 2003. *The Indian Media Business.* London: Response Books Division, Sage Publications.

Labunska, I., A. Stephenson, K. Brigden, R. Stringer, D. Santillo and P. A. Johnston. 1999. "'The Bhopal Legacy:' Toxic Contaminants at the Former Union Carbide Factory Site, Bhopal, India: 15 Years After the Bhopal Accident." Technical Note No. 4/99, Greenpeace Research Laboratories, Department of Biological Sciences, University of Exeter, Exeter, UK.

Mehta, N. 2008. "India Talking: Politics, Democracy and News Television," in *Television in India: Satellites, Politics and Cultural Change.* New York: Routledge.

Moyna. 2012. "Groundwater Contamination Around Union Carbide Factory is Now Officially Confirmed," *Down to Earth,* September 26. http://www.downtoearth.org.in/content/groundwater-contamination-around-union-carbide-factory-now-officially-confirmed. As accessed on August 5, 2013.

Nanda, R. 2008a. "Bhopal Gas Victims' Fight Going in Vain," CNN-IBN, May 5. http://ibnlive.in.com/news/bhopal-gas-victims-fight-going-in-vain/64565-3-1.html. As accessed on December 3, 2010.

———. 2008b. "Chain Reaction: How Bhopal Victims Appealed," CNN-IBN, May 22. Available at http://ibnlive.in.com/news/chain-reaction-how-bhopal-victims-appealed–pics/65690-3-1.html. As accessed on December 3, 2010.

Ranjan, N., S. Sarangi, V. T. Padmanabhan, S. Holleran, R. Ramakrishnan and D. R. Varma. 2003. "Methyl Isocyanate Exposure and Growth Patterns of Adolescents in Bhopal," *JAMA,* 290 (14): 1856–57.

Richards, C. 2004. Interview about the Roger Award, *New Internationalist Magazine,* Issue 368, June 1. http://newint.org/columns/makingwaves/2004/06/01/roger-award/. As accessed on February 20, 2014.

Sasson-Levy, O. and T. Rapoport. 2003. "Body, Gender, and Knowledge in Protest Movements: The Israeli Case," *Gender and Society* 17 (3): 379–403.

Singh, M. P. 2009. "Ministers, Babus Fail to Turn Up for Pest-Fest," *The Hindu,* November 29. http://www.thehindu.com/news/national/other-states/ministers-babus-fail-to-turn-up-for-pestfest/article56914.ece. As accessed on May 5, 2010.

The Hindu. 2010. "Bhopal Victims Demonstrate in Front of MHA," June 21. http://beta.thehindu.com/news/national/article477183.ece. As accessed on May 5, 2010.

The Public Eye Awards. 2005a. "History of Public Eye Awards." http://publiceye.ch/en/about-the-public-eye-awards/history/. As accessed on February 20, 2014.

———. 2005b. "Hall of Shame." http://publiceye.ch/en/hall-of-shame/. As accessed on February 20, 2014.

Thussu, D. K. 2007. "The 'Murdochization' of News? The Case of Star TV in India," *Media Culture Society* 29 (4): 593–611.

Vasudev, S. 2005. "Idiot Sheets?" *Outlook*, October 17. http://www.outlook india.com/article.aspx?228942. As accessed on February 28, 2014.

Vosters, H. 2003. "Bhopal Survivors Confront Dow: They Say Dow Execs Lied to Shareholders," *CorpWatch*, May 15. http://www.corpwatch.org/article.php?id=6748. As accessed on May 10, 2010.

PART III

Case Studies: India and the World

7

A Coming-Out Party for Indian Waste Pickers?

Pondering the Dilemmas of Making Local Environmentalism Global

*Bharati Chaturvedi**

The Context

In the last 16 years since I began working on environmental justice
issues, the landscape has transformed in ways that were hard to predict
at the beginning. My own work both as an environmental activist and
writer, and as part of a formal organization Chintan[1] has focused on
several issues related to environmental justice, consumption, materials
and toxics. In this chapter, I focus on the most contentious aspect of
them all – the issue of the informal waste-recycling sector.

Waste pickers from several parts of the world, more than the
larger informal recycling sector, have drawn global attention in the
last half-decade. There is now a global movement that seeks justice
and inclusion of waste pickers in cities, in waste handling and in the
way urban spaces are designed. The creation of this movement and
its growth has compelled me (and several of my colleagues in similar
spaces) to ask ourselves if such a globalization serves the several local
visions within the movement, and if this is at all a movement. Some of
these discussions have also touched upon how to meet local, regional
and national needs through such global networks. This chapter will
draw out some of the dilemmas I face as an activist and the challenges
Chintan faces (and presumably, other organizations do too); it dwells

on how local issues are best served in global advocacy and whether it is profitable to invest in such work at all. Finally, I glance at how the local change that the waste pickers themselves articulate as their priority can feed into global discourse better.

To make sense of these issues, an understanding of the sector and recent developments of the last five years are important.

Whose Globalization are We Discussing?

This chapter discusses the globalization of the waste pickers' movement for justice. I use the term "movement" as a fuzzy entity comprising multiple actors – some structured into organizations and others not. The term "movement" here is a broad category used to describe a collective thrust towards an idea or a change. In the context of organizations of waste pickers, this alludes to actions organized and undertaken by them around specific issues (such as recognition and the right to work) and organizations that work closely with waste pickers but are largely administered by non-waste pickers.

In India, and in many other parts of the world, waste has always been managed and recycled by indigenous private players. They work in the informal sector, offering (in India) the only mainstream recycling system that exists in the country. Almost 1 per cent of people in cities of the developing world (Medina 2008) are estimated to be involved in recycling, recycling between 9 to 59 per cent (Chintan Environmental Research and Action Group 2004) of the total waste generated in urban India. Waste pickers, itinerant buyers, junk dealers – these are our indigenous waste handlers. Their work includes picking up the waste, segregating it into dozens of different categories (upto 52 for plastics alone[2]), washing and cleaning it, drying it, shredding it and adding value by physical treatment, and trading it to the next higher level. At the end of a long trading chain, there is the preprocessing, often also carried out in the informal sector. For them, waste is lucrative because it generates the next meal. Theirs is an investment of time, labor and acquired skills. The cost is their health, few opportunities to leap into the formal sector and no social security. With no subsidies and low capital investment, over 1.5 million[3] amounting to about 10 per cent of the total waste pickers globally, recycle India's waste.

Currently, in the Indian context, although some waste pickers are organized into various kinds of organizations such as associations, trade unions and co-operatives, a majority of them remain individuals working in the informal sector. Socially, they are primarily illiterate and come from marginalized Muslim, low caste and to some extent, from Dalit communities.

An approximate structure of the recycling sector in India is represented here. Despite being a pyramid-like structure, it does not suggest poverty only at the bottom amongst the waste pickers. Rather, while the largest number is amongst waste pickers, there are several poor at other levels also.

Figure 7.1 How Recycling Works

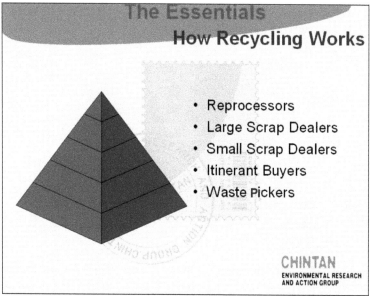

The Essentials

How Recycling Works

- Reprocessors
- Large Scrap Dealers
- Small Scrap Dealers
- Itinerant Buyers
- Waste Pickers

CHINTAN
ENVIRONMENTAL RESEARCH
AND ACTION GROUP

Source: Chintan Environmental Research and Action Group.

Globally, waste pickers are found in several other countries, typically as part of the informal sector. Table 7.1 identifies countries where there has been some form of engagement with waste pickers or their work in the last five years.

In this section there are two issues that are relevant to this discussion. First, that although there is a complex chain of informal sector recyclers, only a small section – that of waste pickers – is part of the global discourse. The most likely reason for this lies in the understanding of the waste recycling and trade chain as one that is inherently most exploitative of the waste pickers, who must therefore be the key benefactors of any movement targeting poverty alleviation and human rights. It is also easier to work, for advocacy purposes, with a single tangible group of people instead of a long, complex chain.

The second issue is related to the actual participation of waste pickers in the overall movement, so to say. Some estimates in Latin America suggest that only 3 per cent (Padilla 2008) of the total waste pickers are actually organized into co-operatives. Table 7.1 explains this further.

Table 7.1 Extent of Recognition of Informal Sector by Municipalities/ Governments in Six Countries

	Formal Sector Recognition of Informal Sector Contribution	Integration of Informal Sector into Formal Sector Activities	Assistance to Informal Sector	Organizing of Informal Sector Labor	Percentage of Informal Waste Sector People Who are Members of an Association/ Co-operative (%)
Cairo	Yes	Yes	Yes	Yes	2.5
Cluj	No	No	No	No	11
Lima	Yes	Yes	No	Yes	7
Lusaka	No	Yes	No	No	0
Pune	Yes	Yes	Yes	Yes	60
Quezon City	Yes	No	No	Yes	37

Source: Scheinberg et al. (2010).

In other words, the movement we discuss is also based on limited organization, but one which is able to be the voice for the sector as a whole. Later sections of this chapter offer a broad understanding of how limited but strategic organizing from amongst large numbers can result in a global presence.

The Many Locals: What is Happening in Six Countries

Before critically examining the movement for waste pickers' inclusion globally, here is a brief overview of the several local movements and policies in the country. I have selected and detailed only such countries where there has been some important or decisive work, and ignored places where the movement is yet nascent.

In Brazil, there has been a strong movement within civil society, including the Catholic Church, to organize waste pickers into co-operatives, starting in the 1980s. There are currently several co-ops working in a range of Brazilian cities, in partnership with municipalities. These partnerships are diverse, and include the right to pick up waste, facilities to recycle waste, and to transport some kinds of waste. A well-known program in Brazil is the Life and Citizenship program. As part of this, every year, there is a festival and conference involving the highest levels of government (former President Lula also attended one of these) where the key issues are discussed and debated. Overall, Brazil appears to be one of the most successful countries in bringing to light this sector and finding tangible ways for their livelihood, enhancement and inclusion on the ground.

In Argentina, the movement appears to be more fragile, because several waste pickers have been drawn into the profession after the financial crisis and did not consistently see their long-term future in it. Therefore they do not necessarily wish to invest in organizing or campaigning. Nevertheless, local gains include the passing of a Zero Waste Law to the advantage of the waste pickers, or "cartoneras."

Overall in Latin America, there is a well-knitted continent-wide network of the various co-operatives, called the Latin American scavengers co-ops. In both Brazil and Columbia, there are now laws that recognize the waste pickers and enable them to carry out their work legitimately.

In Egypt, the waste pickers organized themselves into micro-enterprises that not only picked up waste from the households, but also recycled various streams into plastic pellets, food for swine, etc. In the mid-2000s, they were dislocated when the city of Cairo handed over waste collection to several private companies. Now, some of these companies have discontinued their work while others have hired the waste pickers to implement their contract, albeit at lower work conditions.

In the Philippines, the waste pickers are found at the landfills, themselves highly notorious sites that have buried some of the pickers alive in waste avalanches.[4] Through a number of non-governmental organizations (NGOs) and Church groups, they are now organized into the Payatas Alliance for Recycling Exchange (PARE) which consists of 15 associations whose members are dumpsite pickers. The city recognizes and provides PARE some level of support through the disposal facility contractor, IPM (i.e., setting up of trading centers). PARE follows a system in the recovery of recyclables in the dumping area. Seven associations work during the day while eight work at night. Member waste pickers are allowed to pick recyclables from the dump truck in a period of 30 minutes after dumping. About 2,000 of the waste pickers, called "baraot," are informal members of PARE who sell their recyclables directly to junkshops. Specialized waste collectors of food wastes, textiles, and other specific materials are also active. The dumpsite pickers are able to recover 10,257 tons of recyclables and 1,241 tons of food waste annually before the city contractor does the final soil covering.

The city also provides various facilities to the pickers at the landfill and recognizes the junk shops at the border of the dumpsite. As a result, it is also able to control and upgrade the working conditions and performance standards.

In the Balkans, where most of the waste pickers are Roma, there is a problem of both their work and their historically-marginalized status. Yet, projects funded by multilateral finance agencies, such as the International Finance Corporation (IFC), have been able to produce data, produce small pilots on the ground and even facilitated recognition for the sector. In India, there are several organizations that exclusively or otherwise work on or with waste pickers. These could be through job creation, work with children and direct organizing for inclusion in municipal undertakings in the waste arena. A network of organizations working with waste pickers is also periodically active. In the last five years, the privatization of both waste collection and of technology that uses waste has threatened the livelihoods of waste pickers by competing for recyclable waste. This despite the policy landscape is wide and inclusive, but scarcely reflected in ground reality. Some of the key policies and rules are:

(a) The Union Budget 2013–14, which has a provision for Rashtriya Swasthya Bima Yojana (RSBY), a health insurance for waste pickers (GoI 2013).

(b) The Plastic Waste (Management and Handling) Rules 2011, which mandates that waste pickers be deployed to collect plastic waste (GoI 2011a).

(c) The Electronic and Electric Waste (Management and Handling) Rules 2011, which has provisions that associations (a means by which informal sector organizes itself) be recognized as legitimate actors for collection and dismantling of e-waste. Previously, those not registered as a company were not considered by various authorities for authorization to deliver such services (GoI 2011b).

(d) The National Action Plan on Climate Change 2009, which states:

> While the informal sector is the backbone of India's highly successful recycling system, unfortunately a number of municipal regulations impede the operation of the recyclers, owing to which they remain at a tiny scale without access to finance or improved recycling technologies (GoI 2009: 3: 53).

This is part of the Mission on Urban Sustainability.

(e) The Comptroller and Auditor General of India (CAG) Audit on Municipal Solid Waste in India (2008), which also recommends that "MoEF/states should consider providing legal recognition to rag pickers so that recycling work becomes more organized and also ensure better working conditions for them" (GoI 2008: 3, 3.5: 41).

(f) The National Environment Policy 2006, which states: "Give legal recognition to, and strengthen the informal sector systems of collection and recycling of various materials. In particular enhance their access to institutional finance and relevant technologies" (GoI 2006: 5.2.8 e, 36).

(g) The Supreme Court accepted recommendations of the Report of the Committee constituted by the Supreme Court in 1999 (Solid Waste Management in Class 1 Cities in India). According to this report, in points 3.4.7 and 3.4.8, rag pickers must be converted into doorstep waste collectors as a means of upgradation (GoI 1999).

What do we learn from this global scenario? These examples make it clear that not only do waste pickers exist globally, but that there are concerted local efforts to create inclusive policies for them, in each national or local context. In India, detailing the policies makes it clear that various policies have been consistently in favor of recycling by the informal sector, and their upgradation, specifically, the waste pickers. However, these have been ignored in plans of privatization and waste-to-energy (WtE) plants, including in some of the new urban renewal plans.

Two issues emerge most forcefully from these cases. First, we see the local demand for stable jobs across the world. In many cases, such as in Egypt, India and the Philippines, this is specifically for access to waste that can be legally processed and traded in. A second issue is that while there have been very different models in each country, it is clear that many of them have successfully brought about either policy shifts or that their strategies have compelled their governments to take notice of them, typically through local and national efforts.

This is key to our understanding of the compulsions and the process of coming out as a global movement. Some of the key questions at this juncture are these:

(*a*) What gains could organizations have expected to accrue from globalizing their movement?

(*b*) How much of each country's incomplete tasks/agendas could expect to be further fulfilled via such globalization?

We will critically examine them with a focus on India, in the sections to follow.

The Beginnings of a Global Movement for Waste Pickers' Inclusion

The title of this section is itself worth some thought. It assumes a global goal, although there is none formally declared, except for a resolution passed in Bogota in 2008. However, based on both this declaration as well as the challenges faced in various countries, inclusion seems like a reasonable assumption as goal for the movement. "Inclusion" implies being a formal part of waste management systems with specific spaces assigned for waste pickers as well as for their entrepreneurial skills to be actualized.

More complex is the term "movement." What comprises a movement? Surely it cannot be a large number of people, because this is not the case at the global level, both because of the expenses involved, and the logistical challenge of physically or otherwise making global the grassroots. Most critical is the issue of whether the grassroots-comprising-highly-marginal-populations would have cared to undertake global level advocacy, and to what end? After a brief survey of the recent global initiatives by various actors, we will return to understanding the nature of this movement.

There have been several smaller exchanges between various organizations globally, to see and understand each other's work in the context of waste pickers. In 2004, Chintan in India led a collaboration with organizations in the Philippines and the Community Sanitation and Recycling Organization (CSARO) in Cambodia, to compare and inform countrywide strategies and experiences on waste pickers. In this context they also examined the Extended Producer Responsibility as a tool to benefit waste pickers. Also in partnership was the Global Alliance for Incinerator Alternatives (GAIA), which helped facilitate the process, particularly in the Philippines, where its southern headquarters were located. However, it was only around 2007, with an international conference of the Switzerland-based Collaborative Working Group on Solid Waste Management in Low and Middle Income Countries (CWG) in February 2006 that several organizations were able to meet each other and share ideas for future collaborations on the issue of waste pickers. While there was no distinct outcome (such as a follow-up meeting, etc.) based on this, several organizations began to explore a larger agenda and began networking.

The CWG itself is a platform that comprises diverse individuals and organizations with an interest in issues around solid waste. The initial discussions therefore began between NGOs, consultants and academics; not at the grassroots. Most discussions were related to learning about other local movements.

By 2008, two other aspects of the global movement were underway. The first was the First World Conference of Waste Pickers, held in March 2008 in Bogota, Columbia, which already had a rich history of fighting for waste pickers' rights and where the Third Conference of Latin American Waste pickers was already scheduled to take place. In many cases, there were one or two waste pickers from other countries present, watching and learning about their peers from other parts of the world. A significant absentee was from the Philippines, because it has various waste recyclers initiatives, many of which include waste pickers. As an observer/participant, I believed the meeting to be significant for many reasons.

First, it was an acknowledgement of the worldwide presence of waste pickers and additionally, of their important professional services. Not only did the conference do this as a show of strength, but also because of the diverse actors who participated: donors, representatives from the World Bank and the media. Therefore, it was able to build multi-stakeholder consensus around the issue and its importance. Second, it was significant because it allowed waste pickers to observe, if not always communicate, with each other; it set up the possibility of taking back the idea of a global peer-hood to the grassroots.

I was accompanying a waste picker from the soon-to-be-registered association of waste recyclers, Safai Sena, who frequently expressed both confusion at the outcome of the event and delight at the extent and possibilities of it. While the Latin American groups comprised primarily waste pickers in a position of leadership, who were present, for obvious reasons, in large numbers, the rest of the world's waste pickers played a relatively passive but engaged role. My interviews with several waste pickers from around the world – from Bolivia to Turkey – indicated a common thread of excitement. At the same time, such waste pickers also spoke as observers, offering comments about "them" and "their event," when they referred to the Latin American waste pickers. Nonetheless, this event was important for the attending waste pickers, because it enabled new ways of thinking about both their work and the global spread of it. Additionally, it resulted in wider dissemination back home of what each waste picker saw and experienced during the event. This should not be underestimated, because it opens out other worlds and seems to strengthen the sense of self-worth. In fact, opening up such a new idea at the grassroots, across so many cities and countries, suggests that even if it is not yet a movement in the sense of other mass movements, it is a network that supports the common goals of various waste pickers' groups. From these meetings and efforts to collaborate, it seems that any global collaboration will necessarily be representational, where participants are assumed to be part of a larger, mass-based organization to which they will filter down their learnings and observations.

Barriers such as access to technology, literacy and linguistic differences further set up such collaborations as globalization from the middle, rather than from the bottom. The discussions and negotiations between various actors therefore, are not between the waste pickers and northern NGOs or international organizations, but between civil-society-organizations from the developing world, often represented by middle-class men and women. An exception is the waste pickers' co-operative of Columbia, led by a former waste picker, and some strong leadership shown by Chilean and other waste pickers. Other than that, there is no exception as of now.

Such a model of becoming global requires specific kinds of accountability from the representatives. How do they consult with grassroots organizations, even with limited representation at home? What mechanisms ensure that they are able to convey the key concerns and ideas from the grassroots, rather than present only a more personal view-point? Perhaps the presence of other waste pickers at global forums creates accountability, even if the waste pickers are unable to communicate in the language of the session. In the case of India, the presence of a moderately-active network of organizations working with waste pickers, the Association of Indian Wastepickers (AIW), also functions as a mechanism for collective accountability to the grassroots, as waste pickers and organizations representing them often jointly select representation to international fora. Such pressure on organizations that are part of movements is one mechanism to ensure that local agendas are clearly articulated in global forums.

But globalization also implies organizations from the developed and developing world finding common ground. What is the nature of decision-making and consensus-building in collaborations between organizations from the developed and developing world?

Before diving into the answer, another dramatic persona must be introduced: Women in Informal Employment Globalizing and Organizing (WEIGO). WEIGO's work has been around economic justice and labor rights for women in the informal sector. WEIGO's key work is around organizing and advocating globally around women in the informal sector. Prior to turning to waste pickers, WEIGO has worked with street vendors, garment workers, domestic workers, etc. It was also a key facilitator of the Bogota Conference and was able to secure funds to help set up a global network with several nodes. Clearly then, WEIGO is an important facilitator of several collaborations in the waste picker arena, including building a global network.[5]

The importance of WEIGO in this discussion, apart from its role, is the space it occupies as a repository of multiple viewpoints. Its partners include predominantly organizations – mostly mass-based – from the developing world. One of WEIGO's contributions is to share the story, through its website, Twitter and newsletter, a skill most organizations lack or do not consider worth investing in. This apart, WEIGO undertakes its own research which contributes to available knowledge. Some individuals function in Western academic institutions, remaining part of the wider network and helping to bring voice to global policy-making. More unusual for its work is locating resources for organizations (including my own) to work with organizations of waste pickers and facilitate their self-realization.

Let us compare this with GAIA the global network briefly mentioned previously, with partners from both the developed and developing world. To understand the work of GAIA in this context better, the story of climate change and waste pickers must be told.

Climate Change: The Game Changer

After Bogota, an important arena of global collaboration has been within the climate change discourse.

For waste pickers, the current climate change discourse represents their own marginalization from policy. Recycling, particularly in developing countries, has clear implications for greenhouse gas (GHG) reduction. In Delhi, for example, a study demonstrated that waste pickers saved more GHGs (approximately 3.6 times more) through their work than any project in India that had applied for carbon credits (Chintan Environmental Research and Action Group 2009).

The tools being used globally for climate change, particularly after the Kyoto Protocol of 1997, are based on trading in carbon in the market place as a means of reducing the overall GHG emissions through the Clean Development Mechanism (CDM). In the context of the waste recyclers (not just waste pickers), there are three means by which CDM reproduces injustice.

First, CDM allows a country in the developed world to continue emitting GHGs if it is able to offset them by financing projects that additionally lower GHG emissions. Often, such projects are in the developing world. India and China are important CDM recipients. This therefore incentivizes the developed world to continue to emit GHGs instead of cutting down on consumption and therefore does very little to substantially reduce overall GHGs.

Second, CDM requires formal, highly-structured, documented processes, undertaken by well-organized entities. On account of its structure, it is unable to accommodate other actors like waste pickers, as they are informal, use daily innovation and could change their daily operations to optimize earnings and/or security.

Another issue is that there is only one methodology accepted as yet for computing credits for recycling. Even as these methodologies are further developed and accepted, there is always the fear of large private players moving in, attracted by the carbon funds. In India, there is precedence for this. Case studies show that several waste projects funded via carbon credits have indeed displaced waste pickers.[6] There are no other mechanisms to reward such work that the waste pickers undertake currently.

These two reasons – the informal and flexible nature of their work and the absence of methodologies for recycling any materials (and the inclusion of waste pickers in such methodologies in the future) – make it unlikely that waste pickers will receive direct carbon credits in the carbon market. Yet, they are the backbone of recycling in several parts of the world, particularly the developing world.

A third problem is what the CDM promotes in the solid waste sector. There is a methodology for carbon credits for WtE technologies. Many of these are thermal technologies that require paper, cardboard and plastics in order to function efficiently. This usually implies that they will compete with recycling for such materials. As these plants are set up, it is also unlikely that they will allow waste pickers to continue with free access to waste, their own feedstock. The case of the Okhla WtE plant is a case in point. Already, over 300 waste pickers have lost their livelihood and children have dropped out of school and returned to the work force (Chintan Environmental Research and Action Group 2012). There is a clash between tradition and black letter law here over rights to waste.

In India, there are currently very few such plants, primarily due to their expense but these are increasing, primarily on account of national incentives and national policies, such as incentives announced at the Union Budget, March 2013. These make them viable but make the work of recycling via the informal sector unviable on account of skewed terms.

Given the many links between waste and climate change, it is clear that waste pickers and in fact, the recycling chain per se, has an important stake in the issue. Advocating for justice for waste pickers within the climate change talks and policies has resulted in a global discourse binding together several waste picker groups and their support groups. Consequently, civil society organizations have worked with waste pickers to enable them to understand the issue and to represent their cause at global forums.

Waste pickers have been making their presence felt at climate talks (Conference of Parties, or COP) in Bonn (2009), Copenhagen (2009), Tianjin (2010) and Cancun (2010). In all these, the waste pickers have pointed out the perils of CDM-funding to WtE plants that are likely to require wastes such as paper and plastics to function. There are widespread concerns that CDM for such plants will result in loss of access to such waste for waste pickers, and finally, have severe livelihood implications.

However, examples from all over the world suggest that not only WtE, but also any large project is likely to impact their livelihoods.

In several parts of the world, upgrading landfills is key to reducing GHG emissions, since landfills are an important source of methane. This requires the fencing-off of landfills, and subsequently, blocking access of waste pickers to the waste, which reaches there. While it is undoubtedly undesirable that people forage on mountains of trash, it is also important that the alternative be one that enables them to earn a livelihood and not block it as a reaction to their working conditions. In several discussions with policy-makers, the fencing-off of landfills is often justified not only for projects, but because of the hazardous working conditions of waste pickers. However, such exclusion only worsens their condition.

Waste pickers in Ahmedabad in Gujarat, for example, have faced this first hand in 2010, as their traditional workplace, a landfill, became off limits for them.[7] In fact, in India, there could be greater danger of livelihood loss from landfill upgradation than WtE because of the large number of dumps across the country that urgently require upgradation into engineered landfills. Some of them will seek CDM finance while others are being able to access financing mechanisms other than the CDM for this.

In Pune, the private company Hanjer has made "deals" with the scrap dealers near the landfill, and encouraged a few of them to buy the material that the waste pickers first buy from Hanjer. Only three of the 20 odd scrap dealers at the landfill are operating now. Hanjer has also made appropriate changes in the original concession agreement with Pune Municipal Corporation (PMC) and has access over recyclables now. Waste pickers at the landfill are trying to determine whether it makes more economic sense to work for Hanjer or the scrap dealers, demanding protective gear and minimum wages, or whether to buy material from Hanjer and sell to the scrap dealers. There is agreement over the fact that their earnings have reduced.[8]

The issue in both cases of Ahmedabad and Pune is one of access to recyclable waste, regardless of technology. Extending the argument, the waste pickers would likely find themselves without incomes even if the project was one related to recycling waste. If a large company set up a recycling plant, would that be more beneficial than landfill upgradation or WtE? Unlikely, at least for the waste pickers. In sum, any large waste-handling project that requires either privatizing space where waste is dumped or non-bio-degradable waste itself, will be detrimental to the waste pickers' work and livelihood efforts.

In India, there is one WtE plant in Andhra Pradesh, two in Delhi, and several more proposed across India. Several municipalities are also currently proposing CDM to upgrade landfills. Why then did WtE (rather than the structure of waste projects) enter the discourse as such an important issue for waste pickers? Why was this one of the key statements made by waste pickers at various climate talks? And would the waste pickers live happily ever after if WtE plants all stood cancelled?

Part of the reason for the Indian approach (in the context of waste pickers) to CDM was the outcome of dialogues with another organization, the GAIA. As the name suggests, the key raison d'être for GAIA is to fight off incineration and related burn technologies. It is organized as a network of organizations across the world, with two key offices in the Philippines and in the United States (US). In order to do this, it sees itself as a facilitator for advocacy, providing information and helping organizations without the requisite capacity to learn about the issue. Often, GAIA also undertakes advocacy on behalf of organizations which do not have "the capacity to do this themselves."[9] This is not only in developing countries, but also, in the European Union, where GAIA has robust membership. A staff member from GAIA explains its decision to enter into climate-change issues, something it previously had little experience with, because of the overlaps between incineration, waste and climate change that were clearly emerging. Its proactive interest in waste pickers is relatively recent, although the sector has been acknowledged and strongly supported in its broader vision from the start. One reason for this renewed interest could be linked with the wider global interest in the issue, and that clearly, waste and waste pickers were key to how organizations from the developing world viewed climate justice. Therefore, there was clearly an opportunity to strategically broaden the GAIA programs. Additionally, the same staff member explained during our interview, it was also able to secure funds for building in technical capacity within the waste pickers' groups in India. This also facilitated GAIA's expansion to India and in this arena, rather than any other.

In 2010, GAIA set up in India with a full-time staff member, to work on climate issues. While the initial agenda was evolving, the overall thrust has been related to working with waste pickers' groups to create common cause over the WtE issue and its representation in climate forums. As its own website explains: "[w]aste picker groups from Asia and Latin America have teamed up with GAIA to make a case for recycling rather than burning or burying waste at the UN climate change talks".[10] Asked why GAIA picked India over other countries with fewer resources on both technical issues and organization waste pickers, the GAIA staff member pointed out two important aspects of how a global organization like itself worked. The first, he explained, was that GAIA was a small but global group that did not organize at the grassroots – something that the local NGOs were expected to have done already as a prerequisite to be able to partner with GAIA on waste-picker issues. Therefore, GAIA, he explained, could only work in such countries and cities where there was already a robust organization at the ground. Second, he pointed out, the way GAIA functioned – through the net, an e-list, etc. – presumed literacy, access to the internet and other resources, are rare amongst waste pickers and other informal-sector workers at the cutting edge of grassroots movements in India. Another kind of presence is required. As previously described, most of the organizations working with waste pickers, or indeed, waste pickers' organizations, are organized as a loose network in India, the AIW. GAIA was therefore participating in occasional meetings and trainings of (and via) AIW to build the capacities of the participants about technologies and waste systems.

Another issue that GAIA brought up was related to CDM. While some groups contemplated working with CDM and of demanding a share in the CDM mechanism, GAIA has been advocating a fund entirely separate for waste pickers, a "green fund," since it believes that CDM is a false solution to the climate problem and is therefore a false goal for waste pickers' groups to aspire to be a part of. In part due to GAIA's arguments, the global waste picker movement, largely technically dependent on it, has broadly begun to subscribe to this understanding. Yet, there is also discussion outside of GAIA about pragmatism in demanding waste picker inclusion in CDM as recycling agents, despite CDM being no solution to reducing GHG emissions. Where does such outlier discourse find a place? How does it get discussed in the discourse made dominant?

A striking aspect of GAIA's work, as seen from the case here is the power relations produced/reproduced. As GAIA takes the position of the technical specialist, it therefore, inevitably, positions the others as learners. The polar nature of interaction, the overwhelming (and non-intuitive) nature of knowledge about technical issues and the need to be able to deliver a simple global message leave little space to discuss how local aspirations can be better included in the larger discourse on climate change. In fact, the key issue of large private projects – whatever they may be – as damaging of waste pickers' livelihoods is reduced to opposition to a few technologies. Perhaps GAIA alone is not the only group to be afflicted by this; there are several groups within India who do not work with waste pickers, but who are in fact well-versed about these technical issues, and who could easily have played GAIA's role. Would they have followed a similar approach? To hazard a guess, they would have been under much greater peer pressure to engage more closely, and with greater nuance, with the grassroots. And since they operate in a similar eco-system, they would be more likely to respond to these pressures. Whether this would have been effective or not is not clear. On the other hand, the same local peer pressure is not created in the case of GAIA as the rest of its work is global.

But this is not how GAIA likely sees its role, or its intent. Rather, it clearly sees itself as an unequivocal supporter of the rights of the waste picker movement and sees its contribution in building capacity of groups who have already reached a minimum level of organiza-tion- and resource-access. Perhaps GAIA's pragmatic choice of India, over the equally well-organized Philippines, where it already has an office, may have been a result of available resources, but its investment in environmental justice is not in doubt. Yet, its work on CDM and waste pickers is driven by a few people, with occasional feedback to local groups, frequently as *fait accompli* or less frequently, as requests to read a note with a short deadline. There is little proactive consultation on framing the thinking per se. In the case of GAIA, the assumption is that representation of a large group can be effectively carried out, done via first principles by someone who can traverse the complex-ity of the CDM negotiations. A more participatory process would have likely helped even activists, particularly those who don't follow global processes, to understand these better and possibly use these for local and national advocacy. Contrast this with AIW, where any waste pickers attending global events are expected to be accountable to the network. The question is: is it then the logic of globalization, and contending with multiple languages – of negotiations, of legal language, of technology – and making one's way through the maze of global environmental negotiations that result in trimming the local "voice" to enable it to be global? And is this inevitable?

This gestures to the larger problem of becoming global, of participating in global regimes and governance and developing key partnerships. Global messages must be simplified, lucid and have a global appeal beyond just one country. Local reality is nuanced, complicated and several things must be actioned for any result to become reality. Above all, the global message must be context-relevant.

For Indian organizations working on the waste picker issue, the dilemma is only just emerging. However, there is a strong pragmatic streak, as some organizations have campaigned nationally and globally previously, and are able to find strategic reasons to remain in the global space. A senior representative of the well-known women's organization Self Employed Women's Association (SEWA), which has organized both rural and urban women into co-operatives for improved livelihoods and for enabling them to assert their economic and social rights, believes, from earlier experience in other sectors, that the advantage of global advocacy is to further emphasize the issue at home, and create one more pressure point.[11] Even when global victories are not as grand or precise as campaigners may have hoped for, they become tools for national advocacy. In this context, could the imperfect voice against CDM for WtE technologies become at least one way by which the waste pickers could protect their livelihoods? Current campaigns against WtE plants, including one initially expected to receive carbon credits, are largely led by middle-class residents following the Not In My Backyard (NIMBY) principle, with technical help from local activists. It appears there is adequate technical and legal capital available within India to make the arguments required in most cases. The case for globalization lies elsewhere.

A second and homegrown perspective that waste pickers have voiced is related to being recognized for their work, which, in the climate change context, prevents GHG emissions. Their voices have been able to attract some attention to themselves in a climate-justice context. Can their representation in global fora force a wider recognition of their work locally?

The experience from Copenhagen (2009) suggests it might, but not because of their direct advocacy with officials at the climate talks.

Rather, it is the media, particularly the Indian media, whose stories and reporting emphasize the waste pickers' presence at such talks and often present them as heroic persons with the ability to talk to international audiences. Whether this elicits feelings of national pride or national mortification is not clear, but it gets attention enough to merit a mention at municipal levels. The message to both waste pickers and to officials and others from India is that waste pickers are no aberration. Instead, they are a global phenomenon. This opening of another universe for others (not waste pickers alone) can change perspectives. As in other global instances, it can also "shame" or boost the confidence of officials into acting at home, as the need requires. Although Indian waste pickers have not yet benefitted on this specific attribute of globalization, they are likely to be able to translate their increasing global presence into local pressure. This could happen as direct foreign investment enters into the waste sector, or claims CDM and the local concern is directly tied to international companies, regimes or governments.

For activists, the dilemma of tokenism always looms. Often, only one or two waste pickers are able to attend global meetings. Not only is this on account of financial resources, but also because of barriers like passports, ability to take time off work and child rearing, etc. How justified is it to term a discussion inclusive if only a miniscule percentage of the organized are able to participate in it? If global meetings are held, with only a few people in attendance, how will various benefits, such as knowledge, trickle down? How can such events go beyond exposure visits? This is a challenge. A more positive outcome from such events is that a range of people – activists, waste pickers and others – work in a relatively smaller group to strategize jointly at the meetings. This allows the waste pickers to participate in making strategic decisions, even if the issues and possibilities available at these are limited to begin with. While very little of this experience can be transferred back to the larger group in each city, it creates some degree of leadership within waste pickers to see and think about the process of becoming global. Nevertheless, several members of Safai Sena[12] have mentioned that the experience of going global is not germane to transforming the local landscape but it is an act of solidarity with global peers and offers optimism back home.

In the Indian context, those attending these international talks are part of the AIW and in fact, selected from amongst them. The AIW's process of work both in international fora and domestically is useful to discuss, because of the impact this can have on local and other agendas. By individually bringing up for national discussion other non-WtE projects that negatively impact waste pickers, for example, AIW's members are able to continue keeping nationally important issues on the front burner. In that sense, AIW, through its members, is able to continue to participate in global events, via its members, without being swept over by them. The challenge is to recognize this and consciously ensure this balance is maintained.

Perhaps this two-pronged approach can also solidify into a strategy: be global for a specific narrow issue (such as specific aspects of climate justice) and for building up assets such as technical knowledge and visibility to advocate domestically while focusing on the local for broader issues such as secure livelihoods.

Indeed, if the everyday concerns of the waste pickers have to be addressed through alliances and partnerships, then this bifurcation is an important and strategic route to take. The partnership with WEIGO in this effort to build a national and international alliance is also worth noting for its effort to move downwards to the grassroots in what it supports and the stories it tells. In this case, globalization is at once global presence and solidarity based on local, grassroots-upward decisions. The GAIA and WEIGO partnerships each have a place in the discourse around waste pickers. The former works upwards, into the global, simplifying messaging and picking issues that are already part of its agenda, while the latter combines policy advocacy with supporting grassroots groups.

AIW also has another important role to play as a network; it can and to some degree some of its members are consciously trying to create what I see as a "safe space" for discussion. As it explores its global dimensions, AIW is able to discuss its internal concerns, its differences with global players and points of convergence. This is in fact an important strength of AIW (and perhaps other networks) as the issue itself globalizes. The work with waste pickers as an alliance – national and global – has only just begun, and it is still only a moderately active network, with limited participation. Even so, AIW's members are in an advantageous position of exploring multiple opportunities while absorbing and internalizing the issues brought out through dissenting ideas. This could be a key means for the movement per se to minimize the pitfalls that come with globalizing or at least, articulate them to each other clearly.

New alliances are unchartered terrain. Everyone learns as things unfold. As a participant in many of these fora, and as part of several of these organizations, I find myself asking about being part of an Indian organization, network and alliance (each at different points, in different avatars) and how it is possible to argue for the local, make value-based alliances and not be cowed down to whatever emerges as consensus on technical issues. I am no supporter of perverse technologies like WtE, but I value being able to rethink the global argument to reflect local concerns even deeper. On the other hand, I remain acutely aware that I might serve as a potential spoiler, and that there is perhaps no other way to frame a global argument by consensus but as it is being done already. The two most important and possible manners for an inclusive global framework to operate in, is to create spaces for dissent and discussion, and to constantly tell the local story in multiple media, so it is also able to find its voice in the world.

Notes

*I would like to specially thank Renana Jhabwala National Co-ordinator, SEWA and Chair, SEWA Bharat, for sharing her views through both an interview and discussion of this chapter.

1. Chintan is an environmental justice non-profit based in Delhi. Chintan argues for an urban India that is both sustainable and equitable. It works in partnership with the informal recycling sector to advocate for rights of the city, inclusive solid waste management and equitable consumption. For more information, please see http://www.chintan-india.org. As accessed on November 3, 2010.
2. Gathered from various discussions with informal sector plastic dealers, Delhi, 1994–2010.
3. The Association of Indian Wastepickers (AIW). Note Submitted to Director General Labour Welfare, for Task Force on Street Vendors, Rickshaw Pullers, Auto Rickshaw/Taxi Drivers and Rag Pickers. New Delhi, October 4, 2010.
4. Recall the Payatas Tragedy in 2000, when waste pickers were buried under an avalanche of waste at the Payatas landfill in the Philippines.
5. The information on WEIGO has been gathered from personal interactions, from interviews as cited and from the WEIGO website, http://www.weigo.org. As accessed on November 18, 2010.

6. To understand the issue better, see *Credits Vs Carbon Credits*, a film made by two Delhi waste pickers in 2012–13. It is available online at http://www.chintan-india.org/publications_films.php?action=details&id=12&page=1. As accessed on March 24, 2014.
7. Communication from AIW, October 2010.
8. Communication from Kagad Kach Patra Kashtakari Panchayat (KKPKP), Pune, October 2010.
9. Based on telephonic interview with Neil Tangri, GAIA, November 16, 2010.
10. Available at http://www.no-burn.org. As accessed on October 30, 2010.
11. Telephonic interview with Renana Jhabwala, National Co-ordinator, SEWA and Chair, SEWA Bharat; November 12, 2010.
12. Safai Sena, meaning an army of cleaners, is a registered association of waste pickers, itinerant buyers and small junk dealers. Learn more about Safai Sena at http://www.safaisena.net. As accessed on March 24, 2014.

References

Chintan Environmental Research and Action Group. 2012. "Give Back Our Waste: What the Okhla Waste-to-Energy Plant Had Done to Local Wastepickers." http://www.chintan-india.org/documents/research_and_reports/chintan-report-give-back-our-waste.pdf. As accessed on October 30, 2012.

———. 2009. "Cooling Agents: An Examination of the Role of the Informal Recycling Sector in Mitigating Climate Change." http://www.chintan-india.org/documents/research_and_reports/chintan_report_cooling_agents.pdf. As accessed on October 30, 2012.

———. 2004. "Space for Waste: Planning for the Informal Recycling Sector." http://www.chintan-india.org/documents/research_and_reports/chintan_study_space_for_waste.pdf. As accessed on October 30, 2012.

Government of India (GoI). 2013.The Union Budget 2013–14. http://indiabudget.nic.in/. As accessed on March 24, 2014.

———. 2011a. Plastic Waste (Management and Handling) Rules. http://moef.nic.in/downloads/public-information/DOC070211-005.pdf. As accessed on March 24, 2014.

———. 2011b. E-Waste (Management and Handling) Rules. http://moef.nic.in/downloads/rules-and-regulations/1035e_eng.pdf. As accessed on March 24, 2014.

———. 2009. National Action Plan on Climate Change. http://moef.nic.in/downloads/others/CC_ghosh.pdf. As accessed on March 24, 2014.

Government of India (GoI). 2008. The CAG Audit on Municipal Solid Waste in India. http://iced.cag.gov.in/wp-content/uploads/2013/09/Environment%20auditing%20in%20India.pdf. As accessed on March 24, 2014.

———. 2006. National Environment Policy. http://envfor.nic.in/sites/default/files/introduction-nep2006e.pdf. As accessed on March 24, 2014.

———. 1999. Solid Waste Management in Class 1 Cities in India. https://www.google.co.in/url?sa=t&rct=j&q=&esrc=s&source=web&cd=5&cad=rja&uact=8&ved=0CEEQFjAE&url=http%3A%2F%2Fwww.almitrapatel.com%2Fdocs%2F004.rtf&ei=khAsU7SXOoOnrAfW6I HoBw&usg=AFQjCNG3j21Jwa7KRwvVcGRH_M72l70BjA&sig2=-MAnAiYQxVlsJDXOZo7BVw. As accessed on March 24, 2014.

Medina, M. 2008. "The Informal Recycling Sector in Developing Countries: Organizing Waste Pickers to Enhance their Impact," *GridLines*, October. Note No. 44, The World Bank. https://www.ppiaf.org/sites/ppiaf.org/files/publication/Gridlines-44-Informal%20Recycling%20-%20MMedina.pdf. As accessed on March 24, 2014.

Padilla, N. 2008. Talk at "Waste Pickers without Frontiers," 'First International and Third Latin American Conference of Waste-Pickers,' Bogota, Colombia, March 1–4.

Scheinberg, A., M. H. Simpson and Y. Gupt. 2010. "Economic Aspects of the Informal Sector in Solid Waste Management." Eschborn: German Technical Cooperation (GTZ).

8

Not Politics of the Usual

Youth Environmental Movements

Kartikeya Singh

Concern about their future and the desire to take concerted action on the most challenging environmental issues of our times are putting youth at the forefront of the environmental movement. In a society where youth are often disregarded for their opinions on planning and policy, there are signs that the environmental movement might provide the best avenue in the fight for young people to gain space in political processes. At the climate negotiations in Copenhagen, Denmark, in 2009, more than 1,500 of the participants out of a total of 24,000 registered civil society representatives at the talks were "youth" (Keenan 2010). Though this number may seem small, consider that just two years prior at the United Nations (UN) climate conference in Bali, Indonesia, only 200 youth participated. The figure for official youth participation mentioned above also fails to account for the thousands of unregistered young activists who gathered in the streets and plazas of Copenhagen to signal their concern. Politicians such as President Mohamed Nasheed of the Republic of Maldives have recognized that in the fight for survival in the wake of climate change, youth may prove their nation's strongest allies (Henn 2009). While most countries have regularly disregarded their commitments to Chapter 25.2 of Agenda 21, a framework for sustainable development outlined by the global community (that includes the role of youth in policy decision-making processes), it is unlikely that they will be able to withstand the mounting pressure.

Global climate change presents a challenge for which youth can come together across political boundaries to work towards saving their common future. A big reason is that they place greater importance than older generations on the underlying issue of intergenerational equity with respect to the use of the planet's resources and the health of the biosphere. As such, the International Youth Climate Movement (IYCM), an informal group of youth and youth-run organizations who regularly meet on the sidelines of UN climate negotiations, has spread to over 130 countries on the planet (Keenan 2010). The movement has also transformed from being merely an informal group of youth meeting on the sidelines of climate conferences to establishing a formal constituency recognized by the United Nations Framework Convention on Climate Change (UNFCCC), the chief international body responsible for climate negotiations. Having a formalized constituency in the UNFCCC is a big step towards having youth input in the decision-making process. However, the battle is far from over because nation states are yet to recognize the role of youth in the process and make room for consultations at the national level.

To understand how youth have leapt to leadership, we must take a closer look at the issues attracting youth environmentalists and their methods of organization. Thanks to the internet, youth are using powerful weapons for organizing and defining new spaces to fight environmental battles. In the recent past, the use of simple tools like a "Google Group" or a "Facebook page" has proven useful to unite youth from across a country or across the planet – serving as a vital platform to build capacity and share knowledge on how to organize and which issues to focus on.

The story of the Indian Youth Climate Network (IYCN) thus becomes a story not just of youth using new technologies to excite broad changes and awareness among the already empowered but the story of a unique attempt at what I came to think of as *vertically-integrated activism* and an organization that seeks to create larger systemic change by inspiring a movement. Through an exploration of the history of IYCN, I will discuss the barriers to engaging youth in larger environmental movements and political processes, explore leadership roles in such movements, and also outline the importance of transnational exchanges in empowering youth in creative ways.

The study of this movement in the Indian context is important because of the growing role of India in the multilateral environmental agreements process. Furthermore, nearly 75 per cent of the Indian population of 1.2 billion people is below the age of 35 and classified as "youth." This large demographic has the most to lose regarding intergenerational equity and the environment. The story and growth of IYCN offers many parallels and lessons to be drawn regarding the strengths and weaknesses of youth environmental movements. It also presents an opportunity to look at the role that such movements can play in a continent full of rapidly-emerging economies with diverging geopolitical interests, all of which will have a large impact on the global environment.

The History of the Movement

In December 2007, the UNFCCC hosted a historic conference, where the future of the Kyoto Protocol was to be charted out in good measure. The 13th Conference of Parties (COP) was held in Bali, Indonesia, and delegates were told that because of the heat and humidity they could be a little bit more casual in their attire. The casualness of clothing may have slipped into casualness of effort, leading many critics to say afterward that the conference was somewhat of a beach party as far as the negotiations were concerned (because no concrete climate treaty was established). But something different was happening at the sidelines of this COP: youth in large numbers were gathering and getting their voices heard – in an organized fashion. For them, climate change was an issue of intergenerational equity, as they would be the ones to see the consequences of the inaction of world leaders during the negotiations.

Bali was not the first time that youth had gathered in a noticeable size on the sidelines of a COP. In 2005, youth began by attending COP 11 hosted by the Canadian government in Montreal, Quebec. Since then, they have been demanding their right to influence negotiations and have their policy perspectives heard. Earlier in the year in May 2005, the Energy Action Coalition (EAC) had been born in the United States (US) with the aim of uniting young people across the US for a clean energy future. Its initial base was college campuses where young people could demand clean energy to power their campuses. At the first national gathering in Washington DC, 80 young people convened to help chart out the course of the US youth climate movement. Very quickly, capitalizing on their strength as a network, the coalition was able to launch national campaigns to influence policies of the state and federal governments. By 2009, the annual "Power Shift" summit saw participation of thousands of young people at various venues across the nation, and in Washington DC, 6,000 young people stormed Capitol Hill and demanded a clean energy transition from their representatives in Congress.

COP 12 was held in Nairobi in 2006, and by then similar networks of change had formed in both Canada and Australia with the launch of the Canadian Youth Climate Coalition (CYCC) and the Australian Youth Climate Coalition (AYCC) respectively. But the fact that the conference took place in Africa was an opportunity for youth from these developed nations to be able to share their organizing skills with youth from the continent. Thanks to the second Conference of Youth (CoY) organized by young people prior to the start of COP 12, the African Youth Initiative on Climate Change (AYICC) was born. Young people capitalized on the energy of being able to congregate from many parts of the continent and the world to start this pan-African youth movement. AYICC is an excellent example of the transnational flow of ideas between people from different parts of the world and the possibilities such networking can generate.

At the CoY held just before COP 13 in 2007, the atmosphere was ripe to launch similar youth movements across Asia. In two years' time, youth climate movements from countries like Canada, the US and Australia had matured to a point that their presence dominated the CoY. Only two youth representatives made it to Bali from Africa and none from Latin America. East and Southeast Asian youth were well represented, but there were none from the Middle East or Central Asia and only two young people from South Asia. The young people from Asia attending the conference began their collective campaign by holding small meetings. At the time the group was called the Asian Youth Caucus. Objectives for a pan-Asian youth climate movement were outlined, identifying common resources, mobilizing youth from different parts of Asia on environmental issues, sharing information and building capacity amongst the different regions on how to get organized, and to create greater unity of youth in the world's largest continent.

The vision read:

> For the empowering of youth from across the Asian continent, to encourage greater mobilization to make change happen. In the realm of environmental sustainability, with the help of cross-cultural capacity building, skills and knowledge sharing, it [the Asian Youth Caucus] aims to create a strong network amongst youth from the different Asian nations.

Without adequate representation from many Asian nations, however, the task would be difficult. As the only Indian youth present at the time in these meetings, I was aware that our presence in these transnational youth networks was extremely important. However, it was hard to create a youth network across a continent as vast as Asia, which has so many language and cultural differences. The problem was apparent during the meetings held on the sidelines of the COP where the need to communicate in English amongst members of the group might have meant some information was lost in translation. But while there are many differences amongst the different member nations of the Asian continent, one thing is common in Asian culture: the respect for and importance of elders and the subservient role of youth in society. All members present in these Asian Youth Caucus meetings could readily understand the problems they would face back home when demanding inclusion in decision-making matters of government-officials, members of civil society and industry on topics of environmental change.

For some, these problems started at the COP itself. I walked proudly up to my country-delegates to introduce myself as an Indian youth delegate at the talks. "Youth? Shouldn't youth have the same views as their elders?" I was asked by a high-ranking representative. Recalling all the times I had pondered the question "how old will you be in 2050?" of elder decision-makers, I had to refrain from asking how they could possibly feel the same stake as the young? Had I not spent countless hours preparing policy proposals and submitting them directly to the UNFCCC? Had I not learned about the procedures? Was I not competent to understand the political deadlock that has plagued these negotiations for the last 17 years? I was not yet sure what I would do about the "beach party" that was Bali, but I left the island with an uneasy feeling about what might happen should Indian youth remain outside this process. What worried me most was that not only are Indian youth a significant portion of the global youth population (simply due to the sheer size of the Indian population), but also that they are represented by leaders who are many generations older. This could potentially mean that Indian climate-policy is being dictated by politicians who have only short-term development agendas and who will not live to see the realities of their decisions in the future. As such, the need for young people from India to rise to meet this challenge is important now more than ever.

Youth Leadership

Bob Stigler of the Berkana Institute writes about the rise of "enspirited leadership" in society (2004: 1). Who are these people who are stepping forward to provide "new ways of leadership?" he asks. In most cases, he argues, they are not people in positions of power in any setting but are:

> simply those who see what must be done and are willing to speak, and then to act. Often, as they begin to step forward, their hearts are pounding with fear, but they believe the time has come to offer a new possibility for the future (ibid.:1).

One of the most important characteristics of these "enspirited leaders," as described by Stigler, is that they travel in the company of others. Such leadership is on the rise in India as young people begin to tackle local problems they are witnessing. A group of concerned individuals came together in March 2007 on the North Campus of Delhi University to protest the felling of trees for one of the stadia being constructed for the 2010 Commonwealth Games to be hosted in New Delhi (Singh 2010). The same issue was brought up across the city as Delhi began to lose her green-cover for "world class" infrastructure projects in order to prepare the city for a global audience.

With no other way to document and highlight these events, they launched a blog to reveal the urban development challenges of the city. This was the birth of the *Delhi Greens* blog, and since its launch it has grown in popularity not only in the city but in the nation and certainly provides a window for the world to learn about the environmental issues plaguing the city. Such initiatives are on the rise across the country in different cities. From a vast network of rural youth working to address local natural resource management issues in the form of the Rajputana Society of Natural History (RSNH) to a network of eco-clubs across the state of Chhattisgarh called Nature Bodies, these are the signs of thriving youth networks for change that exist in the country. Later as co-founders we would learn that unifying them is a greater challenge in a country like India.

Several such youth initiatives and individuals came together in India to embody the spirit of the growing international youth movement on climate change – this would be the birth of the IYCN. In the spirit of "traveling in the company of others," IYCN was co-founded by Deepa Gupta, an Indian brought up in Australia, and myself, an Indian who spent half his life in Gujarat and the other half in the US and supported in part by Govind Singh, the founder of *Delhi Greens*. I had first met Govind while on a summer internship at the Centre for Science and Environment (CSE) in 2006. We stayed in touch and reconnected when I moved back to Delhi in August 2007. Excited by the thought of an effort such as *Delhi Greens*, though still an informal blog, but on a national scale, we began some discussions. It was not until I came into contact with youth movements from across the world at the Bali climate talks that I could envision what such an effort might look like in India. Upon returning, I was introduced to Deepa through a member of the AYCC. She was wondering if there had been any Indian youth representation in Bali, and I described to her the conversations I was having with Govind about the launch of a network of Indian youth interested in climate change, and together we created the network. IYCN, thus, is a result of transnational flow of ideas spanning the globe but also an effort by Indians for those living in India. More importantly, it is the result of a collective effort of people who could not have done this alone but needed the company and support of their friends and families to bring this vision to life.

Why Youth?

But before delving further into how the IYCN was founded, one must answer the following questions: why should youth in India care? What is their role? To find answers to these questions let us explore the outcomes of the first Earth Summit hosted by the UN in Rio de Janeiro in 1992. Agenda 21, a framework for sustainable development outlined at the Summit, gave environmentalists hope of a political awakening to address global environmental and developmental challenges. India was one of over 180 signatory nations to the Rio Convention. In this mammoth document there was something more for youth. Hidden among the pages, in Chapter 25, one can find the initial reasons that inspired the creation of IYCN (UN 1992). I will discuss how each clause is relevant for IYCN and the need for youth participation in environmental decision-making.

> 25.2. It is imperative that youth from all parts of the world participate actively in all relevant levels of decision-making processes because

it affects their lives today and has implications for their futures. In addition to their intellectual contribution and their ability to mobilize support, they bring unique perspectives that need to be taken into account (ibid.: 275).

By the sound of this recommendation, the Indian government should have youth engaged in all areas of decision-making as India is presently implementing policies that are resulting in rapid socio-economic and ecological transformation of the country. With all this development, it is certain that the decisions being made today are going to impact our future. Chapter 25 continues:

> 25.3. Numerous actions and recommendations within the international community have been proposed to ensure that youth are provided a secure and healthy future, including an environment of quality, improved standards of living and access to education and employment. These issues need to be addressed in development planning (ibid.).

While it was becoming abundantly clear at the time this document was drafted that there was a link between environment and human health, the link specifically between climate change and human health was made in 2008. In one of its reports, the World Health Organization (WHO) states that climate change puts at risk the "basic determinants of health," which in turn implies that the crisis is one of the greatest risks to human health (WHO 2009). With nearly 200 million climate refugees expected by mid-century, rising numbers of deaths from unpredictable weather and spread of dangerous vector-borne diseases, we can be sure that the future that is being left for youth is one that is unlike that which previous generations enjoyed (International Organization for Migration 2009). Here we are presented with another reason for youth to be involved in the decision-making process.

Why is it that after decades of negotiation, while knowing what is at stake, we still seem to be in the same deadlock of inaction? Let us take a look at who is doing the negotiating: many negotiators are, for lack of better words, on the "far side of 50." While their intellect and their experience are not to be challenged, many would argue that negotiators have fallen out of touch with those whom they are negotiating for. Who is to blame them? After all, the process is much like national politics: short-term political interests of those in office are rarely linked to long-term impacts. But the proverbial question remains for those who have an opinion and who are doing the negotiating: "how old *will* you be in 2050?" Indeed this mantra has become a rallying cry for the international youth movement on the issue, and it is to be taken seriously – because those who are going to be around to suffer the consequences will be young people, not their elders (Singh 2009). The next section of Chapter 25 reads:

> 25.4. Each country should, in consultation with its youth communities, establish a process to promote dialogue between the youth community and Government at all levels and to establish mechanisms that permit youth access to information and provide them with the opportunity to present their perspectives on government decisions, including the implementation of Agenda 21 (UN 1992: 275).

Youth in India need to realize that they can and should have the right to consult the authorities. This section of the Agenda 21 states that the process for consultation of youth must exist in order to promote dialogue. Today people in India have the opportunity to file inquiries to increase transparency and reduce corruption thanks to the passing of the Right to Information (RTI) Act. Perhaps one should be filing an RTI to ask where the youth consultations are that India pledged to take up? India assigns no regular youth representatives to high-level negotiations through organized means. One might wonder what India's position might look like should youth get involved; after all, we would be negotiating our future. Similarly, the United Progressive Alliance (UPA) Government has formed a special "Prime Minister's Council on Climate Change." This council allows for the inputs of civil society, scientists and industries. But I would argue that it needs to have space for youth input as a formal part of the mechanism.

Section 25.7 and Section 25.9 of Agenda 21 are very important parts of the chapter because they mandate the involvement of youth in government delegations representing the country's interests at international fora. Also, the sections state that governments should incorporate "into relevant policies the recommendations of international, regional and local youth conferences and other forums that offer youth perspectives on social and economic development and resource management" (ibid.). Another reason for youth engagement is that this clause provides the right to approach the government with youth policy proposals arising from the myriad youth summits and workshops that are happening across the country at any given time.

Organizing and the Fight for Legitimacy

The sections of Chapter 25 of The Agenda 21 cited here provide the justification for needing to create an entity called the "Indian Youth Climate Network." Our strategy would be to engage various stake holders including youth, business, civil society organizations, the rural population, and government. This vertically-integrated activism would be the key to earn the right to speak up to a higher level of organization and decision-making. While the reasons to establish IYCN were clear, it was quite challenging to establish the network and separate the difference between an organization and a network, both of which the entity was trying to be. We asked ourselves whether we needed to create something entirely new or whether something similar existed. The South Asian Youth Environment Network (SAYEN), a youth environment branch of the United Nations Environment Program, had been operating in the country for several years. However the secretariat was based out of the Centre for Environment Education (CEE), a highly-regarded organization working on environmental education issues in the country for decades. Perhaps the problem was that SAYEN was a "for youth" network but not run "by youth," and as a result lacked the kind of energy and enthusiasm that we hoped to bring by launching a new independent network. Furthermore, at the time we thought our network would not focus on as broad a range of environmental issues as SAYEN focuses on; instead we would focus on those environmental issues that would fit comfortably in the climate–development nexus. We knew that in order to set the agenda for young people on climate change in India, we needed to increase participation while clearly defining the scope of the discussion. We aimed to host such a discussion at the first-ever, Delhi Youth Summit on Climate (DYSoC) in May 2008. This event would launch the movement in the capital city and also signal a launch across the nation.

In order to organize amongst ourselves we used Google Groups, a free online tool provided by the Google Corporation, to share documents and have discussions in the early stages of IYCN's development. This allowed us to include young people from across the country in a conversation that was mostly happening in Delhi at the time. It also allowed us to freely be a network – a loose coalition, which at the time would be supported by different groups across the country, like Delhi Greens in Delhi. To get young people interested, we rallied support from young people at youth environmental conferences being organized by existing non-governmental organizations (NGOs). This helped seed the idea that gathered support from a broader spectrum of young people. The Google Group was a blessing because it provided a forum online where people with enthusiasm who wanted to take leadership and help shape the network could continue the conversation. It was a virtual networking platform for youth and young professionals who were interested in climate change. Slowly we watched the number of participants in the Google Group climb. This did not, however, solve our problem of legitimacy. We knew that if we were to get into conversations with potential established civil society organizations or corporate partners in order to hold events and enter into long-term partnerships, we would eventually require a full-fledged legal entity.

The first step towards achieving legitimacy and at the same time increasing visibility was to create a blog. Being a free online publishing tool, a blog was the ideal platform to begin online discussions about our agenda. Blogs are also flexible enough to be customized and have various forms of embedded media to engage visitors to the website. Having been exposed to the popular North American youth climate movement blog, *It's Getting Hot in Here*, we wanted to have something on a similar scale. Such a platform would be user-driven and provide an organic, open voice for a growing youth movement in South Asia. We hoped that the movement would eventually grow beyond India to encompass all of South Asia, and to do so the brand would have to be strong enough to gain popularity. Therefore, over lunch in Tibet Kitchen near the Shivaji Bus Terminus in Connaught Place, New Delhi, the brand, *What's with the Climate?* was launched. Its tag line, "Voices of a Subcontinent Grappling with Change," would ensure that eventually it would be a platform that youth from across the South Asian region could use. The blog was simple, but publishing it in the public sphere brought in queries from across the nation. A small organization based in rural Andhra Pradesh was the first to contact us. They were working on adaptation for farmers struggling to make ends meet due to an increasingly erratic monsoon. The organization wanted to bring attention to the suffering of the people of the region and seek funds from potential donors, and they wanted to do it by affiliating with the network.

The next several months would be spent trying to recruit members to write for the blog. This was and still is a major challenge. Recruitment is open to all, and some contributors are academics, while others are working for government or think-tanks. Some are representatives of grassroots organizations needing a sounding board to publish information about the work that they are doing in the environmental field. However most are students and members of the network responding to events on the ground. Finally, some contributors are those that have an interest in South Asia but are living abroad. An analysis of the traffic the blog receives reveals that, while most of the readership is from India, the second highest is from the US. In addition, there is a high interest of readers from Canada, the United Kingdom (UK), Australia, many parts of the European Union (EU), China, Russia, Brazil, large parts of southern and eastern Africa, and of course all other countries in South Asia.

The blog has provided a window to the world of the challenges, opportunities and news regarding climate change in India. While the blog was a good platform for the larger youth movement on climate change, it provided very little information on what the IYCN was or how it functioned. For this we wanted to create a separate website to add to our legitimacy as an organization.

To expedite the process, we decided to draw on existing structures of overseas youth climate coalitions. Deepa had been heavily involved in the nearly one-year-old AYCC. Using their governance structure and the model of their website, we were able to quickly establish an online presence. We set the official launch date for the network (and the launch of the website) to coincide with the arrival of former US Vice President Al Gore in Delhi, where the "Climate Project: India" was launched. In the lead up to this event, I found myself working on the ground to seed the idea of IYCN amongst civil society, young people, and business, while Deepa played an equally crucial role of networking with people online and giving the web support that would be required in order to develop partnerships with other organizations and companies.

With the website in place, on March 5, 2008, we were able to launch the IYCN. Thanks to our online presence, people from across the country and the globe contacted us regarding partnerships and potential projects. All of this was without the network being registered as a legal entity. Nonetheless, it became easier to engage potential partners and members with a sense of legitimacy. With this confidence, we were well on our way to building partnerships with companies, civil society, and academic institutions that were required to host the first-ever youth summit on climate change in Delhi. Meetings with organizations like LEAD India, the British Council, and the CEE finally felt productive because we felt that we had an organization we were representing. These were the beginnings of our experiment with social entrepreneurship.

The DYSoC took place on May 28 and 29, and generated a lot of enthusiasm amongst the participants, partner organizations and media. Partner organizations were impressed with our ability to independently organize the event with no direct funding. A 30-minute television segment dedicated to the emerging movement and the event bolstered our confidence while increasing the number of participants at the event. The purpose of the summit was to get young people familiarized with urban planning policies in the capital region in the context of the climate-constrained world. We presented the youth recommendations that came out of the two-day workshop-style summit to the Delhi Government with the hope that they would take us seriously. Some of the suggestions included progressive taxation of vehicles based on horsepower and fuel efficiency, use of information technology for water resource management, expanding the Delhi multi-modal mass transit system, and improving the energy metering system to use "time-of-day" metering that would charge different rates depending on peak and off-peak power production costs. In addition to these suggestions, the event provided a platform for youth and young professionals to discuss projects that they hoped to initiate on their college and school campuses or in the city that would better the environment. This public brainstorming session was inspiring for the members present. The success of the event pushed us to continue to build the movement. We knew that even if the government did not take us seriously at the time, with the attention we were getting by organizing this ground-breaking event, we would rally more support, and one day the government would itself invite youth for consultations.

Organization or Network?

One of the big ideas that emerged at the summit was the need to highlight the solutions to climate change from across the country and to build a solution-based movement. Two recent graduates from the Yale School of Forestry and Environmental Studies in the US, Caroline Howe and Alexis Ringwald, who were working on environmental issues at The Energy and Resources Institute (TERI) at the time, presented a seemingly impossible idea: organizing a "climate solutions road tour," a journey across the country in Indian-made solar-electric vehicles that would highlight the nation's innovations and inspire thousands into action. This would also be the longest electric-car journey in Asia and an opportunity to test-drive an Indian innovation, a lithium-ion battery-powered electric car, produced by Indian manufacturer, REVA. The project was rooted in the idea that "solutions are real, and they exist today." Furthermore, by collectively envisioning a world of solutions, and building a movement based on solutions, we could get much further in solving the climate crisis than we could simply through international climate negotiations. India would be a great laboratory to test this as it is a place that will not only be greatly impacted by changing climate impacts, but it has over 1 billion solutions to climate change (referring to the strength of its human capital). Thus the tour sought to "create, communicate and celebrate" the solutions to climate change by conducting a series of seminars and workshops that would set loose a network of change-makers (IYCN's movement), by communicating existing solutions as well as those being created by members of the network (in order to build capacity and show the world how India is taking action to address climate change), and by using the arts in order to reach out to the broader public and make the movement appealing (*India Climate Solutions* n.d.). The latter would be accomplished with the help of public art projects and music, namely with the help of an American band, "Solar Punch" whose equipment was powered purely through solar energy. Though American, they would master several Bollywood music hits in time for the tour. With this kind of energy and a dynamic team made up of youth, young professionals, entrepreneurs, and artists, it was hoped that the message of solutions would reach a wide audience.

By committing the fledgling network to being the platform for organizing this tour, we took a big gamble. Should we succeed, the network would go down in history, for having conducted this remarkable feat and its membership base could increase sharply as we built the movement along the way: in city after city, new young members would help inspire and it would help us create new centers of change-making activity. The risk was that we were still uncertain about the governance and structure of the network and we did not know how to deal with emerging "chapters" in other cities. The lack of clarity would confuse newly-inducted members of their role and duties in the network shortly after "joining." In addition, we were unclear about how a network might be managed by groups such as Delhi Greens which were separate legal entities (Delhi Greens was registered as a trust in mid-2008) with independent agendas. All of this uncertainty could be potentially detrimental to the overall growth of the network. Imagine the confusion of thousands of people entering a network that was still trying to define its full-range levels on which it should seek to drive systemic change. Regardless, our mission was clear: "to unite the youth of India, towards a clean bright future" (Delhi Youth Declaration on Climate Change, May 28, 2008) and it was with this in mind that we kept the network open to growth and ideation. It became an open laboratory, a place for passionate youth to know that they were a part of "something new, something bold," (New Delhi, DYSoC) and that they could exercise their creative freedoms and entrepreneurship skills.

The climate solutions road tour was one of those ideas; it required institutional backing to raise funds for its mission. While on a fundraising tour in Chennai, we realized not only how important it was to have a legal entity to provide sponsorship but also how difficult it would be to direct the movement from Delhi. A meeting with a businessman and member of The Indus Entrepreneurs group (TIE) in Chennai challenged my confidence in our social entrepreneurship venture. After much probing, he told me flatly: "Sitting here in Chennai, I will never give money to anything that has 'Delhi' in its name." Regionalism is not new in India, and in a country that has often seen too much central government control, people from far-flung states have naturally developed an aversion to Delhi-centric initiatives. It was then that we knew that IYCN would have to be an independent organization and a national network all at once. Being pan-Indian in name meant it was effective at gathering support across the country. But to be an effective platform for raising funds for national projects, it would also have to be registered as an independent organization.

To build the movement beyond Delhi's borders would be just as challenging as trying to build a movement across Asia, for within this country alone, there are several cultures and language barriers. By August 2008, we had organized in partnership with a few organizations from southern India, the first ever for youth, by youth, *national* summit on climate change: the Indian Youth Summit on Climate Change (IYSoCC). This event helped seed the idea of IYCN amongst youth to a wider audience beyond Delhi. It was also a place to introduce the concept of the climate solutions road tour, for it was the passion of these youth that would eventually create spin-off chapters of IYCN. Soon after, IYCN was registered as a separate entity, and with this change came the constant challenge for us to distinguish between the roles of the network and the organization. The network was the loose coalition of affiliated member groups and individuals who made up the larger climate movement, and the organization was the unifying legal entity running coordinated campaigns and projects for all these members to participate in. The organization was also legally liable for its actions whereas the network was broader and, while inspired by the organization, could act independently, driven by individuals and member groups.

In this early phase, we were all learners. Taking a lot of activists and making them responsible managers and operators of an organization was difficult. The greatest challenge was shifting roles from being an activist to being a manager of people, an unexpected role that needed to be filled. One of the biggest tasks was registering the organization with the Indian government, a cumbersome process. Along the way we realized that there would be many such barriers to pass before we were a functioning organization. At least half of our time was spent on creating the organization, which was extremely draining. Administrative duties aside, we began to travel across the country to conduct climate-leadership trainings, modified from existing workshops from Australia and the US. Not having to duplicate some of these techniques and resources proved extremely valuable when working with limited capacity. Here is another example of the power of transnational information exchange that can help bolster initiatives when we did not have capacity.

These trainings would provide a gateway for interested young people on college campuses to learn about climate change and then be motivated by the energy of the workshop to take effective targeted action towards a local environmental issue (perhaps on campus). Focused sessions on identifying the barriers and stakeholders associated with small problems such as waste, transportation, water and energy on campus would allow the students to develop action plans. At Sri Ramaswamy Memorial University in the southern city of Chennai, students decided that they would create an effective waste segregation and management system on their campus. Eventually they would attempt to ban plastic bag use on campus altogether. The group of students organizing these events called themselves the

"Eco-YOUth," emphasizing the "you" in "youth" to highlight the role of the individual in initiating change. Students of Indraprastha University in Delhi were more technical, insisting that a waste paper recycling unit be set up (through use of in-house technology) to create a secondary industry that would employ some of the underemployed staff on campus. At the Indian Institute of Technology, Kharagpur, students wished to install a biogas plant to handle all the food waste and provide clean cooking energy for the school canteen. Pune University students decided that there was too much public through traffic crisscrossing its large campus, so they decided to push for an aggressive policy to limit vehicular traffic. Members of the student group, Pragati, of Sri Ram College of Commerce provided inspiration by probing the use of government-sanctioned funds for sustainable development on college campuses. They would eventually have their demands for the installation of solar hot water heaters met and go further by launching a green publication, creating a public space for posting a "green-tip" daily (for environmental education) and asking for a small lot of land on campus for the creation of an organic garden. Some of these plans would be successful; others would fizzle out over time. At the very least, we saw a potential to create and leave behind a network of "eco-groups" on college campuses to be a part of the larger youth climate network – the movement.

These networks that we were creating prior to the launch of the road tour would help us solve the logistical challenge of conducting the tour. They could organize events during the days that the road tour was in their city and scout out local climate solutions to document and highlight. In the organizing process, the coordinators of the road tour in different cities would have to create their own local network chapter comprising youth, young professionals, companies and civil society groups. Some of these partnerships would be particular to a city, others would be national partnerships. One of the successes of "IYCN the organization" was partnerships it forged early on with companies like Infosys, a leading Information Technology (IT) giant that is dedicated to the environmental cause and that saw the network as a potential source of future employees who would be able to help it fulfill its green mission. Since IYCN expanded so quickly thanks to web-tools, it seemed fitting that the young network would form a partnership with an IT giant which would support not just our creativity but even our organizational growth. Such partnerships are exciting and perhaps reflect how social movements can be supported by the digital age through new partnerships to solve problems as complex as climate change. This example also shows how important it was for IYCN to function not only as a loose network and movement, but also as an organization that could forge bilateral partnerships. A network could not form bilateral partnerships as it would be hard for the partnering organization or company to know who the "person in charge" is with whom the partnership is being forged. In addition, companies might ask, can a loose network give clear shape to the well-defined deliverables and benefits that should come with a partnership? These questions can only be answered when dealing with another organization.

Navigating through the mix of relationships between young people, other non-profit organizations, the government and now industry, required a higher level of professionalism from us. An advisor to the organization suggested that the co-founders take on roles as "Executive Directors" handling the various emerging "portfolios" of IYCN (partnerships, fundraising, programs, memberships, etc.). These roles would help us delegate tasks amongst ourselves and hopefully operate more efficiently. IYCN however, was like an organism, constantly expanding and creating new challenges for us to learn from. As organizers of this movement, we made many mistakes and were constantly adapting to the challenges we were facing. From the very start we were very much what noted American author and Director of the Center for Organizational Learning, Peter Senge (1990), would describe as a "learning organization," one that continues to evolve with time in order to survive and in reaction to the external environment. Although the term refers more directly to companies that must adapt to changing market conditions, I believe it can be applied to social ventures as well.

We faced a tremendous challenge to create a steering committee that spanned the country. The allure of having various geographic regions and both urban and rural voices included was that we could claim to be somewhat "representative" of Indian youth voices. It was inevitable that certain voices would feel left out, some due to communication barriers and others due to bottlenecks created in the process-heavy decision-making structure we were creating. It was almost as if we were trying to constrain the movement within a box as it was trying to grow.

Any decisions that had to be made were through consensus and thus required some form of feedback from every individual on the steering committee. Sometimes the internet connection would be weak in rural Rajasthan which limited the ability of a representative from a member organization in the network to participate. Or a language barrier existed between northern Hindi speakers and those from the south who may have preferred to communicate in English. The problem of choosing which language to communicate in reflects the scenario of the Indian state. Eventually these communication problems led to decisions being made with majority consensus with whoever was participating and gradually resulted in fewer members of the steering committee playing an active role. The lack of participation from the steering committee as it existed then may have also been due to the ambiguity of their roles as steering committee members. At the time they were simply making collective decisions on an upcoming event (the IYSoCC) or having ad hoc discussions on the areas of focus for campaigns as a network. Eventually the steering committee was redundant and repeated attempts by Deepa to resuscitate it after the first IYSoCC in August 2008 failed.

Six months after the launch, we realized the need to restructure the decision-making body. This time, in order to deal with the explosion of tasks (everything from creating programs such as the Campus Climate Challenge, the Agents of Change, and the Climate Leadership programs to increasing membership and raising funds) we limited the number of steering committee members and assigned them with "portfolios" of areas to be covered. This included media, programs, fundraising, partnerships, and volunteers and membership.

Decision-making eventually rested in the hands of a few steering committee members who would be responsible for steering the movement (by ensuring communication between its members) and also manage the organization more efficiently. But as the tasks required increasing amounts of time and commitment from the steering committee, we knew that things would be more efficient if everyone was employed full time (or at least compensated for personal expenses in travel, etc.). This turned our attention to find ways to ensure that the organization would be financially sustainable in the long-run in order to ensure that members could continue to benefit from it. Ensuring the operational sustainability of the platform would eventually take up a larger part of our time, draining the team as they morphed from being activists to managers of a fast-expanding network.

Critics claimed that IYCN was "elitist." This charge came as a result of English being our operating language. The fact that the majority of the active participants of the network were based in urban areas and had access to the internet would imply that the potential of the network to engage the Indian population (solely through online engagement) was at most 6.5 per cent of the total (approximately 71 million people have direct access to internet in India). The nature of our main medium of communication meant that the majority of our participants were urban, middle class, and able to communicate in English. While we recognized that the fact that we were mostly reaching out to this demographic would always be a challenge for us in terms of claiming youth "representation," we should have focused our efforts more decidedly on the urban populace or created strategic partnerships with those civil society organizations that worked in rural areas instead of trying to do both ourselves.

The elitism charge also comes from adults who wish to write off the movement on the grounds that these youth are "co-opted," trying to be a part of the system in order to change it – eventually they may get jobs as negotiators or turn out like the already-established civil society organizations. In doing so, critics believe that these youth might try to restrict access to such levels of decision-making to larger masses. The only example I have of such a charge is through the Agents of Change (AoC) program that was modeled on a similar program established by Sustain US, the US youth network for sustainable development. This program was meant to expose youth to the UN negotiations process by giving them the opportunity to attend climate change conferences and learning to affect policy outcomes. Participation in the AoC program was limited to those between the ages of 18 and 26 in order to keep in line with the UN definition of "youth."[2] However we ignored that the definition of youth was wider in the Indian context with the upper limit being 35.

These misplaced rules forced us to exclude participants who were otherwise capable and strong members within the network but who we felt could not quite "represent" the youth at the international forum. By restricting this access, we were in essence playing the role of gate keeper. We could not of course, stop anyone from raising his or her own funds[3] and attending and engaging with the "Indian youth delegation" or the larger youth movement, but the question of "representation" as youth would create barriers amongst people in the new movement.

In late 2008, IYCN was so focused on being part of the global youth movement, which was trying to attain legal status within the

UNFCCC, that we were blind to these related challenges. So while some government negotiators could write off the youth engaged in the negotiations as "politically immature" and "romantic," others would state that being out of touch with the larger masses or being co-opted into the club is a reason to block their desire for a legal status at the UN for participation in the negotiations.

But it is because youth have traditionally been allowed to participate in a very "tokenized" manner that an increasing number of youth are getting engaged in the official process. By "tokenized" I mean being paraded out to sing or make simple declarations calling on world leaders to act on behalf of the future. These are easy ways for organizations like the United Nations Children's Emergency Fund (UNICEF) and the UN bodies at large to feel like they are "engaging" youth but essentially it amounts to nothing more than youth becoming the "leitmotif" of such conferences. The opposite extreme that is averse to co-option is youth as demonstrators on the streets. These demonstrators can also be used by the establishment, particularly in domestic politics to show which ideologies have more support. At the international level, both are necessary but perhaps a mix, (again in support of vertically-integrated activism), and certainly one that includes youth as being able to make coherent interventions that guide policy decision-making. But in what one might call the current global culture of decision-making an *ageiarchy*, which seems determined to remain in control, why should adult decision-makers want foot soldiers to be in the generals' room?

Something Bold

IYCN has always been a place of many "firsts." Thus, while planning for the road tour, we were also racing against the clock to select and organize the first-ever Indian Youth Delegation to the United Nations Climate Change Conference (COP 14) to be held in Poznan, Poland, in December 2008. This would, aside from ensuring our vision of a vertically-integrated movement, plug Indian youth into the growing international youth movement and be able to offer a valuable perspective of youth from the global South. Specifically this means educating youth from the global North about the complexities of climate change, energy and poverty – issues that plague many developing countries. Consequently it would mean that youth from the North would be able to inform their politicians about this challenge and influence the global climate negotiations. A group of 15 youth were selected initially with wide geographic representation from within India. However getting funding for them was challenging, and eventually only eight youth delegates made it to Poznan. We hoped, however, that these eight would be inspired enough to organize the next youth delegation, and that delegation would then assist in organizing the one after it, and so on. This program, called the Agents of Change, was originally adapted from Sustain US, the US youth network for sustainable development, the organization that gave me the chance to attend the COP 13 conference in Bali, Indonesia the year before.

Exposure to the international youth movement, we hoped, would help Indian youth see the larger picture and visualize how the movement in India is part of a global movement. They could also learn valuable organizing and lobbying and technical skills to strengthen the movement back in India. The experience also provides perspective on the difficulty of solving the climate challenge at the international level and thereby validating the need for grassroots initiatives of change. The mission of the program, however, is to engage youth in policy decision-making as the Agenda 21 clearly outlines. For that we were lucky to have the support of a high-ranking Indian official, Shyam Saran, who was at the time the Prime Minister's Special Envoy for Climate Change. He was very open to having youth be a part of the official Indian government delegation. We were surprised that the request was so easily met – only requiring that government officials recall the country's commitment to Agenda 21. Saran was initially surprised by our request but listened closely as we explained to him the potential role of Indian youth at the COP. This would include not only helping the delegation in its daily tasks, but also showing a different face of India at the negotiations, one that was representative of the majority of its population. The negotiators eventually warmed up to the idea of young faces of India at the international conference that could additionally help them communicate the issue of climate justice and north-south equity to a wider audience.

The Indian youth delegation at COP 14 was successful in injecting the global North–South equity message throughout the workings of the youth movement present at the conference. It was also instrumental in making youth from the global North realize that more should be done to ensure adequate representation of youth from the global South at upcoming COPs in order to help the movement spread equally across the planet. Simply by being present as a network of youth from India, the Indian youth delegation inspired individual representatives of the countries from the global South to realize what they had to do when they returned home from the conference: launch a climate movement for youth. The following year would see the launch of youth climate networks in Bangladesh, Pakistan, Sri Lanka, the Maldives, Bhutan, Fiji, and several nations from Africa and the Middle East.

Back in India, the idea of the road tour, while exciting, was proving increasingly difficult to execute. Originally planned for October 2008, it was delayed due to lack of funds. As the road tour coordinators organized meeting after meeting with potential funders and partners, trying to sell the vision of the tour, it became apparent that while people were excited by its boldness, they were unable to commit many resources. This was in part due to the unfolding international economic crisis and in part due to alternative motives that potential partners had. The latter refers to a problem that we faced navigating through the highly political non-profit scene in Delhi. In a society already crowded by civil society organizations, with limited funding, most of them tend to see youth as volunteers, more interested in getting certificates of participation, rather than having the drive to do something out of genuine interest. In addition, these organizations have their own agendas and they would much rather have youth support their missions.

There would be no funding from existing civil society organizations unless we did projects in line with their missions. They would fail to envision what the possibilities were for youth by participating in youth-run organizations. In addition, we ensured that we had no particular bias in partnerships with any one organization, as the community tends to be divided. As youth, we wished to steer clear of NGO politics; we expressed clearly to the civil society community that we would not be used by others and we would not part take in existing politics. After all, as youth working towards a common future, we could not afford to be divided. So we carried on, driven by a vision to create something new, something bold: a for youth, by youth vertically-integrated movement that would disrupt the traditional civil society space.

The Future

Climate change is a contentious issue and there will always be divisions. As important as transnational flows of ideas and capacity were to the creation of the network and some of its projects, they were also sometimes used to target it. There were a few occasions where individuals targeted the network as having a "foreign agenda" or being influenced by "foreigners." Those leading the charge feared that developed-country interests were trying to urge India to take action on climate change while shirking their own historical responsibilities to reduce emissions. While far from the truth, it was an interesting experience for those of us in the network that had affiliations with foreign countries.

Despite being a passport carrying Indian citizen, I was scrutinized. Self-proclaimed "sons of the soil," questioned whether or not I was truly "Indian," because of my mostly, American education. No one would have thought that perhaps I had retained my Indian citizenship. Why should citizenship even matter? For a politically-sensitive issue such as climate change, it was the only way to attack a movement that threatened to blur the traditional lines of north-south equity and replace it with the challenge of intergenerational equity, which forces all sides to be proactive on taking action on climate change. Mentors of IYCN, respected environmentalists, urged us to keep working and not be discouraged but to also find ways to stop such divisive tactics. Over time of course the only solution would be to ensure that leadership would come from within India. We continued with our work, knowing that we were building a movement based on solutions, not simply on the negative impacts of climate change. The solutions exist, and they are here today. Young India is full of solutions, and could perhaps show the world an alternate path to "development." From youth participation in rural adaptation efforts in Rajasthan through the Rajputana Society of Natural History (RSNH) to youth efforts to push for campus sustainability through technology interventions at the Vellore Institute of Technology (VIT), the solutions exist.

With that message in mind, the Climate Solutions Road Tour launched on January 2, 2009 from Chennai and travelled over 3,500 kms in 40 days to Delhi in solar-electric vehicles to "create, communicate, and celebrate" the solutions to climate change existing in India. During the tour we conducted workshops and interactive sessions on climate change with students from over 200 colleges and 50 schools across the nation with approximately 10,000 students directly impacted (through education and awareness of climate impacts and solutions). With a well-managed media strategy, we ensured that our message calling for the creation of a solutions-based movement reached out to millions across the country and the world. With this, we knew that the movement was launched and no matter what happened to the organization, it would carry on.

IYCN is an idea of what vertically-integrated activism can look like. The fact that it attempts to work at all levels and excite young people on a topic which is so timely makes it appropriate to inspire a larger movement. But like any social movement, it will probably undergo several ups and downs. The challenges remain: can IYCN manage its role between an organization and a movement? Can it avoid traditional NGO politics or will it have to play the game? Most importantly, can it be sustained? For now it continues to be a platform where individuals can come together, engage in climate-development issues and collaborate to create their own projects.

Today it includes members in 18 states, including Jammu and Kashmir, and has a reach of several thousand individuals. It is also trying to build a bridge between urban, internet-using India and rural India through its newly launched "rural climate fellows" program. This flagship program has trained five rural women on climate mitigation and adaptation in order for them to conduct awareness and training workshops in 30 villages in Chhatarpur district of Madhya Pradesh. In April 2008, the Coimbatore Green Wings, a member group of IYCN, leveraged the power of the network to connect local self-help groups with a solar energy start up to create a model for college students to adopt villages and actively partake in sustainable development of the country. News of this endeavor was well received by government, business, and established civil society organizations which recognized that youth were serious and thus should have the right to speak up. Engaging the vast majority of youth who live in rural areas will be the key to achieving consensus on how to take action on climate change within the country.

Along the lines of vertical integration, IYCN also continues to engage youth business and college campuses. The Great Power Race was a competition organized in 2010 between college campuses in India, China and the US to see who could implement the most sustainable practices in their academic institution. The winner was the Indian Institute of Technology Delhi but over 400 other college campuses in India registered and implemented a range of solutions from waste management practices, to increasing tree cover and taking water and energy conservation measures. Similarly, the Eco-Audit program that IYCN has initiated seeks to train young people in how to conduct water, waste and energy audits for companies in order to build a bridge between youth and companies and push for a green jobs-based growth strategy. All of this is earning the right for youth to speak up.

The success of IYCN and the ideas it embodies has allowed it to move beyond its own borders in South Asia by supporting and collaborating with regional networks such as the Pakistan Youth Climate Network (PYCN), the Bangladesh Youth Climate Network (BYCN), the Maldives Youth Climate Network (MYCN), the Bhutanese Youth for Climate Action (BYCA), the Nepal Youth for Climate Action (NYCA) and the Sri Lankan Youth Climate Action Network (SLYCAN). Where the transnational flow of ideas was once happening between nations of the global North and South, we are now witnessing a South–South exchange of ideas and capacity sharing. There have been two regional youth summits organized in South Asia by these youth-run organizations in the last two years.

These connections amongst youth networks are going to prove increasingly vital as the nations of South Asia, often at political odds, find themselves bound closer together by the challenges posed by a changing climate. And while youth may not have much say in the domestic decision-making as yet, they may find ways to strengthen their arguments for being involved by forging ties across national boundaries. In COP 15, youth formally became a UNFCCC-recognized constituency. Their new status, as "YOUNGOs" (youth-run NGOs) is a significant step forward for the international youth environmental movement and provides the support youth need in order to become part of the decision-making process at a national level (Keenan 2010). They must however fight for that right and demonstrate their capabilities. For India, that time may not be too far off: the Indian Planning Commission has finally decided to hold national consultations for its upcoming 12th five-year planning report. By recognizing youth as a constituency, it has approached IYCN and several other youth-run organizations to organize the consultation on several key policy issues including among other things, environment, democratization of information, creation of strategies for inclusive growth and the making of decentralized government work. This is a step towards creating the larger systemic change that IYCN hopes its brand of vertically-integrated activism can inspire. This is perhaps a sign that the movement has entered a new phase. For similar groups in

other countries, until such a day arrives, youth environmental movements will have to continue to evolve with changing circumstances to
gain the space they deserve for safeguarding their future.

✳

Notes

1. There seems to be some confusion as to how many people in India actually
    have access to versus use the internet. The CIA World Fact Book places
    the number at 61 million in 2009 while the Market Statistics website,
    Plugged In states that the range is somewhere between 52 and 71 million.
    Furthermore, *Plugged In*'s analysis reveals that 37 per cent of internet access
    in India happens from cyber cafes. See http://www.pluggd.in/internet-
    usage-in-india-market-statistics-297/. As accessed on March 4, 2014.
2. For the UN's definition of "youth" as between the ages of 15 and 24,
    see http://www.un.org/esa/socdev/documents/youth/fact-sheets/youth-
    definition.pdf. As accessed on March 4, 2014. However, for the purposes
    of IYCN's AoC program, adapted from that of Sustain US, we stretched
    the age limit up to 26.
3. The AoC program was a structured youth-organized delegation to the UN
    climate negotiations. The aim was to select those youth who would be
    able to advance not only the goals of the team but also of the global youth
    climate movement; these individuals had to be dynamic, accomplished
    and representative of youth environmental-action in India. Being selected
    did not however guarantee funding in order for the delegation member
    to be able to attend the conference. The responsibility to source funds to
    pay for the travel was a collective as well as individual effort of the entire
    Indian Youth Delegation team. Funding was by far the biggest barrier to
    participation at the conference aside from accreditation.

References

Henn, J. 2009. "Breaking: The Fight for 350 (President Mohamed Nasheed
    Leads Push for Survival in Copenhagen)," *It's Getting Hot In Here*,
    December 14. http://itsgettinghotinhere.org/?s=breaking+the+fight+f
    or+350. As accessed on March 11, 2014.
India Climate Solutions. n.d. "Climate Solutions Road Tour." http://
    indiaclimate solutions.org/climate-solutions-road-tour. As accessed on
    March 11, 2014.

International Organization for Migration. 2009. *In Search of Shelter: Mapping the Effects of Climate Change on Human Migration and Displacement.* http://www.careclimatechange.org. As accessed on March 4, 2014.

Keenan, A. 2010. *Youth Climate: The Movement's Coming of Age.* Bonn: YOUNGO.

Senge, P. M. 1990. *The Fifth Discipline: The Art and Practice of the Learning Organization.* New York: Doubleday.

Singh, G. 2007. "About Delhi Greens," March 17. http://delhigreens.com/about. As accessed on October 30, 2010.

Singh, K. 2009. "How Old Will You Be in 2050?" *TerraGreen Magazine,* 1 (17), October.

Stigler, B. 2004. "Enspirited Leadership: Landmarks for Uncertain Times," The Berkana Institute. http://www.berkana.org/pdf/enspirited_web.pdf. As accessed on March 13, 2014.

World Health Organization (WHO). 2009. *Protecting Health from Climate Change: Connecting Science, Policy and People.* Geneva: World Health Organisation. http://whqlibdoc.who.int/publications/2009/9789241598880_eng.pdf?ua=1. As accessed on March 13, 2014.

United Nations (UN). 1992. *Agenda 21: Programme of Action for Sustainable Development.* UN Doc A/Conf.151/26, Agenda Item 21, 46th Session, General Assembly Official Records. http://sustainabledevelopment.un.org/content/documents/Agenda21.pdf. As accessed on March 12, 2014.

9

The Environmental Collective of Goiás Youth

Tiago E. G. Rodrigues*

This chapter details a case study of the Environmental Collectives of Youth in Brazil, Coletivos Jovem de Meio Ambiente (CJMAs), and their role in promoting responsible environmental behavior (REB). It is part of my thesis which deals with the social dynamics underpinning the adoption of environmental behavior and how they might be oriented towards achieving an environmentally-engaged citizenry. My hypothesis is that if environmental communication identifies environmental behavior as important to the social development of communities, then citizens' perception of the advantage of adopting REB will be strengthened, leading to the popular conceptualization of REB as a right and duty of citizenship.

Today's youth faces two contemporary phenomena, a connected world and an unprecedented environmental debate. Environmental issues have been widely disseminated, contributing to the social recognition of the degree of environmental degradation and the need to address such issues. Beyond political use and commercial abuse, the environmental debate has a great potential to produce critique of consumption patterns as well as to reaffirm important social values and behavior, which presupposes new relationships with the environment. Notwithstanding inequalities and differences, the quick-networked propagation of certain values allows youth groups to share their reactions to dominant trends and paradigms. Within this context, youth becomes a potential source of social change.

In this interconnected and green world, we must have a clearer idea of the processes and relationships that influence the way social meaning and behavior in relation to environmental issues are shaped. We ought to identify the new spheres of public debate being constructed as well as how the relationships involved are organized. Also, we need to understand the extent to which this process is influencing the overall agenda-setting process regarding environmental issues and collective behavior towards these issues. These are the reasons for conducting this research.[1]

To elaborate on the points I have outlined, data was gathered on a field trip to Brazil which took place over a 10-month period (between August 2009 and June 2010), opening the way for in-depth investigation[2] of the Environmental Collective of Youth movement and the impact it has generated within its particular context. This strategy allowed me to observe how the movement is organized, its objectives, its initiatives, who participates, where support comes from, the extent to which it influences behavior towards environmental issues and how communication takes place at an interpersonal level, as this level of communication has been identified by the literature as being of great importance for the diffusion of new behavior (Rogers 1995; Wejnert 2002).

The National Conference of the Environment

Public policies in the field of youth and the environment start within the government sphere, but may unfold in diverse directions. Even though, there were already government initiatives and projects in place related to youth and the environment, one benchmark was the realization of the First National Conference of the Environment, which carried the slogan "Vamos cuidar do Brasil" (Let us take care of Brazil). It included the integrated organization of the 2003 Children and Youth National Conference for the Environment which took place in November of that year. Beyond that single event, there was youth mobilization and an organization process towards raising awareness of socio-environmental issues, involving delegations of young people between 11 and 15 years of age, from schools from all states of the federation. In addition, young people aged between 16 and 29 participated in the Youth Councils part of the organizing committees in each state.

The National Conference for the Environment in 2003 included two elements: adult and youth. For the youth conference, 16,000 schools were enlisted to have a school-based conference for the environment. The participants of the school conferences elected a male and a female delegate (and a substitute), and defined a proposal around the question, "How are we going to take care of Brazil?" Each produced a poster about the proposal for their community. For this first phase, the federal government claims that the schools mobilized nearly six million people, creating spaces of debate about socioenvironmental issues and the construction of proposals for environmental policies (Brasil 2005b). The next stage of the process, at state level, selected a minimum of eight delegates (four boys and four girls) and a maximum of 14 delegates (seven boys and seven girls) to participate in the national conference. This variation is proportional to the participation and total number of completed proposals forwarded by the schools. This state-level process is coordinated by State Executive Commissions (mostly made of officials from the state-level education secretariat) along with Environmental Collectives of Youth.

The National Conference of the Environment was an initiative of the Ministry of Environment, with the support of the Ministry of Education for its children and youth version. This represented a new way of conceiving and implementing public policies on environmental education through the educational system itself. It was developed by the General Environmental Education Coordination and the Ministry of Education in schools and education secretariats, also originating other programs and projects.

In 2004, a set of continued systemic actions called "Vamos Cuidar do Brasil" (Let us take care of Brazil) was implemented involving the mobilization and training of environmental educators (teachers, youngsters and community leaders) and the constitution of two new spaces for youth action: the Commissions of Environment and Quality of Life in Schools, Comissões de Meio Ambiente e Qualidade de Vida nas Escolas (COM-VIDAs), and the CJMAs (Brasil 2006). While the COM-VIDAs seek to involve and integrate students in their initial years of high school with their teachers and the local community in the construction of the Agenda 21 in the school, the CJMAs aggregate young people between 15 and 29 years of age who might not be members of youth movements or organizations which incorporate the environment topic in their activities. The general objective of both projects is to act, intervene and construct socio-environmental actions and projects from a youth perspective (Brasil 2006).

This process, started in 2003, has unchained a series of interesting initiatives within Brazilian society. Two important initiatives stemming from this process were:

(a) The organization of the CJMAs in a network: the Youth Network for the Environment, Rede da Juventude pelo Meio Ambiente (REJUMA). This is an initiative that strengthens the continuous participation of youth in the Brazilian Environmental Education Network, Rede Brasileira de Educação Ambiental (REBEA) and in the National Council of Youth;

(b) the implementation of the Youth and the Environment Program by the managing agency of the National Environmental Education Policy, Órgão Gestor da Política Nacional de Educação Ambiental, with the objective of contributing to skill-building for young members of the CJMAs. This program evolved based on research which sought to identify the profile, demands, concerns and potentialities of the CJMAs all over the country.

Both initiatives sought to attend to the needs of youth organized around the CJMAs, identified through the 2004–05-survey research on the CJMAs. However, other results originating from this conference process do deserve further investigation, especially in relation to the extent to which this process is influencing the overall agenda-setting process regarding environmental issues as well as collective behavior towards environmental issues.

The Environmental Collectives of Youth (CJMAs)

The CJMAs originated from an initiative of the Brazilian Ministry of Environment with the support of the Ministry of Education in the organization process of the 2003 First Children and Youth National Conference for the Environment in Brazil. The youth were co-responsible for the organization of the con-ference within their states, working in accordance to the principles of "youth educates youth" and "youth chooses youth."

The CJMAs were initially a way of guaranteeing the participation of young people in the organization process of the First Children and Youth National Conference for the Environment, allowing for interaction and partnership among youngsters and institutions that make up the organizing committees in the states of the federation. From the beginning, this initiative has sought to:

(*a*) broaden the scope of the socio-environmental theme in youth organizations which work with the environment;

(*b*) bring the environment topic to several youth organizations;

(*c*) strengthen the youth theme in the collectives and the organizations related to the environment, such as the environmental-education networks, the National Environmental System, Sistema Nacional de Meio Ambiente (SISNAMA)[3] entities, among others; and

(*d*) mobilize and strengthen the participation of youth in the National Conference of Environment (adult version), electing delegates and inserting their proposals and themes of interest in this debate (Brasil 2006; Brasil 2005b).

These collectives are informal autonomous spaces of youth dialogue and action, interested in the development of environmental education. Their participation is voluntary. Some initiatives developed by these youth collectives are the elaboration and development of workshops, promotion of gatherings, creation of internet-based social networks for debating issues relevant to the movement, creation of educational resources and sharing of information. According to the Environmental Education Directing Board of the Ministry of Environment (Brasil 2005a), the CJMAs participate in events, develop environmental-education actions and implement projects of importance to the consolidation of Brazil's Environmental National Policy.

The development of these youth collectives is an interesting example of the involvement of the youth in a civic engagement process in the socio-environmental arena. Besides involving young people who already develop work in the environment field, the CJMAs favor the entry of others in this process following their principles of "youth educates youth" and "youth chooses youth." These collectives operate like local networks that articulate people and organizations, circulate information, disseminate ideas, plan and develop initiatives.

Originally, 27 CJMAs were formed in the organizing process of the First Children and Youth National Conference for the Environment, one for each state of the Brazilian federation (26 states) plus one for the Federal District. After that conference, all 27 CJMAs remained active. However, their degree of engagement in environmental activism varied from one to another. This was due to a combination of factors such as different levels of personal commitment of members as well as different levels of support from local governmental agencies. The influence of the latter can be perceived in a statement from a member of the CJMA in the Amazon state of Pará, who raised the issue of power shift (specifically during the 2010 general elections) affecting the continuity of the CJMA's projects in that state:

> Here (in Pará), the *PT* lost (the labour party which was in power in that state as well as in the federal government since the start of the CJMA initiative under President Lula's government) and the *PSDB* is going to assume the state government (a neoliberal party); we do not really know what is going to happen (CJMA-PA member, 2010).

The CJMAs have been partners in federal programs such as the initiative of the Ministry of Education "Vamos Cuidar do Brasil com as Escolas" (Let us take care of Brazil with the schools), the Youth and Environment Program and the Children and Youth National Conference for the Environment (the first in 2003, the second in 2006 and the third in 2009). The CJMAs also developed their own mobilizing actions and collaborate in projects in their states. As expressed by a member of the CJMA-Cuiabá, in the state of Mato Grosso:

> The Secretariat of Education is our partner since 2006, they recognize our work, sometimes they call us to deal with young people even when the issue is not environment related, above all, in recognition for what we do with the youth at schools (CJMA-Cuiabá member, 2010).

Throughout the organizing process of the First Children and Youth National Conference for the Environment, the federal government perceived the CJMA's potential for mobilization and engagement of the youth in environmental debate and action. They believed it could open channels for political action and possible cultural and socioenvironmental transformation (Brasil 2005b). So, with the intention of gathering subsidies for the elaboration of public policies which strengthen the CJMAs, the federal government, through its Ministry of Environment and Ministry of Education, developed a survey research project entitled "Perfil e Avaliação dos Conselhos Jovens de Meio Ambiente" (Profile and Evaluation of the Youth Councils of Environment) (Brasil 2005c).

The research was elaborated and delivered with the support of the Youth Network for the Environment and the Brazilian Network of Environmental Education. It was a quantitative/qualitative survey involving participants of the then Environmental Councils of Youth of all states of the federation during a two-month period between 2004 and 2005. After the initial period (from the beginning of 2003 to the beginning of 2005) and the completion of that survey, the Councils started to be institutionally recognized as Environmental Collectives of Youth (CJMAs).

The Environmental Collective of Goiás Youth (CJMA-GO)

The Environmental Collective of Goiás Youth, Coletivo Jovem de Meio Ambiente de Goiás (CJMA-GO), was created is 2003 during the process leading to the First Children and Youth National Conference for the Environment. In the state of Goiás, youth were co-responsible for the organization of the three conference processes in the state (2003, 2006, 2009), contributing to the engagement of other young people through its election of delegates to attend the national conference, following the principle, "youth chooses youth."

According to the CJMA-GO (2007), the Environmental Collective of Youth is a social movement that gathers in informal groups of young people concerned about socio-environmental issues. The CJMA-GO claims to have as its objective the promotion and broadening of the socio-environmental debate which refers to the theme "youth and the environment," contributing to the mobilization of children, youth and people of all ages. Some of the themes applied by the CJMA-GO in its activities are sustainable consumption, youth and political participation, sensitization in environmental education, principles of Agenda 21 and educommunication.

Central to the organization and articulation of the CJMA-GO is the use of applications that facilitate interactive-information sharing and collaboration on the World Wide Web (WWW). The movement makes use of social-networking sites, blogs, wikis, video-sharing sites and other web applications that establish spaces for public engagement and networked participation. Networking is an essential part of the everyday of this collective. The CJMA-GO is part of the Youth Network for the Environment (an important space for national articulation of the youth organized around the CJMAs), the Environmental

Education and Information Network of Goiás, Rede de Educação e Informação Ambiental de Goiás (REIA-GO), the Environmental Education Network of the Cerrado, Rede de Educação Ambiental do Cerrado (REA-Cerrado) and the Brazilian Network of Environmental Education. The collective also takes part in different spaces of environmental-education articulation in Goiás, such as the State Executive Organizing Committee – responsible for the children and youth conferences for the environment processes within this state, and the Inter-institutional State Commission of Environmental Education in Goiás. In addition, the CJMA-GO runs its own network, based on the Google Groups e-mailing list.

Through participation in the CJMA-GO's (as well as in the Youth Network for the Environment) google-group for nine months (from March 2010 to November 2010), I observed the importance of on-line networking applications (the so-called Web 2.0 applications) to the organization and development of this youth social movement. I would argue that without web-based communication tools such as Google Groups, the youth environmental movement that arose from the CJMAs initiative would have not reached the level of articulation and mobilization it has.

The CJMA-GO participation in the Program "Vamos Cuidar do Brasil com as Escolas" (Let us take care of Brazil with the schools) is also a highlight. Within this initiative, the CJMA works directly with school students towards the creation of the Commission of Environment and Quality of Life in School, Commissão de Meio Ambiente e Qualidade de Vida na Escola (COM-VIDA). The COM-VIDA draw from the constitution of Agenda 21 in schools, ideally contributing to participation of youth in identifying the needs and demands for developing healthier socio-environments within schools and where possible beyond (Brasil 2004). It is an initiative based on the participation of students, teachers, directors, other school employees and sometimes other members of the broader community to transversally integrate environmental education with actions developed at school.

The CJMA-GO – and another 18 CJMAs around the country – has participated in the COM-VIDAs project along with the managing agency of the National Policy of Environmental Education (Brasil 2009). In 2008 alone, the CJMA-GO had the opportunity to develop a project entitled "Formando COM-VIDAs em Goiás" (Forming COM-VIDAs in Goiás), with the objective of implementing Agenda 21 in 22 state schools in Goiás (Brasil 2009). However, a leader of the CJMA-GO expressed that it is not an easy process to instigate change in the school community, but when that happens, results are more satisfactory. When asked about the difficulties in instigating change in the school community, this interviewee relates this difficulty to the internal organization of schools and their Projeto Político Pedagógico (Political Pedagogical Project). By law, educational institutions are responsible for elaborating and executing their own pedagogical proposals (Brasil 1996). However, as this requires only the presentation of a formal document, not stating the due processes through which it must be constructed, it is often done only for fulfilling the law, thus becoming merely a bureaucratic instrument which lacks the participation of the broad school community.

> There is the school organizational factor, whether the school is already well organized, has a well elaborated PPP which allows for projects like this (the COM-VIDAs), whether the educators and directors provide openness to new experiences in the school . . . there are schools which do not have a clear organization, for example, they have not properly defined their mission in the PPP, they have not defined what the working philosophy of the school is, what educational line to follow and this hinders not only the formation of COM-VIDAs, but any other project to be created at the school (Interview B CJMA-GO, Goiânia, May 2010).

Nevertheless, another member of the CJMA-GO gave a positive example of the initiative developed at a school in the town of São Luis de Montes Belos (GO), where broad participation of the school community took place: apart from students, the Environment and Quality of Life Commission was made up of teachers, the school director and one of the school cooks, who became a leader of that COM-VIDA. According to this interviewee, more than 400 schools have been involved in socio-environmental activities since 2003 in the state, mainly through the formation of COM-VIDAs. Also, the member emphasized that a lot of work takes place through the construction of CJMAs in the interior of Goiás, and continued: "Each local CJMA has been autonomously organized, following its own tracks, realizing or participating in environmental education projects in its community, getting involved with the socio-environmental discussions of the locality it pertains to" (Interview E CJMA-GO, Goiânia, November 2009).

One example of the CJMA's local ramifications is in the town of Ceres, where the CJMA was a partner in the project, "Nossos Rios Nossas Almas" (Our rivers, our souls) – developed by the regional office of the Brazilian Institute of Environment and Renewable Natural Resources, Instituto Brasileiro de Meio Ambiente e Recursos Naturais Renováveis (IBAMA) in Ceres-GO, in partnership with the CJMA-Ceres and other local entities linked to the environmental debate. This project's aim was to sensitize the diverse segments of local society and government officials to the importance of preserving and recovering the Rio das Almas (the Soul River) hydrographical basin. This was done by strengthening inter-institutional partnerships and emphasizing the concept of shared environmental management (Augusto and Damasceno 2007).

Another example is the case of the CJMA-Pirenópolis, which was once involved in a discussion of the town's Agenda 21 project, which this researcher had the opportunity to personally investigate. Unfortunately, the Agenda 21 project in the town of Pirenópolis (which received funds from the federal government) was interrupted due to lack of accountability by the local secretariat of environment. Data I gathered through interviews with local government officials of that town indicated that funds which should have been spent on Agenda 21 initiatives were actually directed to other ends. This shows that even when social mobilization is achieved towards promoting socio-environmental initiatives, obstacles such as weak governance of public resources can hinder social development and motivation for continuous public participation.

Another member of the movement in Goiás I interviewed mentioned that the number of activities developed (including the formation of COM-VIDAs) has decreased in the past year and a half. The member observes that this is due to the fact that the movement has lost connection with participants in the interior of the state by not maintaining continuous contact with them. In addition, the interviewee stated that many of those involved have moved to different locations, concluding "some entered the movement and others left and we have not been able to always engage new members, because of lack of time" (Interview E CJMA-GO, Goiânia, November 2009). Several others mentioned another factor, particularly in 2010, which contributed to this decline in activities realized by the CJMA in Goiás – it was the only year in which they did not hold a CJMA annual meeting which provides space for strategic planning and usually brings together at least one member of each local CJMA in the state. It is usually a time when they establish activities for the whole year in localities and update the remainder of the group on what is happening.

One interviewee indicated that 28 CJMAs had been implemented throughout the state of Goiás since 2003. However, the movement-member highlighted that some CJMAs have a discussion focus while others are action-focused. This is due to reasons such as the numbers of members in that locality, the existence of local support to develop actions and the availability of those members in dedicating time to the movement. He/she claimed that there are currently 13 active CJMAs in the state and concluded:

> Some members apart from studying, they work too, or perhaps are involved with other personal projects which only allow them to participate in the debates in our network or in the annual state conference we organize. Others have more time and are willing to dedicate beyond the participation in discussions, developing local initiatives such as the COM-VIDAS. That is not rigid either. Some members did not have time for developing initiatives at a certain moment, but did latter. Others did before, but are now involved with university, work . . . so are dedicating less time (Interview A CJMA-GO, Goiânia, April 2010).

This also indicates that vulnerabilities such as lack of a stable income and professional initiation do influence their engagement in socio-environmental debate and action. This in turn highlights the need for public policies which better address such social vulnerabilities faced by youth, if the underlying reasons beneath their level of participation in environmental debate and actions are to be addressed.

According to that member of the CJMA-GO, there are currently 66 CJMA members in the state, taking into account the whole of CJMAs in Goiás, which have the CJMA-GO as the central articulating cell of the movement based in the capital city, Goiânia (ibid.). Regarding the articulation among the different CJMAs in the state, the member expressed his/her discontent with the disarticulation among the different CJMAs. He/she mentioned that:

> Since last year, we started to construct the next State Conference of the Goiás Youth for the Environment, and since I became a member, this has been the most horizontal construction I have ever witnessed in the CJMA, but even with many attempts to involve the maximum

number of local CJMAs in the process, that is not what has been happening. I can remember a maximum of six local CJMAs working in the construction of the event and some not even participating that directly (ibid.).

By now, it is worthwhile analysing how the CJMA-GO movement is internally organized as this process reveals its evolving character. According to a member of the CJMA-GO, "horizontality, belonging and autonomy are principles of the CJMA-GO, which seeks in its organization, new ways of viewing and facing the world" (Interview E CJMA-GO, Goiânia, November 2009). I had the opportunity to see these processes in action when I participated in the annual general meeting of the local Environmental Collectives of Youth of Goiás, on July 2, 2010, during the Fifth State Conference of the Goiás Youth for the Environment, Quinto Encontro Estadual de Juventude pelo Meio Ambiente de Goiás (V EEJMA-GO), in the city of Rio Verde – GO.

Since the Third State Conference of the Goiás Youth for the Environment (III EEJMA-GO) in 2008 (an initiative organized by the CJMA-GO), the movement has voted for collegial coordination (instead of a single coordinator, as from the previous years) which seeks to structure and organize the CJMA-GO through the institution of three action axes: communication, management and formation. During the meeting in which I participated, the collegial coordination in charge reported its experiences in the front of the movement for the previous one year, pointing out advances as well as difficulties faced along the way, with a positive balance which culminated in the realization of the Fifth State Conference, the movement's main event. Among other demands, members elected three members to be responsible for each one of those areas for the next one year.

This account shows not only the democratic character of the movement, but also the role that the CJMA initiative (as public policy) can have in promoting civic engagement of youth through participatory governance processes. It can be perceived as an "initiation" process towards how democratic systems of governance work. This can also be said about the election process for the Children and Youth National Conferences for the Environment, previously detailed in this chapter. Here, the role of the CJMAs in each state is, along with the State Executive Commission, to define criteria for the selection of state delegates for representation in the national conference, promote workshops about the school-level conferences, mobilize and capacitate youngsters to act as facilitators in the school conferences and select state delegates (minimum of eight and maximum of 14, divided in equal numbers for boys and girls).

The permanent articulation and construction of this youth environmental movement has made possible the realization of the annual State Conferences of Goiás Youth for the Environment (EEJMA-GOs). From its first occurrence in Goiânia in 2006 (which gathered 150 people from 13 municipalities of the state) to its last in 2010, in Rio Verde (which gathered 70 people from 12 municipalities), this event offers a sphere for mobilization, learning and debate of issues related to youth and the environment. At the last conference, I was able to interact with young people participating in workshops, discussion groups and lectures on such topics as environmental education, political participation, entrepreneurship, educommunication, social organization in networks, organizational strengthening and sustainable consumption.

According to a member of the CJMA movement in Goiás, "the EEJMA-GO is important for the articulation and maintenance of communication within the movement" (Interview F CJMA-GO, Goiânia, November 2009). In addition, as highlighted by another member in relation to the fifth occurrence, "the V EEJMA-GO has been important to strengthen the articulation bases of the movement" (Interview K CJMA-GO, Rio Verde, June 2010).

Another interviewee, who was 17 years old and worked as an apprentice for a Youth Rights Council, indicated the mobilizing character of the event by saying, "I saw that it is not only a matter of me changing. With the event here, I learnt that we have to mobilize others" (Interview H CJMA-GO, Rio Verde, June 2010). In addition, an interviewee mentioned that apart from his/her participation in most annual versions of the event, he/she brought a brother along for the past two events and his/her sister for the last one. This shows that the methodology used by the CJMA-GO to promote environmental education also has the potential for diffusion of environmental awareness and behavior beyond its visible boundaries. One aspect that can have greater social impact is the role of the CJMA initiative to form environmental leaders, such as in the case of a CJMA-GO member who, after participating in the movement in its early stages, has developed work for the Ministry of Environment.

I could also verify the importance of the organizing process for the event in the development of a planning methodology by the CJMA-GO, based on identifying demands in advance to make actions possible. This process started six months before the event took place and led to a relatively successful event. In addition, one of the focuses of the event was the debate of a State Program of Youth and the Environment proposal to be forwarded to legislative authorities. The State of Goiás does not yet have any sort of state government policy directed to this theme and this initiative by the CJMA-GO movement indicates its intention to participate in the elaboration of public policies, showing the potential of this movement to influence the political agenda. Other initiatives that indicate this potential (which deserves further investigation) included:

(*a*) a letter to candidates – an action born within the Youth Network for the Environment to prepare and disseminate (especially among the presidential and governor candidates) information about the work done by youth in community environmental engagement, their beliefs and their expectations of the government. This took place during the general federal and state elections in October 2010. The letter was replicated by the CJMA-GO, who sent it to the candidates in Goiás; and

(*b*) an open letter of the catalão youth – a document stating what the youth from the city of Catalão, in Goiás, expect from their local government in relation to policies directed to the young people in that locality. They claimed the document was to serve as "an informational, political and mobilizing tool for the Catalão society" (Conferência Infanto-Juvenil 2010).

This initiative took place during the Infant-Juvenile Conference "With the word the youth," which had as facilitators members of the CJMA-GO and was held during the First National Meeting and Fourth Symposium of Childhood and Education. It was promoted by the Centre for Research in Childhood and Education of the Federal University of Goiás (Catalão Campus), in partnership with the local council for childhood affairs. It was an initiative that shows the potential of the CJMA movement to converge with other movements based on the ideal of civic engagement and social development as preconditions to achieve sustainable development.

Discussion

The collective identity of the CJMA movement is built around its "youth" character; the principles, "youth chooses youth" and "youth educates youth." Nevertheless, it does not necessarily imply stronger internal solidarity within this social movement collective to the point of resulting in exclusivity, as found in some reformist and radical environmental groups (Saunders 2008). The CJMA's principle, "one generation learns with the other," is indicative of a broader approach. These are the three guiding principles of the CJMA movement as defined by the federal government initiative. It raises the point that initiatives to promote the development of social movements should take into account the paradox observed by Saunders and develop a methodology which addresses the issue:

> The paradox is that a greater degree of internal solidarity within a social movement organization may result in a proclivity for exclusivity and that the process of collective identity and resultant sectarian solidarity can actually divide rather than unite movements (Saunders 2008: 234).

This is not the case for the CJMA-GO. Evidence is in the fact that it developed a partnership with the Citizenship Education Network, Rede de Educação Cidadã (RECID) which does not have "youth" as its central focus. The movement might exclude people from membership on the basis of age, but that does not apply in the case of establishing bonds with other groups. In her case study of three organizations in Britain's environmental movement, Saunders (2008) argues that collective identity (the result of group rather than movement-level processes) is not always beneficial to the broader social movement.

She also observed that "participation in Friends of the Earth (one of the environmental organizations under study) has generally permeated the lifestyles of its members of staff and activists, beyond their working day/group meetings" (ibid.: 238). I would argue that this is also the case for the CJMA-GO, based on different members' statements that their participation in the group has influenced how they perceive environmental issues and their social role in promoting change. As indicated by one interviewee (who has been with the group for more than two years), when asked if his/her participation in the CJMA has influenced the way he/she behaves in relation to the environment:

> It [his/her participation in the group] has changed a lot the way I think, now I look at the environment in a different way . . . I try to change my attitudes, I try to pass on to other people what I know too (Interview H CJMA-GO, Rio Verde, June 2010).

The CJMA movement has its own specificities. It is a movement originating from a government initiative, not a grassroots social movement. However, in the state of Goiás, it has developed into a social movement of its own with some dependency on government initiatives and support, especially in relation to national networking and financial support (such as the organization of national conferences and resources from state-level agencies towards realization of initiatives).

Supporting resources usually come from the government, mostly from state-level and some local-level agencies, frequently secretariats of education. There is rarely any financial support from either the private sector or from members of philanthropic foundations. This indicates the importance of government support to the development of social movements as an alternative source of funding. As pointed out by Barker (2008), it allows movements not to fall into corporate elites' co-option which takes place mainly through the links established by donation from philanthropic foundations.

According to Saunders:

> If there is a collective identity in the group (in relation to the conservationist Chiswick Wildlife Group [CWG] movement), it is defined by the Committee, which is responsible for working out what the "we" will do. To some extent, it is questionable whether CWG volunteers share a collective identity (2008: 236).

The CJMA groups' idea of what "we" will do (according to that author, strongly related to the definition of the collective identity of a social movement group) was originally defined by the federal government initiative. Furthermore, the CJMAs' guiding principles were not formulated within the groups' roots; rather, they were assimilated from top to bottom (from government to movement groups). In this regard, the federal government has created an Orientation Manual for Developing an Environmental Collective.

Despite Saunders' observation in the CWG case study, I argue that the volunteers of the CJMA-GO share a collective identity around: (*a*) the importance of youth in society; (*b*) the role of the youth in promoting social change and (*c*) the strength in unit. The latter could be clearly observed during the state-level conference, where I perceived a feeling of empowerment because it was an event organized by youth for youth.

The local CJMA groups, apart from participating in federal government initiatives such as the development of the COM-VIDAs within schools, also work on local issues, often using their own knowledge, capabilities and local partnerships. In agreement with Saunders' observations in relation to the reformist environmental movement Friends of the Earth (FoE), I argue that it is more accurate to suggest that the CJMAs around the country have a shared concern for environmental justice, while the local CJMA of Goiás has its own collective identity (2008).

The CJMA-GO's active members also commit a generous amount of personal time to it, evidenced by their constant presence in the google-group discussions and the establishment of shared tasks during their general meetings. Solidarity is evident amongst those members who are more active, to the point of establishing emotional bonds. The CJMA-GO members do show rather strong affective bonds with one another, different from Saunders' observation in the reformist FoE movement in Britain. She concludes:

> [A]lthough there is a fair deal of solidarity amongst FoE staff and activists, it is difficult for them to build strong affective bonds with one another because of the sheer size of the organization and the work demands placed upon them (2008: 238).

I argue that the CJMA movement has a shared identity, mostly because the "we" identity (Saunders [2008: 234] sees collective identity as a definition of the "we") was defined and filtered down from the federal government organizational initiative for the movement. This attracted to the movement – people who share those environmental concerns and who identify themselves with the unique niche of the CJMAs within the broader environmental movement – the youth component. Furthermore, the local CJMAs develop similar initiatives to those originally crafted by the federal government. This includes participation in the Youth Network for the Environment, organization of the state-level processes of the national conferences, and development of the COM-VIDA projects within schools. However, they also developed their own projects, based on their knowledge and local partnerships, which have contributed to the formation of a local group level concept of "we."

Even though the federal government originally set the agenda for the CJMAs (including important activities developed by them, in this case the formation of COM-VIDAs), the CJMA-GO culture of organization has been to some extent independent from the federal government influence. It looks more like an organization based on participatory principles and horizontality. Decisions on what to do and how to do it (in relation to campaigns, workshops, partnerships and their state conference) are frequently made by consensus. This is perhaps because without collective support, one has little chance of developing an activity within the CJMA scope. Besides, as previously mentioned, the CJMA-GO has moved from a single coordinator to a collegial coordination system, showing a tendency to evolve into consensus decision-making processes. The CJMA-GO follows a horizontal organizational chart. This differs from what Saunders (2008:246) found in the reformist environmental group Campaign Against Climate Change (CCC). She argues that the "CCC has a hierarchical decision-making structure dominated by a single leader, whereas EDAG (Environmental Direct Action Group) is run by consensus decision-making," putting the CJMA-GO's principles of organization closer to those identified by Saunders in the radical EDAG group (ibid.: 246). This points to an underlying evolutionary process within the CJMA-GO group that can lead to greater autonomy as a social movement.

The concept of "we" as well as the guiding principles of the movement have originally been set by the federal government initiative (through the Ministries of Environment and Education), in spite of being crafted on an idea based on youth participation (perhaps consultation) through the processes of the national conferences (Brasil 2006). Even though local groups have autonomy and may campaign on different issues in different ways, their concept of "we" was filtered by the federal government initiative. This was the case from the beginning of the CJMA movement, under the federal government initiative; however, as we are dealing with young social actors undergoing development in their critical thinking, would the influence of the state in shaping their attitudes to equip them to face socio-environmental challenges not be relevant? Could this not be seen as the state's educational role?

The educational system has been crucial in the process of social-izing people into their roles as citizens (Mann 1970). The educational system is an integral part of the process of ideological shift from indi-vidual freedom to the idea that the actions of an individual directly affect other members of a society, and in turn, him/herself. If REB is the desired social response to counter the long-term nature of environmental problems, then education that addresses this need is a social duty. As Marshall argues, "[t]he duty to improve and civilize oneself is therefore a social duty, and not merely a personal one, because the social health of a society depends upon the civilization of its members" (1977: 90). Education has a direct relation to citizenship because the objective of education is to shape the future adult, thus directly affecting social life. As Marshall concludes, "fundamentally it should be regarded, not as the right of the child to go to school, but as the right of the adult citizen to have been educated" to match his/her needs as well as those of society (ibid.: 89).

Such outcomes can be observed in an account by a member of the CJMA-GO who at a recent annual general meeting of the move-ment became a coordinator of the movement in the state (within the collegial coordination system):

> The people I have met, the paths opened up to me, the broadening of my world vision, the evolution of my critical thought, I owe all this firstly to the CJMA-GO, which always imposed upon me new chal-lenges and obstacles that as I advanced through made me grow within the movement and my social life. And for this, I am always going to see the CJMA as a door which appeared in my life to benefit and put me on the right path (Interview L CJMA-GO, 2010).

I argue that the CJMA initiative of the Brazilian federal govern-ment, as a complimentary initiative to what has been developed within the education system, addresses the educational role of the state in relation to socio-environmental issues.

Different from radical groups, reformist groups "have a collec-tive identity that is often not systemically challenging, and whilst their activism shapes their lifestyles, it dictates it to a lesser extent"

(Saunders 2008: 249). The CJMA-GO fits more into this description, rather than being considered as either conservationists or radicals. From my observations, considering Saunders' (ibid.) conceptual framework based on three types of environmental movement groups – conservationist, reformist and radical – I conclude that the CJMA-GO is a reformist group (perceived as moderate). The CJMA-GO works at creating a climate of opinion to mobilize youth in the public sphere to act responsibly in relation to environmental issues, by equating their behavior to socio-environmental challenges and engaging in the debate and development of public initiatives which seek the achievement of solutions to socio-environmental problems, as well as into alerting decision makers to the role of youth in this process.

The young members of the CJMA-GO I had the opportunity to talk to and interview frequently disagree with the opinion expressed by Araya and Kabakian who argue that "they are the next generation – the future, and therefore, they are keen to guarantee sustainability: their own survival" (2004: 604). The young activists involved in Brazil's environmental movement do not perceive themselves as the future or next generation. This can be observed in one of the interviewees' comments in relation to what influences environmental behavioral change: "when one says the youth is the 'future,' no, the youth is the 'now,' we have to act now. It is necessary to act now so things do not get worse later" (Interview J CJMA-GO, Rio Verde, June 2010).

Even though I agree with Araya and Kabakian (ibid.: 605) that the image that young people have of the future influences their present actions, I would argue, from the experience with the CJMA-GO, that the way they perceive current life-styles and the social system are the main drivers of their concern for social change. They usually express their discontent in terms of the current socio-environmental context and a lack of participatory governance processes as their main reasons for acting.

Conclusion

The future scenarios drawn by the scientific community point to current youth as a strategic generation in their way of facing the challenge posed by what some call the socio-environmental crisis. Due to their potential to learn, mobilize and produce social changes, public policies focused on this generation can be perceived as strategic to match society's life-styles to more sustainable standards. This panorama demands better conditions of development and social participation by young people. As expressed by one youth leader during a CJMA-GO meeting, "youth is not indifferent [to social issues], actually, they are easy to be mobilized. What is lacking is a catalyst to lead them to get organized" (Interview C CJMA-GO, Goiânia, November 2009). And this can come from the state, responsible for developing long-term initiatives such as education to prepare young citizens to face the inevitable socio-environmental challenges.

The results of the CJMA initiative are that in engaging young citizens in participatory processes of environmental education, it contributes to the development of social responsibility as well as REB amongst its members. In addition, this initiative has worked as an avenue for the dissemination of environmental awareness as well as highlighting the importance of civic engagement in social issues, particularly amongst those who participate in activities developed by the CJMAs. In this sense, I argue that the work developed by the members of the CJMA-GO has sensitized other young people to the relevance of environmental issues and contributed to the mobilization of youth to participate in this debate. The young members of the CJMAs can act as multipliers of principles related to civic engagement and socio-environmental responsibility.

Also, there is a great potential for the CJMA movement to converge with other movements based on the ideal of civic engagement and social development as preconditions for achieving sustainable development, as in the case of the partnership between the CJMA-GO and the RECID. The relevance of guaranteeing the continuity of this process of collective construction lies in the influence it has in the dissemination of civic engagement and the promotion of REB.

List of Acronyms

CCC	Campaign Against Climate Change
CJMA	*Coletivo Jovem de Meio Ambiente* (Environmental Collective of Youth)
CJMA-GO	*Coletivo Jovem de Meio Ambiente de Goiás* (Environmental Collective of Goiás Youth)
COM-VIDA	*Commissão de Meio Ambiente e Qualidade de Vida na Escola* (Commission of Environment and Quality of Life in School)

CWG	Chiswick Wildlife Group
EDAG	Environmental Direct Action Group
EEJMA-GO	*Encontro Estadual de Juventude pelo Meio Ambiente de Goiás* (State Conference of the Goiás Youth for the Environment)
FoE	Friends of the Earth
IBAMA	*Instituto Brasileiro de Meio Ambiente e Recursos Naturais Renováveis* (Brazilian Institute of Environment and Renewable Natural Resources)
REA-Cerrado	*Rede de Educação Ambiental do Cerrado* (Environmental Education Network – Cerrado)
REB	Responsible Environmental Behavior
REBEA	*Rede Brasileira de Educação Ambiental* (Brazilian Environmental Education Network)
RECID	*Rede de Educação Cidadã* (Citizenship Education Network)
REJUMA	*Rede da Juventude pelo Meio Ambiente* (Youth Network for the Environment)
REIA-GO	*Rede de Educação e Informação Ambiental de Goiás* (Environmental Education and Information Network of Goiás)
SISNAMA	*Sistema Nacional de Meio Ambiente* (National Environmental System)

❈

Notes

*I am grateful to the School of Humanities of Griffith University for support, and thank the Griffith Centre for Cultural Research for providing additional funding for my participation in the conference leading to this book proposal. Finally, my gratitude to Dr Michael Meadows and Dr Tony van Fossen for their helpful comments on this chapter.

1. According to Neuman (2003), social research is conducted for various reasons, including to answer practical questions, to make informed decisions, or to change society. My research study recognizes those as indirect reasons for the development of this project. However, the main reason for conducting this research is to build knowledge about society.
2. Participant observation took place at events organized by the Environmental Collective of Youth of Goiás (a central state of Brazil). These events included eight general meetings of the movement, one workshop

on sustainable consumption in partnership with the Citizenship Education Network, one workshop focused on preparing "facilitators" for the Fifth State Conference of the Goiás Youth for the Environment and the Fifth State Conference of the Goiás Youth for the Environment. In depth interviews occurred with previous and incoming members of the movement, making a total of 11 interviewees, seeking personal insights on the relationships being developed and the importance of the processes taking place. In addition, secondary source methods of inquiry for this research include extensive reading of a body of relevant Brazilian federal government documents as well as analysis of locally-produced articles and internet material presented in blogs, social network sites and e-mail lists. The former allowed the identification of government initiatives in the area of youth and environment. The latter permitted an analysis of the content produced by the movement and how it is disseminated.

3. The SISNAMA, Sistema Nacional de Meio Ambiente (National Environmental System) was created by law in 1981 (law n.6.938). The foundational idea of this system is to share among government actors (federal, state and municipal) the environmental management in the country. In this way, responsibilities have been divided among the national environmental agencies, the state level environmental agencies and the municipal agencies.

References

Araya, Y. N. and V. Kabakian. 2004. "Young People's Involvement in Global Water Issues," *Futures*, 36 (5): 603–09.

Augusto, J. and D. Damasceno. 2007. "A educação ambiental em Goiás no contexto da juventude." Goiânia. Unpublished article.

Barker, M. 2008. "The Liberal Foundations of Environmentalism: Revisiting the Rockefeller-Ford Connection," *Capitalism Nature Socialism*, 19 (2): 15–42.

Brasil. 2009. "Ministério do Meio Ambiente," *Agenda 21 e Juventude: Experiências de todo o Brasil*. Brasília: DF.

———. 2006. "Órgão Gestor da Política Nacional de Educação Ambiental. Ministério do Meio Ambiente e Ministério da Educação," *Juventude, Cidadania e Meio Ambiente: Subsídios para a elaboração de políticas públicas*. Brasília: DF.

———. 2005a. "Ministério do Meio Ambiente e Ministério da Educação," *Apresentação dos Coletivos Jovens de Meio Ambiente*. Brasília: DF.

———. 2005b. "Ministério do Meio Ambiente e Ministério da Educação," *Coletivos Jovens de Meio Ambiente: Manual Orientador*. Brasília: DF.

Brasil. 2005c. "Ministério do Meio Ambiente e Ministério da Educação," *Perfil e Avaliação dos Conselhos Jovens de Meio Ambiente*. Brasília: DF.

Brasil. 2004. "Ministério do Meio Ambiente e Ministério da Educação," *Formando Com-Vida: Construindo Agenda 21 na escola*. Brasília: DF.

———. 1996. "Lei de Diretrizes e Bases da Educação Nacional." http://portal. mec.gov.br/arquivos/pdf/ldb.pdf. As accessed on February 12, 2011.

CJMA-GO. 2007. "Coletivo Jovem de Meio Ambiente – Goiás," *Juventude e Meio Ambiente*. Goiânia, Brasil.

CJMA-PA member. 2010. REJUMA Google Groups. As accessed on November 11, 2010.

CJMA-Cuiabá member. 2010. Interview for the blog "Página do E." http:// www.youtube.com/watch?v=K5LLlmvFxpc. As accessed on November 14, 2010.

Conferência Infanto-Juvenil. 2010. "Com a palavra: as crianças e os adolescentes," *Carta Aberta da Juventude Catalāna*. Catalão, Brasil.

Mann, M. 1970. "The Social Cohesion of Liberal Democracy," *American Sociological Review*, 35 (3): 423–39.

Marshall, T. H. 1977. *Class, Citizenship, and Social Development: Essays*. Chicago: The University of Chicago Press.

Neuman, W. L. 2003. *Social Research Methods: Qualitative and Quantitative Approaches*. Boston: Allyn and Bacon.

Rogers, E. M. 1995. *Diffusion of Innovations*. New York: Free Press.

Saunders, C. 2008. "Double-Edged Swords? Collective Identity and Solidarity in the Environmental Movement," *British Journal of Sociology*, 52 (2): 227–53.

Wejnert, B. 2002. "Integrating Models of Diffusion of Innovations: A Conceptual Framework," *Annual Review of Sociology*, 28: 297–326.

About the Editor

Somnath Batabyal is Lecturer, Media in Development at the School of Oriental and African Studies (SOAS), University of London, United Kingdom. His other works include *Making News in India: Star News and Star Ananda* (2012) and an edited volume *Indian Mass Media and the Politics of Change* (2011). Batabyal's critically acclaimed debut novel, *The Price You Pay*, was published in 2013.

Notes on Contributors

Bharati Chaturvedi is an environmentalist and writer. She is the founder and director of Chintan Environmental Research and Action Group.

Smita Maitra has a Master's degree in English literature and has spent 10 years as an anchor, reporter and producer with India's leading news broadcaster NDTV. She is now following her dream of making vintage toys and bespoke designer cakes. Maitra is also the co-editor of the online literary journal *Cerebration* (http://www.cerebration.org. As accessed on May 12, 2014).

Pratap Pandey is an avid television watcher and is trying to muscle into the glocal commentariat.

Matti Pohjonen is a visual and media anthropologist completing his doctoral thesis at SOAS, University of London, United Kingdom. He is a filmmaker, digital activist and writer.

Tiago E. G. Rodrigues is a Brazilian doctoral candidate at Griffith University, Australia. His research explores the role of responsible environmental behavior as a right and duty of citizenship in the long-term sustainability of collective environmental behavior.

Shalini Sharma currently teaches at Tata Institute of Social Sciences, Guwahati, India. Prior to this she was a Felix PhD scholar and senior teaching fellow at SOAS, University of London, United Kingdom. Her PhD thesis examined the relationship between the New Social Movements, Media and Memory, through the case of the Justice for Bhopal Movement. She has been a member of the International Campaign for Justice in Bhopal since 2006 and currently also coordinates the Remember Bhopal Trust.

Kartikeya Singh is a PhD candidate at the Fletcher School of Law and Diplomacy, United States. The focus of his research is climate, energy and innovation. A co-founder and former Executive Director of the Indian Youth Climate Network, Singh has also been involved in the UN climate negotiations since 2007.

Hanna Werner obtained her PhD from Humboldt University, Berlin, Germany, where she currently teaches as well. From 2008 to 2011, she received a scholarship from the Cluster of Excellence "Asia and Europe in a Global Context: Shifting Asymmetries in Cultural Flows," Heidelberg University of Heidelberg, Germany. Her research focuses on modernity, development, governmentality, social movements and the dynamics of knowledge systems in a cross-cultural perspective.

Index

For Product Safety Concerns and Information please contact our EU
representative GPSR@taylorandfrancis.com
Taylor & Francis Verlag GmbH, Kaufingerstraße 24, 80331 München, Germany

www.ingramcontent.com/pod-product-compliance
Ingram Content Group UK Ltd.
Pitfield, Milton Keynes, MK11 3LW, UK
UKHW021632240425
457818UK00018BA/363